I santi : fratelli e sorelle nostri, innamorati di Gesù
e della vita . Diventa loro amico e saranno i tuoi grandi
compagni di viaggio.

Francesco

The saints, our brothers and sisters, greatly love Jesus and life.
Become their friend and they will be your travel companions.

Francis

APPEAL FOR DONATIONS

If you can and wish to contribute financially to the initiative
Tweeting with GOD we would be very grateful. You can transfer
your donation via the website www.tweetingwithgod.com
or directly to the following bank account:

Bank: ING Bank
Account holder: JP2 Stichting Leiden
Mention: "Tweeting with GOD"
IBAN: NL31 INGB 0005717224
BIC/SWIFT: INGBNL2A

Address of the bank:
ING Bank NV Foreign Operations
P.O. Box 1800
NL-1000 BV Amsterdam
The Netherlands

The JP2 Foundation, based in Leiden, The Netherlands,
was set up to cover the financial and contractual aspects
of our projects. For its income, this non-profit organisation
depends entirely on the help of sponsors.

All donations are used for funding our projects only.

We thank you in advance for your generosity!

www.tweetingwithgod.com/donate

FATHER MICHEL REMERY

Online
with
Saints

Discover **friends** and **companions**
on your path to **God**

DEVELOPED BY

www.onlinewithsaints.com

Nihil obstat: Rev Mgr Gerard J Diamond STD, diocesan censor

Imprimatur: Rev Mgr Greg Bennet MS STL VG, vicar general

Melbourne, 11 December 2018

Developed by Tweeting with GOD

www.tweetingwithgod.com

Graphic design & layout by Gustavo Huguenin

Illustrations by:

Gustavo Huguenin (1.3, 1.6, 1.8, 1.12, 1.15, 1.16, 1.17, 1.18, 1.21, 1.22, 1.26, 1.28, 1.30. 1.32, 1.34, 1.35, 1.38, 1.39, 1.41, 1.42, 1.43, 1.44, 1.45, 1.46, 1.48, 1.51, 1.52, 2.1, 2.2, 2.9, 2.10, 2.11, 2.12, 2.13, 2.14, 2.15, 2.18, 2.20, 2.24, 2.27, 2.29, 2.30, 2.32, 2.35, 2.36, 2.40, 2.41, 2.43, 2.46, 2.47, 2.49); **Ambar Calvo** (1.5, 1.7, 1.9, 1.19, 2.3, 2.23, 2.26, 2.28, 2.50); **Gleydston Barba** (1.4, 1.13, 1.20, 1.23, 1.29, 1.31, 1.33, 1.36, 1.37, 1.40, 1.47, 1.50, 2.4, 2.6, 2.7, 2.16, 2.17, 2.22, 2.31, 2.34, 2.38, 2.42, 2.45, 2.48); **Fernando Nazário** (1.10, 1.11, 1.14, 1.24, 1.25, 1.27, 1.49, 2.5, 2.8, 2.19, 2.21, 2.25, 2.33, 2.37, 2.39, 2.44);

Photo page 18: Mazur/catholicnews.org.uk

Many thanks to:

D. Boruta, J. Bullat, R. Burgaj, R. Cocut, R. van Dijk, A. Golemi, F. Goulart, G. Huguenin, D. Loos, B. Schoo, K. Schoo, L. & L. Schäfer, P. & J.W. Severijnen, I. Spruit, M. Svobodova, M. Szaplonczay, L. Tax, R. Tolmik. The experts: Father Marc Lindeijer sj, Bollandist; Father Jeroen Smith, pastoral expert on the saints

Scripture quotations have been taken from the New Revised Standard Version of the Holy Bible, Catholic Edition, or translated by the author

www.onlinewithsaints.com

Online with Saints

Discover *friends* and *companions*

on your path to *God*

TABLE OF CONTENTS

PART 1: SAINTS ON HOLINESS AND VOCATION IN DAILY LIFE

SAINTS

GOD'S WILL

VOCATION

MISSION

MULTIMEDIA

MULTIMEDIA

LIFE & FAITH

FASHION

CREATION

SOCIETY

CHURCH

PART 2: SAINTS ON OUR RELATIONSHIP WITH GOD AND OTHERS

PRAYER

SUPPLICATION

SACRAMENTS

DOUBT

BIBLE

DESOLATION

RELATIONSHIP

FORGIVING

MARY

APPENDICES

ABOUT THIS BOOK

VIRTUAL ENCOUNTER

Imagine you could meet and greet a saint, which saint would you choose? The multimedia content of this book offers a virtual encounter with 100+ saints from all around the world. Women and men, carpenters and scholars, mothers and popes, princes and paupers: their inspiring life stories are linked to real life modern questions, and together with them answers are found.

APP

Let the saints tell their story in the first person by video: use the free app *Online with Saints (see page 23)* to scan the image of the saint in this book. Then the app will take you to their social media profile. The app contains 100+ saints, with interesting facts, quotes, prayers, and captivating stories of personal faith, love, and sacrifice. You can even take a selfie with the saint of choice. Obviously, it is possible to share discoveries on social media. Also, you can personalise the app through your *Online with Saints* profile.

REFERENCES

In this book you will find several types of references in the running text:

- References to Bible texts, e.g. *(Gen 1:1)*. For the abbreviations see Appendix 1.
- References to other saints in this book e.g. *(see Saint 2.5)*.
- References to the book *Tweeting with GOD*, e.g. *(see #TwGOD 3.4)*.

TWEETING WITH GOD

The book *Tweeting with GOD* (#TwGOD) is related to all your favourite social media channels and contains the answers to 200 questions by young people, covering the essential elements of the faith *(see page 16)*.

YOUR PATH TO SAINTHOOD

Anyone can become a saint! Every saint is different, with their own unique personality and destiny. Each of them found their vocation in a different way — demonstrating that God has a special plan and vocation for each individual. *Online with Saints* invites you to discern your own personal journey towards sanctity. The empty profile of **Saint 3.0** may be helpful for doing so.

ONLINE WITH GOD

What if communicating with God were as simple as posting or liking on social media? Whether your favourite tool is Instagram, Facebook, or Twitter, the multimedia initiative *Tweeting with GOD* helps you to see how simple it is to relate to God, even when you are offline!

MODERN TECHNOLOGY

Through a close integration between social media, modern technology and printed books, *Tweeting with GOD* (#TwGOD) wants to help you discover answers to your questions about the faith. The project was brought to life by young people with many questions, who keep searching for the meaning of their relationship with Jesus in their lives.

GET STARTED

Are you curious about the faith? Want to know more? Are you looking for the reasons behind what we believe? Alone or in a group, you can find answers to your questions using *Tweeting with GOD*.

TWEETING WITH GOD

Finding God on Instagram, Facebook, Twitter...

1. DOWNLOAD THE FREE APP TWEETING WITH GOD

Use this interactive tool to discover more about the faith on the go:

- Follow Mass or concelebrate in 15+ languages
- Pray the rosary and many other Catholic prayers in 15+ languages
- Find a brief answer to 200+ burning questions
- Scan the book *Tweeting with GOD* to find online extras

www.tweetingwithgod.com/app

2. GET THE BOOK

Tweeting with GOD (available in 30+ languages)

- 200+ questions of young people answered, searching for the reasons why

- Fun facts, prayers, and thought-provoking quotes

- M. Remery, *Tweeting with GOD. Big Bang, prayer, Bible, sex, Crusades, sin, career...*, Freedom Publishing Books 2017

www.tweetingwithgod.com/book

3. EVERYONE CAN BE A YOUTH LEADER

**Download the free Manual for speaking about the faith in your youth group.
Find fun and interactive ways of presenting and discussing faith-related topics**

- Lead your group using the tips and step-by-step instructions

- No previous experience needed

- No need to be a theologian or priest

- Free access to Specials with a series of detailed programmes

www.tweetingwithgod.com/everyoneleader

4. FOLLOW US ON SOCIAL MEDIA

 /TweetingwithGOD

 @TwGOD_en

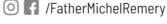 /FatherMichelRemery

 @FrMichelRemery

WORDS OF **POPE FRANCIS**

The saints now in God's presence [in heaven] preserve their bonds of love and communion with us *(GE4)*. We do not need to think only of those already beatified and canonised *(GE6)*. I like to contemplate the holiness present in the patience of God's people: in those parents who raise their children with immense love, in those men and women who work hard to support their families, in the sick... Very often it is a holiness found in our next-door neighbours, those who, living in our midst, reflect God's presence. We might call them 'the middle class of holiness' *(GE7)*.

We should not grow discouraged before examples of holiness that appear unattainable. There are some testimonies that may prove helpful and inspiring, but that we are not meant to copy... The important thing is that each believer discern his or her own path, that they bring out the very best of themselves, the most personal gifts that God has placed in their hearts *(1 Cor 12:7)*, rather than hopelessly trying to imitate something not meant for them. We are all called to be witnesses, but there are many actual ways of bearing witness *(GE11)*.

To be holy does not require being a bishop, a priest or a religious. We are frequently tempted to think that holiness is only for those who can withdraw from ordinary affairs to spend much time in prayer. That is not the case. We are all called to be holy by living our lives with love and by bearing witness in everything we do, wherever we find ourselves. Are you called to the consecrated life? Be holy by living out your commitment with joy. Are you married? Be holy by loving and caring for your husband or wife, as Christ does for the Church. Do you work for a living? Be holy by labouring with integrity and skill in the service of your brothers and sisters *(GE14)*.

A Christian cannot think of his or her mission on earth without seeing it as a path of holiness, for 'this is the will of God, your sanctification' *(1 Thess 4:3)(GE20)*. Not everything a saint says is completely faithful to the gospel; not everything he or she does is authentic or perfect. What we need to contemplate is the totality of their life, their entire journey of growth in holiness, the reflection of Jesus Christ that emerges when we grasp their overall meaning as a person *(GE22)*.

You too need to see the entirety of your life as a mission. Try to do so by listening to God in prayer and recognising the signs that he gives you. Always ask the Spirit what Jesus expects from you at every moment of your life and in every decision you must make, so as to discern its place in the mission you have received *(GE23)*. The Lord will bring it to fulfilment despite your mistakes and missteps, provided that you do not abandon the path of love but remain ever open to his supernatural grace, which purifies and enlightens *(GE24)*.

Franciscus

From the Apostolic exhortation Gaudete et Exsultate, *19 March 2018. Numbers refer to paragraphs in the document (GE).*

INTRODUCTION: **THE SAINTS IN OUR LIVES**

Q: What can I learn from the saints? Why ask for their prayer?

The saints are a fascinating company. You find all kinds of people among them: former sinners, crooks, lapsed Catholics, addicts, prostitutes, murderers, enemies of God... Others were devoted Christians and friends of God from the beginning. What unifies them is that they have overcome their earthly impulses and selfish desires. They managed to turn to God alone. Gradually, they were able to fulfil the unique vocation that we all share: to become holy in our lives.

I see the saints as witnesses of hope! Their example shows that anyone can become a saint, even me! Some saints seem to have been holy from the very beginning of their lives, like Saints Dominic Savio and Aloysius Gonzaga. Others have had to struggle with their sins and kept falling over and over again, like Saints Paul the Apostle and Augustine of Hippo. Some of them have a very dark past and rejected God or fellow human beings at one point. All of them made mistakes in their lives and have sinned. So they are just like me and you! The saints are human and have been struggling with God's call to sanctity. But they were open to God's supernatural grace and won the race of human life! (*2 Tim 4:7; see Saint 1.12*). We can do the same!

REAL HEROES

I love to consider the saints as our heroes of the faith: they have contributed to making the world a better place, closer to the ideal of the kingdom of God (*Rom 14:17*). They made it to their final destination with God in heaven. They are great inspirations for us: we can follow their lead and seek to grow in holiness. Looking at their utterly perfect examples, sometimes I am a little discouraged. Thankfully, there is no need to follow every saint in everything. That would not only be impossible,

but it might above all deflect us from our personal path towards sanctity. Inspired by the example of the saints we are called to find God's Will for ourselves.

Note that we do not adore or worship the saints, not even Mary (*see Saint 2.50*). We worship God alone. But just as with earthly heroes, we can honour or venerate them if we want to. Also, we are not worshipping statues or images (*Ex 20:4-5*). When we pray in front of a saint's statue, light a candle, or kiss an icon, we do not intend to adore the saint, but God. Nor are we calling on the spirits of the dead (*Lev 19:31*). The saints are alive in heaven with God (*Jn 11:25-26; Heb 12:22-24*). That is why we celebrate their feast often on the day of their death: it was the beginning of their life in heaven. God gave them the grace they needed to run the race and win (*1 Cor 9:24-25*). So when we honour the saints, we intend to honour God, who made their sanctity possible (*Eph 2:10*).

ONLINE WITH SAINTS

Whenever I can, I ask the saints to pray with me. Strictly speaking, we do not need the saints, as we can pray directly to God. Jesus is the only mediator between us and God (*1 Tim 2:5*). However, the saints are with him in heaven, where they are aware of us and can hear us (*Lk 15:7*). They are very close to God. Their prayer is more powerful than ours, which is always limited by our sinfulness. For many of us it is quite normal to ask friends to pray for us (*Rom 15:30-32; Jas 5:16-17*). The saints are our friends in heaven, and you can ask them to pray for you too! On earth we cannot pray all the time, but the saints in heaven can (*Rev 5:8; 8:3-4*). Your prayer can take many forms and does not need to be elaborate. A spiritual tweet or post is enough. Asking the saints to pray for you is as simple as online interacting on social media!

YOU ARE NOT ALONE

You are never alone when you pray. The saints in heaven join you in your prayer. I find it very soothing to realise that they are all part of our spiritual family. They are witnesses of the faith, martyrs, examples for each of us *(Heb 12:1)*. This is why we speak of the 'communion of the saints' in the Creed. Together with all the faithful in heaven, in purgatory, and here on earth, we form a community, one single body with many members: the Church *(1 Cor 12:12-27)*.

Anyone in heaven is a saint: those who have been formally declared saints, but also your grandparents, parents, and all other people who have died before us and made it to heaven. Those who are in purgatory are on their sure path to heaven, and thus on their way to being saints. Our communion of love is so strong that even death cannot break it. Provided we have not consciously and permanently rejected God, after our death we continue to be part of the same Church, while being in another 'place or state.' This is why we can pray for the dead, that they may soon pass through the phase of purgatory and enter heaven to join the saints. And this is also why the saints can pray for us that we may become holy too! Reason enough to go online with the saints in your prayer!

fr Michel

Father Michel Remery
Author of Tweeting with GOD
& Online with Saints

HOW DO SAINTS **BECOME SAINTS?**

In all ages there have been Christians with a particular openness to the grace of God. From the very beginning, the Church sees such Christians as an example to others and declared them to be saints. Over the centuries, a special procedure developed to make sure that people considered saints really were holy. When the Church officially declares somebody a saint, we can be sure that person is in heaven. And that can be very useful to know, because it means we can ask the saint to pray for us *(see Introduction; #TwGOD 4.15)*. After all, the saints in heaven are far closer to God than we are here on earth!

CANONISATION

Someone is declared a saint through the process of canonisation. Part of this process includes gathering objective evidence that somebody has lived a truly good and virtuous life. In addition, future saints need to have performed a miracle after death, as proof that they are interceding with God for us *(see #TwGOD 4.18)*. Such a miracle is often the recovery of a person from a serious sickness, without there being any possible medical explanation for it. A commission of doctors and scientists critically examines such cases, because there must be no room for any doubt: the healing must be impossible to explain scientifically. On the basis of such evidence, the pope can decide to declare somebody a blessed or a saint.

STEPS TOWARD SAINTHOOD
There are several steps to be taken in the process of being declared a saint:

- First, a diocese or religious order puts together a file of evidence about the person proposed for canonisation. As soon as the file is accepted for an inquiry by the Congregation for the Causes of Saints, which is the official Vatican organisation tasked with these matters, the person under investigation becomes a **servant of God** *(see #TwGOD 2.5)*.

- If the evidence confirms that the person in question tried to live as a good Christian and led a life of heroic virtue, he or she is declared **venerable**. Note that there is no official date of liturgical celebration for servants of God and venerables. Therefore, in this book the date of their death has been indicated between square brackets as a possible future date of formal public veneration (if ever they will become blessed or a saint).

- If a miracle happens through the intercession of the person declared venerable, the pope can decide to declare that person **blessed**, through an official liturgical celebration. On 19 October 2003, for example, Venerable Teresa of Calcutta was beatified. For martyrs, who died because of their faith, a miracle is not required. The liturgical celebration of a blessed is limited to a certain area of the world.

- If yet another miracle happens, the case is put before the pope again, and he can then decide to declare the blessed person to be a **saint**, an example and an intercessor for all the Church. So, on 4 September 2016, Blessed Teresa of Calcutta was canonised and became a saint. Saints are venerated publicly all around the world.

From: M. Remery, Tweeting with GOD, Freedom Publishing Books 2017, Question 4.17.

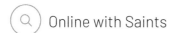

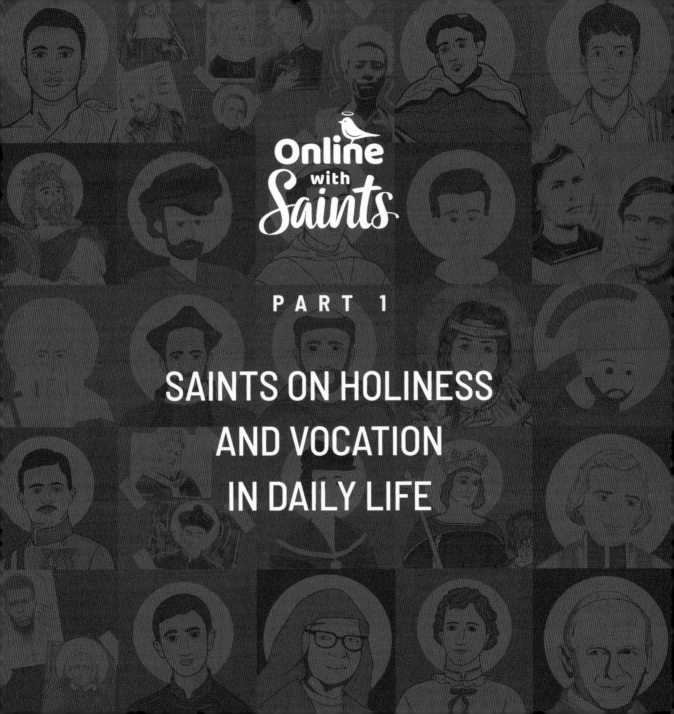

Online with Saints

PART 1

SAINTS ON HOLINESS AND VOCATION IN DAILY LIFE

ALL SAINTS IN HEAVEN

🌍 ALL THE WORLD

🕯 1 NOVEMBER;
1ST SUNDAY AFTER PENTECOST (EAST)

SCAN

Q: WHAT COMMON CELEBRATIONS ARE RELATED TO CATHOLIC SAINTS?

On 1 November, we celebrate the memory of All Saints, without naming them individually (see #TwGOD 3.27). The next day we celebrate All Souls: we pray for all the deceased, that they may soon pass through purgatory and enter heaven (see #TwGOD 1.45 & 1.47). In many countries there are traditions such as visiting the cemetery for blessings, prayers, or lighting candles on this day. You can easily imagine how these customs blended together into the secular celebration of Halloween — which should not be confused with the Catholic celebration. In old English, 'saints' is 'hallows', and All Hallows' Eve soon became Halloween. Mexico celebrates the Day of the Dead at the same time, with pagan traditions like *Santa Muerte*, which is not a Catholic saint at all. Similarly, in spite of its popularity in the Caribbean and Latin America, *Santería* is not a Catholic rite, but a mix of traditional religions. These customs should be approached very carefully, also because of the connection with black magic and satanism. The following feasts are linked to truly Catholic saints.

O God, all saints have found the way to be with you forever in heaven. Help me to grow in sanctity and become myself a saint in heaven one day. All saints in heaven, pray for us!

VALENTINE, PATRICK, AND MARTIN

Saint Valentine's day, on 14 February, is well known around the world (see Saint 2.39). Saint Patrick's Day, 17 March, became a national feast for all the Irish around the world (see Saint 1.43). Public parades, festivals and Irish folk songs are part of the secular celebrations. The shamrock originally refers to Saint Patrick's lecture on the Trinity, which he explained with reference to the three leaves that together form the 'trinity' of a single shamrock (see #TwGOD 1.33). Saint Martin is commemorated on 11 November (see Saint 1.37). In the dark winter weather of Northern Europe, children go out with lanterns of hollow beetroots with carved faces. Singing songs of Saint Martin, they collect sweets in their neighbourhood.

THREE KINGS

On 6 January we celebrate the feast of the Epiphany: the message of Jesus's birth was made public and was visible to all who could see (see #TwGOD 3.28). Three kings or magi read the news in the stars and set off on a long journey to adore the newborn Lord. In some European countries their feast is celebrated by baking a cake with a bean in it. Whoever finds the bean will be king for the remainder of the day. In other countries children go around the houses to collect sweets with their songs. There also is a tradition of blessing houses on this day (see #TwGOD 3.28). In southern countries there are parades where sweets are distributed. Also, in some countries, swimming competitions are held.

SAINT NICHOLAS

6 December is the feast of Saint Nicholas (see Saint 2.36). In many countries there are traditions around his birthday. On the eve of his feast, or during the night, he brings sweets and presents to children. In the Netherlands, for example, his yearly arrival in November is an official event, and he is welcomed by the local mayor. When Dutch settlers brought the feast of

---

IN THE COMPANY OF THE SAINTS

'Of what profit to the saints are our prayers and the honour we pay them? Of what use is this feast day?... The saints have no need of honour from us; neither does our devotion add the slightest thing to what is theirs. Surely, we are the ones to benefit, when we venerate their memory. I confess that at the very thought of them I feel myself inflamed by a tremendous yearning to be with them... We long to share in the citizenship of heaven... When we celebrate the saints, we are inflamed with another yearning: that Christ, who is our life, may manifest himself to us as he did to them and that we may one day share in his glory.'

[Bernard of Clairvaux, Disc. 2, Opera Omnia Cisterc. 5]

Sinterklaas to New Amsterdam (today's New York), he soon became famous as Santa Claus. Saint Nick is dressed as a Catholic bishop with a red cope, a red mitre, and a long white beard: can you see the parallels with Santa Claus? In certain countries, the Christ Child brings the children presents for Christmas, which may be the reason Santa Claus started to operate at Christmas, rather than the liturgical feast of Saint Nicholas. These are just a few examples: in many countries other saints' days gave rise to popular feasts. What common celebrations of saints can you list?

A surprising number of holidays and traditions originate from saints' feasts, including Halloween, Valentine's Day, and Santa Claus.

GUARDIAN ANGELS & ARCHANGELS

 HEAVEN

🕯 2 OCTOBER (GUARDIAN ANGELS),
29 SEPTEMBER (ARCHANGELS);
8 NOVEMBER (EAST: MICHAEL AND GABRIEL)

SCAN

Q: WHAT IS THE DIFFERENCE BETWEEN ANGELS AND SAINTS?

DO WE BECOME ANGELS WHEN WE DIE?

Angels are intelligent beings created by God. The Bible often mentions angels, and they can be divided into various groups or choirs *(see #TwGOD 1.41)*. Like people, God created them with a free will, so that they could freely choose to accept God's love. Since they did accept his love, they live forever with God in heaven. It is incredible to imagine, but some angels decided in their freedom not to accept God's love, and turned against him. These are the 'fallen angels' or 'angels of darkness', led by Satan, the enemy of God *(see Saint 2.25; #TwGOD 1.42)*. Angels are, as it were, a step ahead of us, just as the saints are, for they have made their final choice for God already. We too can choose to accept God's love during our lives; our choice becomes definitive at the moment of our death. The word 'angel' comes from the Greek *angelos*, meaning messenger. They can bring our prayers and petitions to God. And they are more than that.

O God, you send the angels to watch over me and help me. May I collaborate with your grace at every moment, and continue to grow in holiness. Holy angels of God, pray for us!

GUARDIAN ANGELS

The angels are sent by God to help us as travelling companions. Jesus said that even the smallest among people have angels assigned to them, who are with God in heaven (*Mt 18:10*). Everyone has a guardian angel. Our guardian angel has the task of helping us in our faith and finding the way to eternal life with God (*Heb 1:14*). From conception to death your guardian angel prays for you and cares for you. You can pray daily to your guardian angel: 'Angel of God, my guardian dear, to whom God's love commits me here: ever this day be at my side, to light and guard, to rule and guide. Amen' *(see Tweeting with GOD app > Pray > Catholic prayers > 4. Other prayers).*

ARCHANGELS

The only angels whose names are mentioned in the Bible are the three Archangels Michael, Gabriel, and Raphael. Each of them plays an important role on our path to God. Michael is mentioned several times throughout the Bible as the defender of God's people against the enemy of God, and the leader of the heavenly host or 'army' *(Dan 12:1; Rev 12:7)*. Gabriel brings God's message to Mary, telling her that she had been chosen to be the mother of God, and receiving her answer in his name *(Lk 1:26-38)*. Raphael was sent to help Tobit and his son Tobias. He travelled with Tobias and helped him find his wife. Finally, he healed Tobit from his blindness *(Tob 3-12)*.

ANGELS AND SAINTS

The essential difference between angels and human beings is that angels are pure spirits: they do not have a body — and never had one. When we die, our eternal soul is temporarily separated from our body, and can go to heaven (*see #TwGOD 1.43-1.47*). Just as true love cannot simply disappear, our soul cannot die. God's love for each of us is for eternity, and he promises that at the end of time, our soul shall be united with an 'updated version' of our own bodies.

GOD HELPS US THROUGH ANGELS

'We have...received a truth which must be profoundly important for every Christian: that there are pure spirits, creatures of God, initially all good and then, through a choice of sin, irreducibly separated into angels of light and angels of darkness. And while the existence of the wicked angels requires of us that we be watchful so as not to yield to their empty promises, we are certain that the victorious power of Christ the Redeemer enfolds our lives, so that we ourselves may overcome these spirits. In this, we are powerfully helped by the good angels, messengers of God's love, to whom, taught by the tradition of the Church, we address our prayer.'

[Pope John Paul II, General Audience, 20 August 1986]

So, our bodies make us different from angels. This difference remains in heaven, simply because we are different kinds of creatures. Human beings never become angels and the saints have not 'earned their heavenly wings.' To complicate matters, we often refer to the Archangels as, for example, *Saint* Michael, or the *holy* Archangels. This is because anyone in heaven is holy, and therefore worthy of the term saint. Did you ever pray to your angel?

Angels are messengers of God, sent to help us. When we die we do not become angels, for they are a different kind of creature. They have been in heaven from their creation.

BLESSED **CHIARA LUCE BADANO**

 1971 – 1990 ITALY 🕯 29 OCTOBER

SAINT **JOHN BERCHMANS**

 1599 – 1621 🌍 BELGIUM 🕯 13 AUGUST

SCAN

Q: **WHAT DOES IT MEAN THAT I SHOULD BECOME A SAINT?**

HOW CAN I DO THIS?

Chiara was an ordinary teenager from Sassello, Italy. She loved modern music, singing, and dancing. For sports she enjoyed tennis, swimming, and hiking. She was not the brightest of her class, and failed her first year of high school. She loved her parents, but could be very obstinate and could easily get into arguments with them, for example over her habit of hanging out late with friends. Chiara had a great love for Jesus, and sometimes was teased at school because of her faith. At the age of 16, she was diagnosed with a rare and painful form of bone cancer. After the first shock, she was able to say with great faith: 'For you, Jesus; if you want it, I want it too!' On her sickbed she became a source of consolation to those visiting her. One of her doctors said: 'Through her smile, and through her eyes full of light, she showed us that death doesn't exist; only life exists.' She died at the age of 18, and her last words were: 'Bye, Mum, be happy, because I am.'

O God, Chiara and John became saints by living their ordinary lives with extraordinary love. Help me to grow in sainthood too. Blessed Chiara Luce Badano and Saint John Berchmans, pray for us!

DOING ORDINARY THINGS WITH LOVE

John came from Diest, Belgium, where his father was a shoe merchant. He felt a desire to become a priest, inspired by Aloysius Gonzaga (see Saint 1.8). At school, he was a boy like the others, joking, running and shouting. At the same time he stood out because he was able to do every odd job like setting the table, cleaning the house or shopping with such a positive and kind nature. He joined the Jesuit novitiate, where he learned the spiritual wisdom that would make him a saint: holiness is not in extraordinary deeds, but in doing ordinary things in an extraordinary way. He tried to serve God in everything, especially in his daily tasks. John was sent to Rome, where he threw himself with dedication and joy into his studies, in which he excelled. No-one noticed how he slowly declined because of an illness, which he bore with great patience. When he finally was admitted to the infirmary, those who visited his sickbed were strengthened in their faith and encouraged by this young man who received everyone with great love and joy. He died a week later, 22 years old.

YOUR SAINTHOOD

Just as Chiara and John's path to sainthood was very different, your path too will be different. Still, you are also called to grow in holiness. Their example shows that this is not impossible. Chiara became a saint by simply living her life, and accepting the unavoidable with faith and a smile.

John became a saint by doing ordinary things with love, seeing everything in relation to his relationship with Jesus. Your call to become a saint does not require you to do the impossible. Rather, you are called to do whatever you can with love and a smile. But how do you go about this?

STEPPING STONES TOWARDS SAINTHOOD

- Use every opportunity to grow in your relationship with God. Resolve to accept unavoidable difficulties and suffering with patience and love.

- Try to do ordinary daily tasks with extraordinary dedication and love. Be cheerful and be open to the needs of other people.

- Take a brief moment for prayer every day (see Saint 2.1-2.6).

- Search for the will of God in everything. A spiritual director can help you (see Saint 1.9-1.10).

- Learn about your faith and let yourself be inspired by the example of the saints. Do you want to become like them?

Becoming a saint means living your ordinary life in an extraordinary way. Search for God in everything, pray, ask forgiveness, accept the unavoidable, and help others with joy.

SAINT **PETER THE APOSTLE**

📅 CA. 64 AD   🌍 HOLY LAND, ITALY

🕯 22 FEBRUARY (CHAIR OF PETER),
29 JUNE (PETER & PAUL),
1 AUGUST (PETER IN CHAINS); 16 JANUARY (EAST)

SCAN

Q: DO SAINTS NEVER SIN?

WHAT IF I AM TOO HUMAN AND FLAWED TO BE A SAINT?

Simon Peter was a fisherman from Bethsaida in the Holy Land. He was a very unlikely saint! Although he was an enthusiastic follower of Jesus, he often spoiled things because of his impetuous behaviour. Jesus made Peter the first pope, calling him the rock on which he wanted to build his Church — the Greek word 'petra' means 'rock' (Mt 16:18-19; see #TwGOD 2.17). But immediately afterwards, Jesus found reason to strongly rebuke him, for he was obstructing God's saving mission by focusing only on human reasoning and desires (Mt 16:22-23). Peter knew of his many mistakes, and told Jesus at one point: 'Go away from me, Lord, for I am a sinful man!' (Lk 5:8). The evening of the Last Supper, Peter assured Jesus passionately that he would never leave him (Mk 14:18-31). But only a few hours later he felt how dangerous it was to admit his faith, and three times he denied that he knew Jesus (Mk 14:66-72). Although he wept bitterly when he realised what he had done (see #TwGOD 3.38), these examples demonstrate that Peter was deeply flawed.

O God, Peter became a saint, in spite of his many flaws. Help me to see that my weaknesses can be ways in which your greatness becomes clear. Saint Peter the Apostle, pray for us!

IMPATIENCE

One of the biggest problems in spiritual life can be the patience you need in order to learn to pray and discern God's Will *(see Saint 1.9)*. The temptation is to get up and start doing things, even when you do not as yet know God's Will. Yet Peter shows how his impetuous behaviour leads him into trouble time and time again. He follows his first impulse without checking how it corresponds with God's Will. How often is this true for you too? One day, Peter was waiting for Jesus to tell him and the others what to do. But he got tired of waiting and decided to go fishing. Obviously, he did not catch anything, as his actions did not correspond with God's Will. Only when Jesus appeared and told Peter to throw out his nets, did he catch many fish, so many that the nets were overflowing *(Jn 21:3-6)*. It will be the same for you. Be patient and keep searching: when you find God's Will for you, you will be able to bear many fruits.

A NEW MAN

After receiving his mission to go out into all the world and preach the gospel *(Mk 16:15)*, Peter seemed like a new man. He preached with fire, seemingly without fear for himself or his life, even when he was arrested and beaten because he confessed that he loved Jesus. He was even able to perform miracles, although he did not claim them for himself: Jesus acted through him *(Acts 3:6)*. It can be the same for you! Probably you will perform no visible miracles, but indeed Jesus can work through you too, as long as you allow him. This is the best way to become a saint yourself: be ever closer to Jesus and try to do his will at every moment. You will probably fall, but the important thing is getting up again and again.

TOO FLAWED?

Saint Peter's unlikely example can console us all: no-one is too human or too flawed to become a saint! On the contrary,

---

QUO VADIS – WHERE ARE YOU GOING?

'Peter came to Rome!... Perhaps the fisherman of Galilee did not want to come here. Perhaps he would have preferred to stay there, on the shores of the Lake of Genesareth, with his boat and his nets. But guided by the Lord, obedient to his inspiration, he came here! According to an ancient tradition... Peter wanted to escape Rome during Nero's persecution. But the Lord intervened: he went to meet him. Peter spoke to him and asked. "Quo vadis, Domine?" "Where are you going, Lord?" And the Lord answered him at once: "I am going to Rome to be crucified again". Peter went back to Rome and stayed here until his crucifixion' (see #TwGOD 2.18).

[Pope John Paul II, Homily for the inauguration of his pontificate, 22 October 1978]

Jesus calls us all to follow him and become saints in the process — each in our own way, with our qualities and flaws. Becoming a saint is more than living a life in accordance with the commandments: it has to do with growing in closeness to God and in recognising his will for you. Peter's experience shows us how: by loving Jesus more than anyone. Three times Peter denies Jesus. Three times Jesus asks Peter whether he loves him *(Jn 21:15-23; see #TwGOD 4.2)*. He also asks you: do you love me, more than anyone?

Everyone is human and flawed, and everyone can become a saint! Becoming a saint is not first of all about living correctly, but about opening yourself to God's Will. Keep trying!

SAINT
JOHN BOSCO

 1815 – 1888   🌐 ITALY   🕯 31 JANUARY

SCAN

Q: WHAT DOES HAVING A RELATIONSHIP WITH GOD REALLY MEAN?

John Bosco was born in Piedmont, in the north of today's Italy. His mother Margaret infused in him a great love for God and a strong faith at a time of poverty and hardship. He entered the seminary, where he trained for the priesthood. As a priest, he became chaplain of a girls' boarding school. But he did not limit himself to the school compound. Visiting a prison, he was deeply struck by the number of young boys he encountered there. Together with his mother, he began to shelter boys, educating them in the faith and in a profession, desiring to change their fate. His actions were frowned upon by the upper classes, who feared the spread of revolutionary ideas. In Italy, diocesan priests are referred to as 'Don', which is why John came to be known as Don Bosco.

O God, Don Bosco placed his relationship with you at the centre of his life. Help me to do the same and recognise your help in the sacraments. Saint John Bosco, pray for us!

SALESIANS

Several times during his life, Don Bosco faced serious opposition, including from his bishop, but he never gave up. He continued to work at bettering the lives and prospects of young people. Soon he was joined by others who shared his ideals. This was the beginning of the Salesians of Don Bosco (SDB), officially called the Society of Saint Francis de Sales (see Saint 1.10). Saint Francis had a deep prayer life and defended the Catholic faith in a peaceful way. Don Bosco was inspired by his example and wanted to have such a profound relationship with God. He became known for his joyful and optimistic approach to life, while taking his Christian responsibility very seriously. In all his projects he gave evidence of a great trust in God, and frequently called out to him in his daily prayer.

SACRAMENTS

While Don Bosco provided the boys with the primary needs of life — shelter, food and education — he especially wanted to help them grow in their relationship with God. He called his approach 'the preventive system', since he wanted to prevent the boys falling out of society and into sin. He urged them to frequently look back over their lives and ask God's forgiveness for everything they did wrong. He taught them that the confession of sins is the best way to grow in a relationship with God. Every sin disrupts this relationship, which can only be repaired by receiving the sacrament of reconciliation. This is also true for you: frequently looking back over your behaviour will help you grow in holiness, and thus in your relationship with God. Step by step you will learn to recognise your sins more quickly and even to prevent them. Having thus prepared them to meet Jesus in the sacrament of the Eucharist, Don Bosco also urged the boys to receive Communion. There is no closer way to be with Jesus on this earth, for in the Eucharist, Jesus is truly and bodily present (see Saint 2.13).

WHAT DO YOU WANT?

'Do you want the Lord to give you many graces? Visit him often. Do you want him to give you just a few? Visit him seldom. Do you want the enemy to assault you? Rarely visit Jesus in the Blessed Sacrament... My dear young people...often go to visit Jesus, and the enemy will not win out against you!'

[Don Bosco, in: G.B. Lemoyne, Vita di S. Giovanni Bosco, Torino 1972, Vol. II, 241]

RELATIONSHIP

Having a relationship with God means reaching out to him and finding him in everything. God loves you from the very beginning of your life. But do you truly love him back? Do you search for him in prayer, and tell him about your day, thanking and praising him, asking his help for you and others? Do you serve him by doing good to others? Do you ask for his forgiveness when you sin? Do you visit him in church? (see box). Do you try to live in 'communion' with him, especially by attending Mass and receiving Communion as Don Bosco urged? While you try to find an answer to these questions, you will grow in your relationship with God. Growing in your bond with him will not only give you the confidence that you are not alone, whatever happens, but also bring you true and lasting happiness! What could you do first?

Every relationship is two-sided: God loves you, and if you try to love him back you are working on your bond with him. You can meet him especially in prayer and the sacraments.

SAINT
STANISLAUS KOSTKA

 1550 – 1568   POLAND, ROME   13 NOVEMBER

SCAN

Q: WHAT IS THE SECRET OF HAPPINESS?

Stanislaus was born at Rostków Castle, Poland. His father was a wealthy nobleman and close advisor to the king. He sent his sons to Vienna, Austria, to study with the Jesuits. Stanislaus was bullied by his brother Paul, who teased him for his piety and devotion to God. For Stanislaus had discovered a great joy in getting to know more about the faith and the person of Jesus, and he spent much time in prayer. He loved life with the Jesuits, but realised that his family would never allow him to join them. The Jesuits in Vienna did not dare to accept him, out of fear of his father's power. Thus, Stanislaus decided to run away in pursuit of his heart's desire to become a Jesuit.

O God, Stanislaus found true joy in doing your will. Help me to discover your will for me and find my happiness in living accordingly. Saint Stanislaus Kostka, pray for us!

PURSUIT OF HAPPINESS

Dressed as a beggar, he walked almost 500 kilometres to get to Dillingen, Germany, narrowly escaping his brother Paul, who pursued him persistently. Stanislaus met Saint Peter Canisius, and told him of his inner joy in following Jesus. Peter was impressed and expected great things of the young man. He sent Stanislaus to Rome in the company of two fellow students, a walk of another 1000 kilometres with many hardships. In Rome, Stanislaus was admitted as a Jesuit student. He received a furious letter from his father, which he responded to in filial terms saying that this was the will of God for him, but that he had no wish whatsoever to offend his parents. Nine months after his entry to the novitiate he fell seriously ill, and died shortly after making his final vows as a Jesuit on his deathbed. He was 17 years old. Paul arrived in Rome about a month later. First he did not want to recognise the holiness of his brother. However, over the years, something changed in Paul, and eventually he even asked to be admitted as a Jesuit himself. The day of Paul's death, 13 November, is the feast day of Saint Stanislaus.

TRUE JOY

It is sometimes said that the only secret to happiness is in accepting that it does not exist! Stanislaus would disagree violently. He sacrificed everything for the deepest desire of his heart to become a Jesuit, which he profoundly recognised as God's Will for him (see Saint 1.9). In pursuing this desire, he found his deepest joy. He was willing to go through many hardships to achieve his goal. Therefore, it may seem that his efforts were ill-rewarded by his early death, which prevented him from becoming a full Jesuit as he had set out to be. But Stanislaus found his most profound joy precisely in doing the will of God from day to day, and not so much in achieving his goal, however worthy a cause that was. He was aware that he would only find his ultimate joy upon arrival in heaven, and all his life was but a preparation for this perfect happiness (see box).

UNCONTAINABLE JOY

'Consider how hard it is for a person to be separated from any place he has loved deeply... But think of the great joy the good will feel at the thought of the service they have paid to God. They will be glad because they have suffered something for love of him... Think of the joy that the soul will feel... How much greater its uncontainable joy and complete satisfaction when it arrives in its own country to enjoy the vision of God with the angels and the blessed... I shall reflect on myself and ask: "What have I done for Christ? What am I doing for Christ? What ought I do for Christ?"'

[Stanislaus Kostka, Journal, in: B. Ghezzi, Voices of the Saints, Chicago 2000]

YOUR DEEPEST DESIRE

The secret to happiness is doing what you truly desire, and dedicating yourself to this. In other, more Christian words, the secret to happiness is in finding and doing God's Will. As Catholics, we know that our deepest desire corresponds with God's Will for us (see Saint 1.9). Stanislaus' example shows that we can find true joy, here and now, in living with God and seeking his will in everything: 'Seek your happiness in the Lord, and he will give you your heart's desire' (Ps 37:4). Do you want to find this happiness?

The secret of happiness is in finding and doing God's Will in everything. Only by surrendering to Jesus's love can you fulfil your heart's desire and find everlasting joy.

BLESSED **MARIA ROMERO MENESES**

 1902 – 1977   NICARAGUA, EL SALVADOR, COSTA RICA

🕯 7 JULY

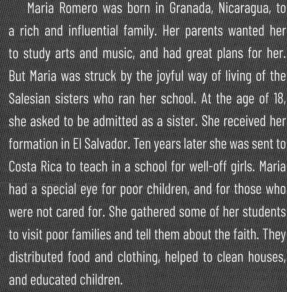

Q: I AM A GOOD PERSON; WHY DO I NEED GOD AND RELIGION?

Maria Romero was born in Granada, Nicaragua, to a rich and influential family. Her parents wanted her to study arts and music, and had great plans for her. But Maria was struck by the joyful way of living of the Salesian sisters who ran her school. At the age of 18, she asked to be admitted as a sister. She received her formation in El Salvador. Ten years later she was sent to Costa Rica to teach in a school for well-off girls. Maria had a special eye for poor children, and for those who were not cared for. She gathered some of her students to visit poor families and tell them about the faith. They distributed food and clothing, helped to clean houses, and educated children.

O God, Sister Maria had a great heart for Jesus and Mary. Help me to reach out to you and to serve my neighbour while learning ever more about you! Blessed Maria Romero, pray for us!

FROM COFFEE TO CHAPEL

When Maria realised that there were many children whose families could not care for them, she set up recreational centres, where poor children could pass their day and be educated. She was inspired by Don Bosco, the co-founder of her Congregation (*see Saint 1.5*). The teaching of the faith to young and old was very important to her. In front of her convent in Costa Rica she saw a beautiful coffee plantation. She dreamt that one day, a chapel would be built there, together with a clinic and a pharmacy, as well as housing and school for poor girls. Eventually, she would be able to realise her dream and set up many more projects. Maria did not simply work to be 'good', but to become holy and to help others to do so. This is also the reason why she was able to face hardships with confidence and a smile: she left the ultimate responsibility in God's hands.

THE KINGDOM OF GOD

Prayer was essential for Maria. She had a close bond with Jesus and tried to help people grow in friendship with him and with Mary, the Mother of God (*see box*). Maria Romero always saw the good in people, especially in those who were underfed and under-educated. She tried to help the rich too — for starters by convincing them to share from their wealth. In all this, she was very much like Jesus, who inspired her every good act. The first aim of our lives is not to do good but to be good. Being good is more than living in a good relationship with others and doing good. We have been created good by God for a purpose and a future: he loves us and wants us to be with him forever. This future life is not far away: it has already started! Jesus calls us all to do good and share with others so that we contribute to the building up of God's Kingdom, which starts on earth (*Lk 17:21*).

GOD'S PERSPECTIVE

Do you need God and religion to be good? The short answer is no, people without faith in God can also do much good.

> **LOVE AND FEEL LOVED**
>
> *'Mary my Mother! I truly believe that I am one of the happiest Sisters on earth; because I fully enjoy what I once read: "the greatest happiness in this world is to love God and feel loved by him" (and I add: "to love the Virgin Mary and experience being loved by her").'*
>
> [Maria Romero, Letter to Mother M. Ausilia Corallo, 7 July 1975]

But just doing good will leave you with a lot of questions. Why would you do good? How much good is enough? What is the purpose of doing good? When a man came up to Jesus and called him 'good master', Jesus answered: 'Why do you call me good? No one is good but God alone' (*Lk 18:19*). The purpose of life is not just being good but being good in the sight of God. At the creation, he made us in his image and likeness (*Gen 1:26*). Jesus's cryptic answer reminds us that whatever is good in us is a reflection of the goodness of God rather than our own doing. The good we do reflects his love, whether we are aware of it or not. Everyone who does good to others is on the right path. But this path is not complete without reaching out to the ultimate author of the good we do, namely God. You too are invited to reach out to God every day in your prayer (*see Saint 2.3*), by receiving the sacraments (*see Saint 1.5*), and in the way you treat other people and are good to them. Where do you want to start?

> Being good is not enough, for your life is not complete without God, the author of all goodness and love. Without him you cannot find the true happiness he intended for you.

SAINT
ALOYSIUS GONZAGA

 1568 – 1591   ITALY   21 JUNE

Q: WHY SHOULD ANYONE WISH TO GIVE UP THEIR CAREER AND LIVE ONLY FOR GOD?

Aloysius was the eldest son of the powerful duke of Castiglione in Italy, who wanted his son to succeed him as a ruler and diplomat. A career of great wealth and power lay before Aloysius — if only he chose to work for it. At the age of nine he was sent to the court of the Medici in Florence to receive his education. The greatest rulers and minds on earth visited this famous court. But Aloysius was not impressed by the glitter and glory he saw there. He tried to withdraw from the fake smiles, the gossiping, the lust, the dishonesty and disloyalty he encountered at court. He made a vow to live one hundred per cent for God. He received his first Holy Communion from the Cardinal of Milan, Saint Charles Borromeo, who was touched by his earnest conviction to live with God.

O God, may I live for you alone, like Saint Aloysius, and let you heal my brokenness, helping me to find your will for me. Saint Aloysius Gonzaga, pray for us!

 SCAN

1.8

A NEW CAREER

Aloysius's greatest desire was to become a missionary priest, a Jesuit. His father strongly disagreed, and insisted that he not throw away his bright career and future. After years of struggle, at the age of 18, Aloysius won. He gave up his birthright and became a Jesuit novice in Rome. The only career he desired was to be with God. He could be a little too fervent in his desire to fast and to pray at every moment. His spiritual director helped him to develop a healthy balance in his religious life by eating enough and dividing his time between prayer, study, and social time with his fellow students (see Saint 1.10). Aloysius made it a habit to look down, in his desire not to be tempted by what he could see around him. He wanted to live only a Godly life. As the plague broke out in Rome, Aloysius cared for sick and dying patients and carried them to hospital. Soon he caught the disease himself, and fell fatally ill. The last word on his lips was "Jesus."

TWO QUESTIONS

We are all called to live one hundred per cent for God and steer away from gossip, lust, dishonesty and disloyalty. But why would someone throw away a good career in society? The answer is found in two questions that are asked of everyone. First, are you willing to give up everything for God? Second, what is God's Will for you personally? You can only find the answer to the second question if the answer to the first is yes. Maybe God will not ask you to give up everything, but to be fully free, you need to be ready to do so, free from all attachment. The Jesuits speak of 'holy indifference': only when you are willing to accept anything as long as it is the will of God, will you be open to finding his plan for you. Note that God's plan is different for every person. It was Aloysius's vocation to give up everything and live the short but intense life he did. Your vocation can be very different, but just as rewarding!

> ## LOVE FOR GOD
>
> "Saint Aloysius loved God very much. Whenever God was spoken of in his presence, his emotion was visible in his countenance, and this at all times and everywhere. His charity for his neighbour was remarkable. He loved to serve the sick in the hospitals, and when he went there he made their beds, brought them their food, washed their feet, swept their rooms, and urged them to be patient and to go to confession. He had obtained general permission to visit the sick at home; and no one was more attentive or more diligent in fulfilling this office of charity to all.'"
>
> [Virgilio Cepari, De vita Beati Aloysii Gonzagae, Ch. XVIII]

NO COMPROMISE

Aloysius's great desire to live for his ideal — and give himself completely in order to achieve this — makes him a great patron saint for youth and students. As indicated, not everyone is called to make exactly the same choices as Aloysius Gonzaga. But we can all learn from his passion for God, his spiritual life, and his service to the people who needed him most. He did not let himself be defined by the plans of his family or his career possibilities. Aloysius used to say: 'I am a piece of twisted iron and entered religious life to be made straight.' If you allow it, God will heal every brokenness and make straight every twistedness. He will help you to overcome every obstacle in the faith. Are you ready to let him do so?

> Everyone has a different vocation. To find God's Will for you it is important to be ready to give up everything, even though he may not ask you to do so.

SAINT
JOHN PAUL II

 1920 – 2005   POLAND, VATICAN CITY

 22 OCTOBER

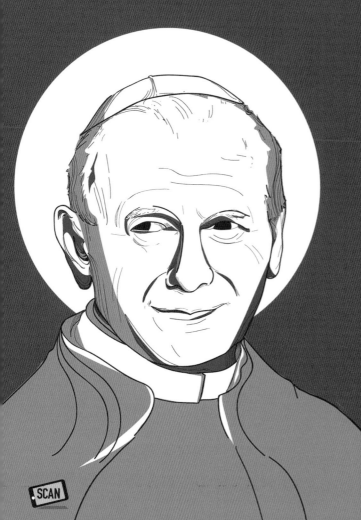

Q: HOW CAN I KNOW WHAT GOD WANTS ME TO DO WITH MY LIFE?

Karol Wojtyła was born in Wadowice, Poland. As a boy, he loved athletics, football and swimming, had a large group of friends, and a beautiful girlfriend. He moved to Cracow with his father to study languages. The Nazi occupation forced the university to be closed. When some of his friends intended to take up arms to fight the enemy, Karol strongly spoke up for a non-violent resistance. For example, he was one of the driving forces of a secret theatre group and he hoped to help people keep faith and morale through their intellectual performances. Not long after the death of his father, Karol intensified his prayer life and discerned that God was calling him to become a priest *(see box)*. He studied in a clandestine seminary in his free time, while also working in a stone quarry and later in a chemical factory. In spite of these hardships, Karol felt confirmed in his choice to pursue his vocation, and was ordained a priest in 1946 *(see box)*.

O God, John Paul II discerned your will in prayer. Help me to grow in intimacy with Jesus and learn to recognise his voice, especially in my own prayer. Saint John Paul II, pray for us!

CHRIST

As a priest, he would often take young people out into the mountains for hiking, skiing, and kayaking. When they set up camp, they gathered around their 'uncle', as they called him. He listened attentively to their questions and always gave them a candid answer. He was appointed auxiliary bishop and later cardinal of Cracow. As such, he became an important force against the evils of communism. In 1978 he was elected pope. From the beginning of his pontificate, he spoke to the heart of the faithful. 'Do not be afraid' he cried to the crowds gathered in Saint Peters' Square, urging them (and the communists) to 'Open wide the doors to Christ.' He had a special message for young people, telling them: 'You are the future of the world and the hope of the Church. You are my hope!' (22 October 1978). He would often repeat this message in different words, inviting his listeners to open themselves to God's voice and answer to his will for them personally. Pope John Paul II is the founder of World Youth Day, which he instituted after a successful international youth gathering in Rome in 1984.

PERSONAL RELATIONSHIP

But how to find the will of God? First of all, you will need to grow in your relationship with Jesus (see Saint 1.5). This relationship sheds a fully new light on your life, especially through your prayer (see Saint 2.3). If you learn to pray, you will gradually grow in intimacy with God, and learn to recognise the way he speaks to you. Thus you can learn to discern God's Will for you. You do not have to do this alone: it would be good if you can find a sister, priest, or someone else with a good relationship with God to accompany you.

LISTEN

In spite of his busy schedule as pope, John Paul II set aside ample time for his daily prayer. You may follow his example! He did this not only to be with God, but also to listen to him. As you grow in your relationship with God, you will learn to listen better

> ## MY VOCATION
>
> 'I am often asked, especially by young people, why I became a priest... It is impossible to explain entirely, for it remains a mystery, even to myself... Yet, I know that at a certain point in my life, I became convinced that Christ was saying to me what he had said to thousands before me: "Come, follow me!" There was a clear sense that what I heard in my heart was no human voice, nor was it just an idea of my own. Christ was calling me to serve him as a priest... I would like to invite each of you to listen carefully to God's voice in your heart. Every human person is called to communion with God. That is why the Lord made us, to know him and love him and serve him, and - in doing this - to find the secret to lasting joy.'
>
> [Pope John Paul II, Teleconference with young people, 15 September 1987]

to the way he speaks to you. He does so especially in the depth of your heart, where your conscience sits. Find your deepest desire, your most profound longing, and you will also have found your vocation! But be aware that there are many more superficial desires that are crying out for your attention, and possibly trying to draw you in the wrong direction. That is why it is important to take enough time when discerning your way to God: God's sense of timing is different from ours. Be faithful to your prayer, learn to listen to your conscience, and search for that one direction that will give you lasting and profound inner peace. What will be your first step?

> Finding your vocation starts with opening yourself to God: learn to pray, ask to grow in your relationship with God, and gradually discern his will for you.

SAINT
FRANCIS
DE SALES

 1567 – 1622 FRANCE 24 JANUARY

Q: HOW CAN I FIND HELP IN MY SEARCH FOR GOD AND HIS WILL FOR ME?

Francis de Sales was born in the Castle of Sales. He was a man of great faith and nicknamed the 'gentleman saint' because of his friendly and gentle ways. He became a priest in a time of turbulence in the Church. The people in his region, and especially in Geneva, had largely converted to Calvinism. Although he was convinced that the Calvinists would be much happier as Catholics, Francis did not force his views upon them. Still, he used every opportunity to speak about the love of God for his people and his Church. Francis' clever use of pamphlets — the means of social communication of the period — earned him the title of patron of journalists and writers. The result of his humble and erudite approach was that many in the region converted to Catholicism again. When he was made bishop of Geneva, and the Calvinists did not allow him to settle in his diocese, he quietly set up his residence in Annecy and urged the people there to treat the Calvinists peacefully and respectfully.

O God, Francis was fervent and gentle in his relationship with you. Help me find a good spiritual director and be open about my experience with you. Saint Francis de Sales, pray for us!

SCAN

DEVOTION

One of his professors said of Francis: 'Those who judged him more devout than learned were astonished that he was as learned as he was devout.' His devotion to God and his spiritual life with him was clear in everything he said and did. In an inspired speech to Catholic clergy he once cried out: 'At last the day has dawned! We must reconquer Geneva, the ancient seat of our assembly.' But he was not calling for a war. To the great unease of his listeners he continued saying that Catholics first had to examine their own conscience and turn again to God alone. He concluded: 'Breach the walls of Geneva with our ardent prayers and storm the city with mutual charity. Our front lines must wield the weapons of Love!' Thus he subtly led his listeners to trust more in God than in their own strength. This reference to our conscience is the key to discerning God's Will *(see Saint 1.19)*.

SPIRITUAL DIRECTION

So, how to find help in discernment? For Francis the answer was spiritual direction or accompaniment. The idea of this is that someone with great faith and profound experience in prayer accompanies you on your way to God. Francis gave spiritual direction to many and wrote over 10,000 letters helping people on their way to God *(see Saint 2.32)*. A good spiritual director listens carefully to your experience with God, in order to help you recognise the chief thread of God's guidance. Ultimately, God is your spiritual director: the human spiritual director should not decide for you or push you in a certain direction. Rather, he or she helps you to grow in your relationship with the Lord, and helps you recognise — step-by-step — how God is calling you.

FINDING ACCOMPANIMENT

An important point for Francis was that holiness is a calling for everyone, not just for bishops and nuns. Each of us can be greatly helped by spiritual direction. But how do you find a good

---

> ## *SEEK A HOLY PERSON*
>
> *'If you want to walk the paths of the spiritual life, seek a holy person to guide and conduct you... Pray most earnestly to God to give you a guide after his own heart ... Deal with him in all sincerity and faithfulness, and with an open heart. Manifest your good and your evil, without pretence or dissimulation. This way, your good will can be examined and confirmed, while your evil can be corrected and remedied. You will be soothed and strengthened in trouble, moderated and regulated when things go well.'*
>
> [*Francis de Sales*, Introduction to a Devout Life, ch. 4]

spiritual director? First of all, pray to God to help you find the right person. Ask around and go and talk to a possible spiritual director, a sister, a priest, a mother... You'll want someone with experience in accompaniment, and above all with a strong relationship with God. If you think you have found someone, start a 'trial period'. It is important that you feel that this can work: you'll be speaking about some very personal stuff! When you both agree to continue, do not change any more, as the danger exists that you will only look for voices that confirm your superficial desires. But God's plan for you might be very different! Try to be completely open with your spiritual director *(see box)*, and trust that eventually you too will find the will of God for you. Are you inspired to search for a spiritual director?

Find a spiritual director: pray, search, try. When you have found someone, be faithful and open about your experiences. Thus you can be helped to grow in your bond with God.

SAINT
JOAN OF ARC

📅 CA. 1412 – 1431   🌐 FRANCE   🕯 30 MAY

SERVANT OF GOD
HENRY DORMER

📅 1844 – 1866   🌐 ENGLAND   🕯 [†2 OCTOBER]

SCAN

Q: CAN YOU EVER BECOME HOLY IN THE ARMED FORCES?

Joan came from a Catholic farming family in Domrémy, France, during the Hundred Years' War. At the time, her country was occupied by the English. One day, she felt called by Saint Michael the Archangel and other saints to help crown Prince Charles VII to drive the English from French territory. Eventually she managed to see the prince, and urged him to take the throne to which he was entitled. Inspired by her enthusiasm, Charles decided to fight the English. Joan insisted on joining him as a female knight, a rarity at the time. Led by Joan, the French army freed the city of Orléans, and other victories over the English followed. Joan was the heroine of France, and was called 'the virgin of Orléans.' Charles was crowned king in Reims cathedral. Not long afterwards, Joan was imprisoned by the Burgundians who opposed the French king and handed her over to the English. She was falsely accused of heresy and condemned to be burned at the stake in Rouen. On the day of execution she was around 19 years old. She placed a small cross on her dress as a sign of her dedication to Jesus. Her ashes were thrown into the Seine.

O God, Joan and Henry lived for their duty to fight evil. Help me to stand up against wrong while listening to my conscience. Saint Joan of Arc and Servant of God Henry Dormer, pray for us!

EVANGELISATION AND CHARITY

Henry came from a long family tradition of military service to his country. He was born near Warwick in England. When he was 19 years old, Henry discovered his personal faith and his relationship with God during a retreat preached by a Dominican friar *(see Saint 1.18)*. He was gazetted ensign in the 60th Regiment *(King's Own Royal Rifles)* and in 1866 he was sent to London, Canada, to guard the Canadian border against Fenians and Americans. Here, his fellow officers soon discovered Henry's great devotion to God. When off-duty, he often spent the night in prayer, and took care of poor, sick, and elderly people in his neighbourhood. He shared his faith with children, soldiers and officers who were interested in the gospel. He started wondering whether he had a religious vocation to join the Dominicans, but continued his military service with diligence. He was 21 years old when he fell ill with typhoid fever, which he caught from a woman he was caring for. He died in uniform and was buried with military honours. Local newspapers reported: 'The saint is dead!'

SOLDIER SAINTS

Joan and Henry show that there are different ways to become a saint in the armed forces. Joan listened carefully to divine inspiration in her prayer, and showed her dedication to God in the battlefield. She also shows that women and men are of equal value *(see Saint 1.47)*. Henry lived his life as a soldier while demonstrating a great love for God: both on and off-duty he was a Christian even before being a soldier.

JUSTIFIED VIOLENCE

Also today, you can live closely to God while serving in the armed forces. The key is in dedication to God first, and then to your duty, obeying your superiors while always listening to your conscience first *(see Saint 1.44)*. Christian military service embodies our duty to stand up against evil and injustice

---

ACTION AND PASSION

'Joan's...compassion and dedication in the face of her people's suffering were intensified by her mystical relationship with God. One of the most original aspects of this young woman's holiness was precisely this link between mystical experience and political mission. The years of her hidden life and her interior development were followed by the brief but intense two years of her public life: a year of action and a year of passion... The liberation of her people was a work of human justice which Joan carried out in charity, for love of Jesus. Her holiness is a beautiful example... Faith is the light that guides every decision, as a century later another great saint, the Englishman Thomas More (see Saint 1.44), was to testify.' [Pope Benedict XVI, General Audience, 26 January 2011]

(see Saint 2.26). Sometimes this means that a just measure of violence needs to be used. Unjust aggressors and enemies of peace need to be stopped to protect our families, and the weak or innocent — with force if necessary. If a war is fought, it must be a 'just war' *(see #TwGOD 4.43-4.44)*. As long as evil exists, we will need our armed forces. How can you stand up against evil?

Also in the armed forces you can become holy, by growing in your relationship with God, seeking his will in everything, and carefully listening to your conscience.

BLESSED
PIER GIORGIO FRASSATI

 1901 - 1925   ITALY   🕯 4 JULY

SCAN

Q: COULD SPORTS BE A VOCATION TOO?

HOW DO I NOT IDOLISE SPORTS?

Pier Giorgio was a great lover of sports and was born in Turin, Italy. His mother was a painter and his wealthy father a liberal newspaper mogul, politician, and diplomat. As a child Pier Giorgio was known as 'terror' for the little practical jokes he liked to play. He was an average student, who struggled to get on at school, and even had to resit a year. For the last 4 years of his life Italy was run by the fascist regime of Benito Mussolini. During his studies to become a mining engineer, Pier Giorgio was active in the opposition to fascism. He had a deep spiritual life, with his devotion to the Eucharist and Mary as two fundamental elements of his daily life. He joined Catholic Action *(see Saint 1.20)* and the Saint Vincent de Paul Society *(see Saint 2.19)*. He dedicated much of his free time to helping sick and needy people, sacrificing time and energy to them, desiring as he did to be close to Jesus in everything. He loved to read texts of Saint Paul and Saint Catherine of Siena *(see Saint 2.38 and 1.48)*. She inspired him to become a lay member of the third order of the Dominicans.

O God, Pier Giorgio loved sport, but loved you even more. Help me to find a just balance between sport and charity, winning and helping. Blessed Pier Giorgio Frassati, pray for us!

SPORTS AND DEATH

Pier Giorgio was known as a good mountaineer, and regularly brought a group of his friends into the mountains of northern Italy. They often spoke of the faith, or went to Mass together. He also was a good skier and strong swimmer. Among other sports he was involved in were soccer, hiking, fencing, rowing, and horse riding. One day he was rowing with friends on the river when he felt a sharp pain in his back. He was diagnosed with a fatal disease, poliomyelitis, probably contracted from one of the sick he cared for. He died within a few days aged 24.

NO IDOLISING

Saint Paul, one of Pier Giorgio's favourite authors, said: 'Do you not know that in a race the runners all compete, but only one receives the prize? Run in such a way that you may win it' (1 Cor 9:24). In many ways, sports are like real life, where one often has to win in order to advance. But, a defeat in sports should not set you back completely. That would mean idolising sports, which brings you away from God. In fact, you could even argue that you are closer to the suffering Christ in defeat. Paradoxically, this applies only if you have given yourself fully in your attempt to win. But never at the cost of everything: just as God's commandments are reflected in sportsmanlike behaviour in the field, in sport too, love is the highest norm. Seen in this light, sport can definitely be a vocation, as we are to use all our gifts to the best. But remember that vocation is about the calling of God: make sure to discern carefully what he is asking you, with the help of a good spiritual guide (see Saint 1.9-1.10).

TEAMWORK

We are in this race of life together. While trying to excel in our personal life with God, we can only truly excel if we care for others on the way. Pier Giorgio often played sport together with others, and was happy to help a competitor who could

---

TRUE HAPPINESS

'In recommending heartfelt prayer to you, I am including all the practices of piety, first of all the most Holy Eucharist... then you will be able to thank with greater awareness the Lord God who has called you to be part of his flock and you will enjoy that peace which those who are happy according to the world have never tasted. Because true happiness, young people, does not consist in the pleasures of the world and in earthly things, but in peace of conscience which we can have only if we are pure in heart and in mind... In order for our life to be Christian, it must be a continual renunciation, a continual sacrifice which however is not burdensome... compared with a happy eternity, where joy will have no measure nor end, and where we will enjoy a peace beyond anything we could imagine.'

[Pier Giorgio Frassati, To the members of 'Catholic Youth', 29 July 1923]

not run as fast as he could. In the evening he went to care for the needy. Life is indeed about "winning the race", but this is the race of our entire life rather than that one match or game. An important lesson of Jesus is that we can only win the race as a team, as a Church community, working and advancing together, strong and weak alike. Thus there will be a prize at the end: eternal happiness with God in heaven. Do you want to win that prize?

Sport can be a vocation if that is what God calls you to do: discern your calling carefully. Sport is not just about individual winning, but about advancing together as humanity.

SAINT **JOHN THE BAPTIST**

 CA. 30 AD   🌍 HOLY LAND

🕯 24 JUNE (BIRTH); 29 AUGUST (DEATH)

Q: IS IT WRONG THAT I AM AMBITIOUS?

John the Baptist is often called the bridge between the Old and the New Testament. He was a cousin of Jesus: his mother Elizabeth and Mary were related *(Lk 1:36)*. The way in which he was conceived and born shows that he was chosen by God for a very special mission *(Lk 1,5-66; see #TwGOD 1.27)*. He prepared the people for accepting that Jesus was the Saviour whose coming had been announced throughout the ages in the Old Testament. John was called the Baptist because of his desire to baptise people as a sign of their conversion. One day, Jesus came up to him and asked to be baptised. That was the beginning of Jesus's public life, during which he spoke about God and preached the gospel. John's end was rather sad, as if his role was over when he had baptised Jesus. He was arrested by Herod, the local ruler. Because of a whim of Herod's wife and daughter, John was beheaded, and buried by his disciples.

O God, John was the greatest, Jesus said. Help me to be great in my ambition for Jesus to become greater, and myself to become smaller. Saint John the Baptist, pray for us!

 SCAN

THE GREATEST

John was the greatest of all people on earth, Jesus said (Mt 11:11). He was chosen by God to prepare the world for the coming of Jesus, a mission that was announced in the Old Testament (Isa. 40:3; Mal 3:1). He was the greatest...but Jesus relativised this, by saying that the least in heaven was greater than John (Mt 11:11). That is because people in heaven have arrived at their final destination, where they are gathered around God and spend their time with him forever. John had not yet arrived at that destination and his ambition was to get there! He is so great and important for our destiny as Christians that we celebrate both his birth and his death.

AMBITION AND HUMILITY

Ambition is a strong desire and determination to achieve something. As long as it is not directed only to your own advancement in life, ambition can be very good and very different from careerism (see Saint 1.50). John the Baptist was very ambitious. He had a strong determination in his preaching and building up of his small community of followers. He was ambitious in his plan to bring them together, to baptise them, to instruct them. At the same time, he was very humble in his willingness to give it all up for Jesus. He had put a lot of effort into building up his community. Still, he did not wish to claim ownership and keep the result for himself as we often do with our projects. As soon as Jesus passed by, he told his disciples to follow him. He did not want to keep anything for himself and gave it all to Jesus.

IT'S NOT ABOUT YOU

John shows how you too can be ambitious in a good way. He was very well aware that his task was not to be important himself, but to prepare the heart of people to recognise Jesus. That was his only ambition. Without a hint of careerism, he said that he was not even worthy to do the work of a simple

---

RELATIONSHIP WITH GOD

'John the Baptist...had the profound humility to hold up Jesus as the One sent by God, drawing back so that he might take the lead, and be heard and followed... Precisely for love of the truth he did not stoop to compromises and did not fear to address strong words to anyone who had strayed from God's path... He understands that the only steadfast reference point is God himself. John the Baptist, however, is not only a man of prayer, in permanent contact with God, but also a guide in this relationship... Prayer is not time wasted, it does not take away time from our activities, even apostolic activities, but exactly the opposite is true: only if we are able to have a faithful, constant and trusting life of prayer will God himself give us the ability and strength to live happily and serenely, to surmount difficulties and to witness courageously to him.' [Pope Benedict XVI, General Audience, 29 August 2012]

---

slave for Jesus, for example by undoing his shoe-laces (Mk 1:7). As long as your ultimate desire is to follow Jesus, your ambition can do a lot of good! But be aware that whatever you manage to build up or achieve is not yours, but belongs to God. If you have such an ambition, you can give it all up when asked, and say about Jesus, just as John the Baptist did: 'He must become greater, but I must become less' (Jn 3:30). What is your greatest ambition?

Ambition and drive to achieve something good while avoiding egoism is great! Everything that promotes the coming of Jesus's Kingdom is to be stimulated.

SAINT
THOMAS BECKET

📅 CA. 1119–1170 🌍 ENGLAND 🕯 29 DECEMBER

Q: HOW TO SAY 'NO' WITHOUT SHUNNING YOUR DUTY?

HOW DO YOU HELP WITHOUT LETTING OTHERS TAKE ADVANTAGE OF YOU?

Thomas was not a kind man, in spite of his good looks and intellect. This arrogant and ambitious English cleric had a taste for expensive clothes and wealth, but did not like to share them. Infamous is the story of how he refused to help a beggar on the streets of London. He became very close to King Henry II of England, and was given the powerful position of chancellor, as was Thomas More later (see Saint 1.44). He was immensely rich. When he realised that a private fleet of three ships was a little over the top, he gave one of his ships to the king. When the most important ecclesiastical post in England, Archbishop of Canterbury, became vacant, Henry wanted Thomas to take the position. Probably the king hoped that having a friend in that powerful position could only be to his advantage.

O God, when the moment came, Thomas was ready to sacrifice everything for you. Help me to say 'yes' to you and discern what is good and right. Saint Thomas Becket, pray for us!

SCAN

A RELUCTANT MARTYR

In spite of his initial refusal, Thomas was ordained and appointed as Archbishop of Canterbury. Soon, a surprising change came over him. He started to live an ascetic life without grandeur, prayed more, and was careful in his religious duties. He personally helped the poor, and resolved disputes in a fair and just manner. He was just also in matters related to the king, which gave rise to a series of bitter disputes. At one point, Thomas was even forced into exile, and only returned after years of diplomatic negotiations. Thomas's death has inspired great works of literature. Famously, the king was said to have exclaimed in irritation one day: 'Will no one rid me of this turbulent priest?' Some of his vassals heard these words and saw an opportunity for their own advancement. Four knights rode out to Canterbury that same night. Thomas was brutally slain in front of the utterly shocked monks as recorded by an eyewitness *(see box)*.

DRAWING THE LINE

Jesus said: 'Give to everyone who begs from you' *(Lk 6:30)*. It is very Christian to share from what we have, whether it concerns time, skill, or possessions. It is also Christian to risk being cheated or misused, rather than refusing bluntly. But Jesus also said that we need to be careful, for we are like sheep among wolves *(Mt 10:16)*. Discernment is needed all the time. Something may be good in itself, but it may not be your task to do this. Thomas was used to saying 'no.' He may not seem to be the best example, since this is a man who refused to help a beggar in spite of his great wealth. However, also after his conversion he often said 'no', and with good reason. Obviously, we have to say 'no' to whatever is wrong. But you also will have to say 'no' to things that are laudable and important in themselves. You have your own personal vocation to pursue, and that should come first. By saying 'no' to certain requests, you are able to say 'yes' to your duty. As always, discernment is very important *(see Saint 1.34)*.

MURDER IN THE CATHEDRAL

'After the monks took [Thomas] through the doors of the church, the four... knights followed behind... On one side was the altar of the blessed mother of God, on the other the altar of the holy confessor Benedict... "I," he said, "am prepared to die for my Lord, so that in my blood the Church will attain liberty and peace... He had barely finished speaking when the impious knight... suddenly set upon him and, shaving off the summit of his crown which the sacred chrism consecrated to God... The third knight inflicted a grave wound on the fallen one... placed his foot on the neck of the holy priest and precious martyr and (it is horrible to say) scattered the brains with the blood across the floor, exclaiming to the rest, "We can leave this place, knights, he will not get up again."' [Edward Grim, Vita S. Thomae, in: J. Robertson, Materials for the Life of T. Becket, Vol. II, London 1875-1885]

THE ART OF REFUSING

- Begin by having real interest in the person before you. Listen carefully and say neither 'no' nor 'yes' in advance.
- Pray God to help you discern his will for you *(see Saint 1.9)*. If it is an important decision you may ask for some time.
- If your answer is 'no', say it clearly without leaving any doubt *(Mt 5:37)*, but be gentle and kind.
- If possible, give reasons for your refusal, and suggest an alternative solution.
- Don't feel guilty: remember you said 'no' in order to continue to work on your big 'yes' to God.

Are you ready to say 'no' for his cause?

Saying 'no' to something in order to keep your 'yes' to God is very Christian, while it is also true that we would rather risk being taken advantage of than refuse help if we can give it.

SAINT **CHARLES** **LWANGA** AND 21 MARTYRS

📅 1860 – 1886   🌍 UGANDA   🕯 3 JUNE

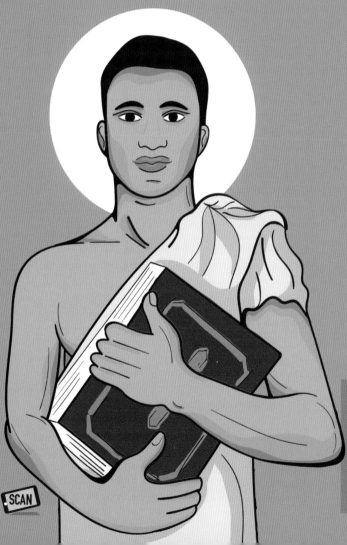

Q: WOULD IT NOT BE BETTER TO LEAVE PEOPLE WITH THE RELIGION THEY WERE BORN INTO?

WHAT ABOUT RELIGIOUS FREEDOM?

Charles Lwanga was the chief page at the court of King Mwanga II in Buganda, Uganda. Together with some other pages he had become a Christian, thanks to the preaching of the first Catholic missionaries. These 'Missionaries of Africa' had no power, apart from the message of the gospel. They suffered many hardships and illnesses while often being misunderstood. Eventually, some people recognised the importance of their message and — of their own free will — asked to be baptised. Probably because he did not wish to give up his lavish lifestyle, King Mwanga did not like Christianity and called it a foreign interference. The king was used to being obeyed blindly. He became extremely angry when some of his pages refused to participate in sexual acts with him because of their Christian conviction.

O God, Charles considered his life less important than living and proclaiming his faith. Help me to share my faith with others in a just way. Saint Charles and companions, pray for us!

SCAN

SIN OR DEATH

King Mwanga rounded up Charles and the other Christians in his court and gave them the terrible choice between renouncing their faith or being put to death. Although some of them were only recently baptised, they all chose death rather than deny their love for Jesus. In his rage, the king killed one of them on the spot and ordered the others to be executed at a traditional place of sacrifice, Namugongo. Witnesses told how the convicts sang and chatted on the long walk to Namugongo, and seemed almost proud to give their lives for God. They were forced to build a pyre and were burned alive, together with a group of Anglican Christians (see #TwGOD 2.39). The last words of Charles were: 'Katanda! – My God!' The love of these Christians for God was greater than anything else. No one could have forced them into making such a terrible sacrifice: they freely chose to die for Jesus rather than commit a sin.

RELIGIOUS FREEDOM

The argument of King Mwanga that Christianity would be linked to a foreign power has been used at various moments in history, just as other arguments have attempted to stop the preaching of missionaries. Arguments usually made by emperors, dictators and oligarchies who wished to maintain their own rule. They did so at the cost of religious freedom, which is one of the most fundamental freedoms, for it has such an impact on all other areas of life. Everyone should be free to choose and exercise their religion. It is very sad and greatly wrong that at certain times in history, people of the Church despised other religions, forced people to convert, and suppressed free will and free choice. Recent popes have strongly condemned such wrongdoings (see #TwGOD 2.13 & 2.31-2.32). And they have spoken up for religious freedom time and time again. 'The truth will set you free', said Jesus (Jn 8:32; see #TwGOD 1.8). He spoke of the truth of the gospel and wanted to let all the world know of God's love.

> ### PRIORITY OF TRUTH
>
> 'Saint Charles Lwanga and his companions are the special witnesses of [our] calling to share in the redemptive mystery of Christ's cross and resurrection. They stand for the essential priority of the truths and demands of the gospel, over all other interests, in determining Christian behaviour. The memory of the martyrs serves to assure us in every circumstance that 'the sufferings of the present time are not worth comparing with the glory that is to be revealed'. The Christian message…is a message of hope and courage…you are never alone as you face the trials and dangers of this earthly pilgrimage.'
>
> [Pope John Paul II, Address to Ugandan bishops, 20 June 1988]

ONE MESSAGE FOR ALL

Jesus ordered his disciples to preach the gospel to all people everywhere (Mk 16:15). He knew that only by embracing God's love could they find true happiness. The reason why we continue to preach the gospel in deed and in word is Jesus's commandment, and our conviction that life as a Christian is the best possible way of living. While respecting the freedom of every human being, Christians feel obliged to offer everyone the possibility of freely choosing to follow Jesus. For that reason, so many missionaries have gone around the world. Also today we need many missionaries to bring the gospel to everyone without force, but with great conviction! Do you wish to be one of them?

Jesus gave us the important mission to tell everyone about the love of God. While everyone should be left free to choose, we wish to share with all people the joy of being Christian.

KATHARINE DREXEL

 1858 –1955   USA   3 MARCH

LAURA OF ST CATHERINE

 1874 –1949   COLOMBIA   21 OCTOBER

JEAN DE BRÉBEUF

 1593 –1649   CANADA   19 OCTOBER

PETER CHANEL

 1803 –1841   FUTUNA   28 APRIL

1.16

Q: WHAT ARE SOME GREAT EXAMPLES OF MISSIONARIES PREACHING TO NATIVE PEOPLES?

Katharine came from Philadelphia, USA. Her father was a successful investment banker. When Katharine visited the West of the USA, she was profoundly touched by the living circumstances of the native Americans. Upon the death of their father, his three children inherited his millions. They visited Pope Leo XIII to ask for missionaries to run the missions they were supporting. Looking at Katharine, the pope suggested she could be a missionary herself. She almost ran away, but after discerning her vocation with her spiritual director *(see Saint 1.10)*, she joined the Sisters of Mercy. The remainder of her life was dedicated to the aid of native and African Americans. She used part of the family fortune to found a religious congregation, set up schools, and to start a university dedicated to these people. She died after a long life of service to God.

O God, your missionaries desired to share your love with the world. Help me to do the same. Saints Katharine Drexel, Laura of St Catherine, Jean de Brébeuf, and Peter Chanel, pray for us!

SCAN

LAURA OF ST CATHERINE OF SIENA

Laura was born in Jericó, Colombia. The death of her father left her family without resources. Laura was sent to an orphanage, and trained to be a teacher with the intention to support her mother financially. Gradually she grew in affection for Jesus and had a desire for the religious life. While she had a private longing for a contemplative religious life, she also wanted to spread the gospel to people in her country who had never heard of Jesus. She started to work with native Americans and promoted an equal treatment of all people in opposition of the racism she encountered around her. Together with some other women she started to live with native Americans in Dabeiba, where they began a new Congregation. She died after a decade-long illness.

JEAN DE BRÉBEUF

Jean was a French Jesuit who was sent to the missions in Quebec, Canada. He spent most of his missionary life with the Huron natives. After several unsuccessful attempts to reach out to them, he managed to learn their language. Gradually, his great passion for Jesus touched the heart of the Huron people. Several of them asked to be baptised. After some 15 years with the Huron, rival Iroquois natives attacked the Huron mission. They subjected Jean and some others to terrible ritual torture before killing them. He suffered silently and without complaint, while supporting his fellow prisoners. The Iroquois drank his blood in the hope of gaining his strength and mocked the baptism he preached by pouring boiling water over his head. This man of peace died because he wanted to share his love for Jesus with others.

PETER CHANEL

Peter was a Marist priest from France who was sent as a missionary to Western Oceania, where he arrived after a journey of almost a year. Peter was dropped on the island of Futuna with two companions. They were well received by King Niuliki and his people, who had recently banned cannibalism. The mission work asked for much patience, but started to advance when the missionaries had learned the local language. Gradually they managed to win the trust of the people. But the king feared losing his status and prerogatives. When his own son asked to be baptised, the king ordered Peter and his companions to be clubbed to death. Their blood proved to be fruitful, however, for within a few years the entire island was Catholic. Would you be willing to risk your life for such cause?

HUMAN PROMOTION AND LOVE

'I say this to you with regret: many grave sins were committed against the native peoples of America in the name of God... I humbly ask forgiveness... I also would like us to remember the thousands of priests and bishops who strongly opposed the logic of the sword with the power of the cross... I also ask everyone, believers and non-believers alike, to think of those many [missionaries] who preached and continue to preach the Good News of Jesus with courage and meekness, respectfully and pacifically...who left behind them impressive works of human promotion and of love, often standing alongside the native peoples or accompanying their popular movements even to the point of martyrdom.'

[Pope Francis, Address to indigenous leaders in Bolivia, 9 July 2015]

These missionaries truly gave themselves to bring the good news to people who had never heard of Jesus, risking hardships, rejection, and even their own lives for the gospel.

BLESSED
ANDREW OF PHÚ YÊN

📅 CA. 1625 – 1644   🌐 VIETNAM   🕯 26 JULY

BLESSED
ISIDORE BAKANJA

📅 CA. 1887 – 1909   🌐 CONGO   🕯 15 AUGUST

SCAN

Q: HOW CAN I BE A WITNESS TO MY FRIENDS AND STILL BE ACCEPTED?

DO I REALLY HAVE TO PREACH TO THEM?

Andrew was born in the Phú Yên province in Vietnam. He studied with Jesuit missionaries, and was baptised when he was around 16. Soon, he joined the catechist's association, and promised to spend his life spreading the gospel and helping priests in their mission. His love for God was great. In 1644 the local king ordered that Christianity be prevented from spreading further. Andrew was arrested and dragged before the authorities, who tried to make him give up his faith. Andrew said he would rather suffer than betray the love of Jesus. In prison he was serene and even joyous because of his suffering for the Lord. Those who visited him were fortified and helped by his faith. He asked them to pray that he would have the strength to be faithful to the end. Just before he was beheaded at the age of 19, he cried out the name of Jesus.

> O God, Andrew and Isidore were true to you. Help me to live as a Christian and demonstrate my love for you in everything I do and say. Blessed Andrew and Isidore, pray for us!

MISTREATED FOR PRAYING

Bakanja was born in Bokendela, Congo, when it was under Belgian control. He asked to be baptised when he was around 18 years old, thanks to the quiet work of Trappist missionaries, and received the baptismal name Isidore. He always carried his rosary with him, and often prayed. His fellow workers at a rubber company were intrigued and asked him to tell them about the gospel and teach them to pray. His Belgian superior did not like missionaries, for they preached that black and white people were equal. Isidore was told to stop praying and sharing the faith. He was severely beaten, and his legs were chained. A passing inspector was horrified at the sight of the mistreated man with his back torn apart by deep wounds covered with filth and flies. Isidore was taken in and cared for. He said that he had already forgiven his aggressor. He died after several months of agony as a result of his wounds, with his rosary in his hand, aged around 22.

WITNESS

Like Andrew and Isidore, every Christian is called to be a witness of the love of Jesus. This does not mean that we are all forced to face trial (see Saint 2.23). Being a witness may be simpler than it sounds: if you try to live as a Christian at every moment, you are already a powerful witness, probably without realising it. You can pray silently for your friends, that they will recognise how great life is with Jesus. So, there are many things you can do, even without opening your mouth. Preaching may not be the best way to convince them! There is nothing more irritating than a friend who is nagging. Your friends will already know what you want to say. It seems better to wait for a moment when they are ready to listen, for example when they ask you genuinely why you go to church or why you pray before meals.

RETURN LOVE FOR LOVE

"'Everyone who acknowledges me before others, I also will acknowledge before my Father in heaven" (Mt 10:32). Andrew of Phú Yên in Vietnam made these words of the Lord his own with heroic intensity. From the day he received baptism at the age of 16, he strove to develop a deep spiritual life. Amid the difficulties to which all who adhered to the Christian faith were subjected, he lived as a faithful witness to the risen Christ and tirelessly proclaimed the gospel... The words he repeated as he resolutely advanced on the path of martyrdom are the expression of what motivated his whole life: 'Let us return love for love to our God, let us return life for life.'

[Pope John Paul II, Homily at the beatification, 5 March 2000]

BE ACCEPTED

We all want to be accepted and all need good friendships. Thankfully, true friends will accept you just the way you are. If your faith is part of who you are, they will accept this — although they may have another conviction. This might be different in the case of less good friends or acquaintances. Also Jesus had the experience of friends leaving him because they could not accept his words (Jn 6:60-68). You may come to a point where you notice that you have grown too far apart. Do not worry about this: even if you were to lose all your friends, Jesus would still be with you. But as we said, true friends will not leave you that easily. Especially when you try to live in the love you receive from Jesus! Do you want to be a witness of that love?

Jesus needs you as his witness, first of all by living your life as a good Christian. Words may not even be necessary. True friends will accept you as you are, also with your faith.

SAINT
DOMINIC

📅 1170 – 1221

🌐 SPAIN, FRANCE 　🕯 8 AUGUST

.SCAN

Q: WHY WOULD I WANT TO SHARE MY FAITH?

WHAT IS THE DIFFERENCE BETWEEN APOLOGETICS AND POINTLESSLY ARGUING?

Dominic came from Caleruega, Spain. After many years of study, he was ordained a priest. On a journey with his bishop through the south of France, he encountered the Albigensians or Cathars. They proclaimed a distorted form of Christianity, saying among other things, that matter and the body is of evil origin. Suicide by starvation, for example, was not considered problematic (see Saint 2.33). Dominic saw the impotence of the Church to respond. The Catholic missionaries were not able to react with the truth of the gospel to the misled convictions of the Cathars. Together with some Cistercian monks he started patiently to explain the faith, while themselves living a convincing life as followers of Jesus in holiness, humility and simplicity. After ten years, he founded a house in Toulouse, which was the beginning of the Order of Preachers (OP) or Dominicans. Their ideal was to live very close to God through study and prayer, while preaching the word of God in a way that people could understand. Some Dominicans were severely misled themselves when they played an important role in the horrors of the inquisition (see #TwGOD 2.32). In spite of this dark period of the Order, also today Dominicans try to live in the spirit of Saint Dominic while sharing the love of Jesus with everyone who wants to listen.

FOR ALL CATHOLICS

Sharing the faith is not just for priests and nuns! *(see Saint 1.17)*. For starters, they are just a tiny percentage of the 1.2 billion Catholics in the world *(see Saint 1.48; #TwGOD 2.1)*. Also, they do not come to the places where many laypeople come. When was the last time you saw a priest in your office, classroom, or workspace? Just imagine if every Catholic in the world were to bring a non-Catholic friend to church next Sunday. And that ten percent of them remained interested in hearing more. That would mean 100 million people interested on one Sunday! Such results would be impossible to achieve for priests alone. However, sharing the faith is not about numbers, but about helping people to find happiness because they get to know the love of Jesus for themselves. If you know that love yourself, you will want to give everyone a chance to meet him!

APOLOGETICS

Faith involves the whole person. You may experience God's love in your heart, but to share your joy with others you will need to apply your intellect and reason too. Apologetics refers to the art of explaining the faith in a rational manner through systematic argumentation. It is based on the biblical invitation: 'Always be ready to give explanation *(apologia)* to anyone who asks you to account for the hope that is in you' *(1 Pet 3:15)*. The approach of *Tweeting with GOD* is an example of this. You may enjoy the argumentation, but be careful not to forget the aim, which is to explain the faith in a rational and understandable manner. When that aim is lost, you end up speaking just for argument's sake, and the discussion easily ends in pointlessly arguing.

> O God, Dominic saw that his words were only convincing when he lived accordingly. Help me to apply my faith in everything and share it wherever possible. Saint Dominic, pray for us!

> ## GOD-LIKE ZEAL
>
> 'His successor...gives a complete picture of saint Dominic in the text of a famous prayer: "Your strong love burned with heavenly fire and God-like zeal. With all the fervour of an impetuous heart and with an avowal of perfect poverty, you spent your whole self in the cause of the Apostolic life" and in preaching the gospel. It is precisely this fundamental trait of Dominic's witness that is emphasised: he always spoke with God and of God. Love for the Lord and for neighbour, the search for God's glory and the salvation of souls in the lives of Saints always go hand in hand.'
>
> [Pope Benedict XVI, General Audience, 3 February. 2010]

STEPS TO SHARING

Sharing the faith with others combines a lot of what can be learned from other saints:

- Pray daily and grow in your personal relationship with God *(see Saint 1.5)*.
- Be a good witness in your daily life, loving God and people *(see Saint 1.17)*.
- Learn more about the faith and the reasons why we believe *(see #TwGOD 1.7)*.
- Be ready to stand up for the faith when the occasion might arise *(see Saint 1.19)*.
- Share your faith, explaining the reasons. Be convincing but leave people totally free to accept God's salvation *(see Saint 1.15)*.

> The most important thing is to live your Christian life in a convincing way: pray, love and speak reasonably. Apologetics is a rational explanation without arguing pointlessly.

SAINT **JOSELITO SÁNCHEZ**

 1913 – 1928   MEXICO   10 FEBRUARY

SCAN

Q: HOW DO I STAND UP FOR MY FAITH WITH FRIENDS OR FAMILY? AT SCHOOL OR AT WORK?

Joselito was born in Sahuayo, Mexico. When he was 11 years old, the Mexican government initiated a strong persecution of Catholics. Churches, schools and convents were closed, while priests and religious were exiled or cruelly executed. When two years of peaceful opposition to the anticlerical measures did not produce any result, the Mexican people rose up violently against the government. The rebels called themselves Cristeros after Christ the King. They fought for their religious freedom. When his brothers joined the rebel forces in 1926, Joselito wanted to follow their example to defend Jesus and the Church, but he was considered too young. Joselito insisted, and finally was allowed to be the flag bearer of the standard of the Virgin Mary of Guadalupe *(see Saint 2.23).*

O God, Joselito was faithful to Jesus and his faith even in the face of death. Help me to find the courage to stand up for my faith also when confronted by others. Saint Joselito, pray for us!

FAITH AND FIDELITY

Young as he was, he encouraged his fellow rebels by his confidence in God and with his prayers. One day, when his general's horse was shot, Joselito gave him his own horse. On foot, the boy could not get away in time and was captured by government troops, who imprisoned him in his parish church. His capturers offered him freedom if he would renounce his faith, but Joselito cried out: 'Never, never! I would rather die! I do not want to join the enemies of Christ the King! Shoot me!' He was tortured to make him change his mind. They cut the soles of his feet and he was forced to painfully walk to the cemetery. He was violently chopped with a machete, but still he would not renounce his faith. Just before he died, he drew a cross in the dirt on the ground and kissed it.

STANDING UP

Joselito's example shows that embracing the love of God and standing up for your faith is a matter of life and death. Thankfully, most of us will not be tested in this extreme way. Still, standing up for your faith can be very difficult and scary. The following tips may be useful.

- Know why you stand there: if it is because of your personal relationship with God, he will surely assist you.

- Your words about the faith are only convincing if you always try to behave as a Christian (living in love, forgiving, sharing, while avoiding gossip, immorality, and discrimination...).

- Keep it personal: your testimony is not so much about knowledge, but about your relationship with Jesus: do not be afraid to say "I do not know."

- Be simple and humble in your opposition: remember that this is not about you but about God.

- Only God can convert hearts: there is no need for provocation and everyone has the free right to their religion or opinion.

THE WILL OF GOD

'My dear mother, I was taken prisoner in combat today. At present, I believe that I am going to die, but it does not matter, mother. Accept God's Will. Do not worry about my death, which is what mortifies me. Tell my brothers to follow the example left by their youngest brother. And you must do God's Will, have courage and send me your blessings together with my father's. Say hello to everybody on my behalf for the last time and receive the heart of your son who loves you so much and had wished to see you before dying.'

[Joselito, Letter to his mother, 6 February 1928]

JESUS ABOVE ALL

The most important question to answer if you wish to stand up for your faith is whether you are ready to place your love for Jesus above everything else. In other words, are you prepared to admit that you are Christian and obey God rather than people, as Peter said? (Acts 5:29). The same Peter had denied three times that he knew Jesus, but later thoroughly regretted his cowardice (Lk 22:54-62). This may console you when sometimes you do not have the courage to stand up. Also, it simply may not be the right moment. But you will be ready when the moment comes if you do like Joselito and stay always closely connected to the love of God in your heart. Are you ready to stand up for your faith?

> Be a convincing Christian throughout your life, keep it personal, without the need to have an answer to everything, be loving, simple, and humble, and above all trust in God!

BLESSED
LUIGI & MARIA
QUATTROCCHI-CORSINI

 1880-1951 (LUIGI), 1884-1965 (MARIA)

 ITALY   🕯 25 NOVEMBER

Q: HOW TO PASS ON MY FAITH TO MY (FUTURE) CHILDREN?

HOW CAN *GOD* BE PART OF MY PARENTHOOD?

Luigi and Maria were ordinary people at first glance. He came from Catania, Italy, and studied law in Rome. After some years at the Revenue Department, he worked on the board of various banks. Maria came from Florence, Italy, and was of noble birth. Contrary to Luigi, she was very pious. She served as a nurse in Ethiopia, and during the Second World War. In fact, both she and Luigi were very active during the war, helping refugees and sheltering Jews. The couple had four children, although Maria admitted in her letters that she dreaded every pregnancy. When she was pregnant with their fourth child, a serious condition prompted the doctor to propose an abortion, but both Maria and Luigi refused, for they did not want to intervene with the life God had given them *(see Saint 1.38)*. Thankfully, all went well.

O God, Maria and Luigi saw you as the foundation of their family life. Help me to be an example to my family too. Blessed Luigi and Maria Quattrocchi, pray for us!

SCAN

MARRIED WITH CHILDREN

Gradually, Luigi had warmed to the faith. As a family they began the day with Mass, prayed the rosary together, and tried to be charitable to everyone they could help. He and Maria were active in many ways, helping to found important Catholic organisations like the Italian scouts, Catholic Action, and an organisation arranging pilgrimages to Lourdes. Not only their children, but also many friends were impressed and inspired by their faith (see box). Their two sons became monks, while one of their daughters became a Benedictine nun. They were glad that their children found happiness by fulfilling their life's vocation. However, as parents it was hard to part from them: they experienced these vocations also as a painful loss. They died aged 71 and 81 after a life of ordinary sainthood, prompting us to realise that holiness is attainable for everyone who pursues their life's vocation with diligence and dedication to God and fellow human beings.

GODLY PARENTHOOD

Luigi and Maria showed how God can be part of your parenthood almost without effort when you try to grow in your personal faith first. The family is the most important environment for passing on the faith. Obviously, it is not necessary for all your children to enter religious life: that fully depends on their personal vocation. But in the case of Luigi and Maria, it is a sign of their successful education to faith. Obviously, in every household there must be rules, and sometimes you do things because you have to. But it is very unfortunate when children come to see faith solely as an obligation rather than an answer to the love of God for them. There is no set recipe for passing on the faith to your children, just as we are not to copy the saints but find our own vocation. Still, the following general points may help.

EXTRAORDINARY IN AN ORDINARY WAY

'Luigi and Maria kept the lamp of the faith burning...and passed it on to their four children... [They] also handed on the burning lamp to their friends, acquaintances, colleagues.... And now, from heaven, they are giving it to the whole Church... With full responsibility they assumed the task of collaborating with God in procreation, dedicating themselves generously to their children, to teach them, guide them and direct them to discovering his plan of love... Drawing on the word of God and the witness of the saints, the blessed couple lived an ordinary life in an extraordinary way. Among the joys and anxieties of a normal family, they knew how to live an extraordinarily rich spiritual life.' [Pope John Paul II, Homily at the beatification, 21 October 2001]

PASSING ON FAITH

- State the obvious: you can only pass on what is yours, so keep advancing in your personal bond with God and your knowledge. Also, spend time with your children.

- Make it visible without ostentation: above all, mean it when you pray. A crucifix, statue of a saint, rosary, holy water, palms, all are concrete signs that can help.

- Let faith be part of normal family life, not something separate or just obligation. Have a good laugh together, pray together, go to church, read the Bible and talk about it...

- Be honest, even about possible doubts, but do not dwell on them. Stick to the core message of God's love, which should be your guide rather than just duty or rules.

- Have faith. You don't need much knowledge but much passion. When you have done all you can to pass on the faith, relax, and leave the outcome in God's hands.

It all starts with your personal faith: above all it is your passion for Jesus in everything that makes you an inspiring parent for your children — not just your obedience to the rules.

VENERABLE
FULTON SHEEN

📅 1895 – 1979   🌍 USA   🕯️ [†9 DECEMBER]

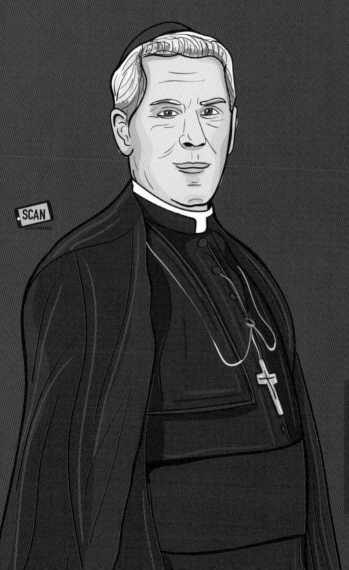

.SCAN

Q: IS THERE A CHRISTIAN WAY OF COMMUNICATING ONLINE? SHOULD WE BE INVOLVED IN SOCIAL MEDIA?

Fulton was born in El Paso, Illinois, USA. He trained for the priesthood in Minnesota, and as a young priest was sent to study canon law in Washington D.C., philosophy in Louvain, Belgium, and theology in Rome, Italy. He had an intimate relationship with God in his spiritual life, based on daily prayer in front of the tabernacle *(see #TwGOD 3.21)* and a search for living in holiness. He credited God for everything that was good in his life. He was a gifted speaker with a great sense of humour, who enjoyed especially laughing at himself *(see Saint 2.14)*. This made him a pleasant man to meet and listen to, even for those who might not agree with his message. Not long before his death, Pope John Paul II said to him: 'You have written and spoken well of the Lord Jesus. You have been a loyal son of the Church.'

O God, Bishop Fulton used every means to speak of your love to everyone. Help me to use social media well for the sake of myself and for others. Venerable Fulton Sheen, pray for us!

MEDIA EVANGELISER

Bishop Fulton was an evangeliser at heart and used every means of communication for explaining the faith. He was known for his expressive preaching, and wrote dozens of books on various topics. He gave Lenten reflections and began a weekly radio broadcast called *The Catholic Hour*, which became very popular and ran for several decades. He also broadcast Mass on the new medium of television. In 1951 he was ordained a bishop and began his first weekly television programme, in which he spoke to a live audience. He appeared in his full episcopal outfit, speaking without notes, sometimes using a chalkboard. Other popular TV programmes followed, reaching up to 30 million people at the peak of this ministry. In the 1970s he introduced a pre-podcast-like ministry by distributing his talks on cassette tape. He did not avoid political topics, speaking against Nazism, Communism, discrimination, and the Vietnam War, for example. Above all, he used every opportunity to speak of Jesus.

ONLINE COMMUNICATION

Online communication has the same basis as every form of communication. Fulton was known for the generous and authentic way in which he addressed people and communicated. He had an optimistic approach to life, and showed concern for the people he met. He also had a deep love for the Church and a great desire to lead people to the truth. He demonstrated important communication skills, that are also valid online: optimism, concern for your public, desire to present the truth, and above all authenticity, be yourself! Christian communication will never minimise or exclude people, but rather is it inclusive and radiates love — without having to be soft or romantic.

GET INVOLVED?

Bishop Fulton showed how we can embrace new means of communication as Christians. He used every form of communication that was available to him to reach out to people

---

AN INCOMPLETE HEART

'Look at your heart! It tells the story of why you were made. It is not perfect in shape and contour, like a Valentine Heart. There seems to be a small piece missing out of the side of every human heart... When God made your human heart, he found it so good and so lovable that he kept a small sample of it in heaven. He sent the rest of it into this world to enjoy his gifts, and to use them as stepping stones back to him... In order to love anyone with your whole heart, in order to be really peaceful, in order to be really wholehearted, you must go back again to God to recover the piece he has been keeping for you from all eternity.'

[Fulton Sheen, Remade for Happiness, Ch. 1, pp. 13-14]

and tell them about Jesus. He is not unique; Saints Paul, Francis Xavier and Francis de Sales did the same, for example *(see Saint 2.38, 1.29 & 1.10)*. And you can join them, especially using social media, for at least a third of the world population spends hours on social media every day, and many more are online almost continuously. They may not know it, but just as in the time of Bishop Fulton, people are craving for a positive message of salvation, full of hope and love, brought cheerfully and with a light touch by genuine and authentic witnesses. Jesus needs you to join in and help announce his gospel online and offline today *(see Saint 1.17)*. In what way can you contribute to that?

Also online we should behave as Christians. We need to use every means of communication to speak about God's truth, so also social media, in an authentic, positive, and loving way.

VENERABLE
CARLO ACUTIS

📅 1991 – 2006   🌐 ITALY   🕯 [†12 OCTOBER]

SCAN

Q: HOW DO YOU AVOID AN ADDICTION TO SOCIAL MEDIA?

I AM MORE OF A GEEK; CAN I SERVE GOD ON MY COMPUTER?

Carlo was a computer geek. He was born in London, England, and grew up in Milan, Italy. His great passion was computers, and he had a vast knowledge of programming. He created websites, designed leaflets and edited films or comics. He also found time to do volunteer charity work in an orphanage and with elderly people. He loved to joke and laugh, but also tried to treat everyone well. The most important thing for him was: 'To always be close to Jesus, that's my life plan.' From an early age, he had a great devotion to the Eucharist and tried to attend Mass every day, first surprising his parents, then taking them with him. He called the Eucharist 'my highway to heaven.' Before or after Mass he prayed in front of the tabernacle, where the sacrament of the Eucharist is preserved *(see box; Saint 2.13)*. He also had a great love for Mary, and often prayed the rosary. Probably this is why, in 2006, he was able to accept his diagnosis of acute leukemia with such faith and calmness. In his prayer, he offered his pain to God for Pope Benedict XVI and the Church. He died a few days later at the age of 15.

O God, Carlo loved your presence in the Eucharist above all else. Help me to discern carefully between what is urgent and what is important. Venerable Carlo Acutis, pray for us!

ADDICTION

There are various reasons why social media can be addictive, for example:

- You can feel obliged to interact because of real or presumed peer pressure.
- With so much going on online, it is easy to fear missing out on something.
- A 'like' can make you feel good, but the lack of it can make you uncertain.
- Seeing others on an outing without you can make you feel excluded.
- Comparing yourself to others can boost your self-esteem, but the contrary is also true.

Do you notice that most of these reasons are linked to your ego and your self-image? It is good to realise who and what you are in yourself, and in the eyes of God, before comparing yourself with others *(see Saint 2.28)*. Carlo said: 'All people are born as originals but many die as photocopies.' You are unique, so a comparison with other people only brings you part of the way. Be yourself! When you are happy with the way God created you, you will look at yourself, the world – and social media – in a different way. It is easy to spot what you could have had, but much more gratifying to look at all you are and have right now.

URGENT OR IMPORTANT?

Another point Carlo made is that we spend so much time on superfluous things, while often forgetting what is really important – your relationship with God, or visiting someone who is lonely, for example. Reacting on social media seems urgent, for your phone gives you notifications all the time. But is it really that important? Only you can answer that question. Considered calmly, you might have wanted to spend some of the time you used to check out new posts or interact online differently.

THE VALUE OF THE EUCHARIST

'I believe many people do not really understand the value of Holy Mass. Because if they were to realise the great treasure that the Lord gave us - offering himself as our food and drink in the Holy Eucharist - they would go to church every day to participate in the fruits of the Sacrifice which is being celebrated there. And they would renounce so many superfluous things!'

[Carlo Acutis, www.carloacutis.com]

NOT ONLY GEEKS

Carlo had a great desire to share his faith with others. For example, he built a website about Eucharistic miracles. He used his computer skills and experience with modern means of online communication to speak of the love of God online. You can do the same — in your very own way. Every Christian is called to help share the faith with others, wherever you are. When you spend a lot of time online, it is only logical to speak of the faith there too. You can like, share and retweet contributions by others, for example by Pope Francis or *Tweeting with GOD*. Or share an impressive quote by your favourite saint, like those in the app *Online with Saints*. Be inventive, for social media develops so quickly that your input is very much needed. What contribution can you give right now?

Be happy with who you are, without comparison with others, and choose consciously how you use your time. Your computer skills can be of great use for proclaiming the gospel online.

SAINT
CECILIA

 CA. 229   ITALY   22 NOVEMBER

Q: IS MODERN MUSIC EVIL?

IS THERE SUCH A THING AS TRULY CHRISTIAN MUSIC?

Cecilia was a young girl from Rome, born in a Christian family at a time that Christians were often persecuted (see #TwGOD 2.19). Historically, not much is known, but her legend is a very intense example of faith. Cecilia loved Jesus so much that she promised him to remain a virgin during all her life (see Saint 2.37). This was her way to keep her faith pure in the midst of the pagan culture of Rome. However, her parents married her off to a rich young man, Valerian, who was not a Christian. She was devastated: what was to come of her private vow to Jesus?

O God, Cecilia was able to find you in the beauty of music; help me to discern which music is helpful in my relationship with you and which is not. Saint Cecilia, pray for us!

SCAN

SHARING THE FAITH

Cecilia did not give in to her despair, but spoke intensely to her future husband of her love for Jesus. Eventually Valerian asked to be baptised. He and his brother Tiburtius became fervent Christians. He respected the virginity of his wife and even took upon himself the dangerous task of burying Christians who were executed because of their faith. Not much later, the two brothers were arrested and executed. Cecilia had to bury her own husband. She did not lose her strong faith, and instead spoke about Jesus to everyone she met, resulting in the conversion of hundreds of people. She turned grief for her husband into a powerful urge to evangelise and speak about Jesus (see #TwGOD 4.49-4.50). Eventually, she too was arrested and put to death as a martyr for the faith.

MUSIC

So, how can Cecilia help us to answer the question? An ancient tradition says that on her wedding day 'While the profane music of her wedding was heard, Cecilia was singing in her heart a hymn of love of Jesus, her true spouse.' This 'profane music' was the music of the ancient Romans, who were serving the Roman gods while fighting the Christians with force. The only music Cecilia wanted to make and listen to was music that would praise God, her only true love! Even today, that argument is the most important element in choosing what music is good for you. Cecilia's song is a good example of truly Christian music, as it praises God and speaks of Jesus's love. Also today we need really good musicians who make great Christian music.

TRUE BEAUTY

So, how you can discern the difference between bad and good music? We do not speak here of the lyrics alone (see Saint 1.24) or of the purely artistic quality. For starters, as long as it is true music, it can serve to praise God. The keyword for true music is beauty.

MUSIC, FAITH, LOVE

'Music...gives a voice to the testimony of faith in Christ... The words of faith need deep inner silence, to listen to and obey a voice that is beyond the visible and tangible... Faith follows this deep voice wherever art itself alone cannot arrive: it follows this voice on the path of the witness, of offering oneself out of love, as did Cecilia. Then the most beautiful work of art, the masterpiece of the human being, is his every act of authentic love, from the smallest in daily martyrdom to the extreme sacrifice. Here life itself becomes a hymn: an anticipation of the symphony we shall sing together in heaven.'

[Pope Benedict XVI, Address at a concert, 1 October 2010]

This means that in principle every style of music can be good. Obviously, certain styles of music are better suited than others, for example, for the liturgy or quiet prayer. An important point is the effect the music has on you, for music can be something very powerful. You'll need to make conscious choices here too. A good question to ask is: 'What does this music do: does it bring me closer to God, or does it, for example, arouse me physically or give me strange thoughts?' So, there is no reason that music would be devilish or unworthy simply because it is modern. Neither modern nor ancient music are automatically bad, but discernment is necessary. Christian words, music, or melodies help you grow in your relationship with God. What is truly Christian music for you?

Truly Christian music praises God in word and melody. In principle, this is independent of the style of music. The most important thing is whether this music brings you closer to God or not.

SAINT **DAVID** THE KING

📅 CA. 1000 BC 🌍 HOLY LAND

🕯 29 DECEMBER; SUNDAY BETWEEN 26-31 DECEMBER (EAST)

SCAN

Q: WHY IS CHURCH MUSIC SO BORING?

WHAT MAKES LYRICS SUITABLE FOR CHRISTIANS?

David was a simple shepherd boy in the Holy Land. The Bible records that 'he was ruddy, had beautiful eyes, and was handsome' (1 Sam 16:12). All his life, he loved music and dancing. He was even famous for it (Am 6:5). David composed and wrote numerous lyrics, many of which still survive today (2 Sam 1:19-27; 22:2-51). In fact, many of the 150 Psalms in the Bible are attributed to him (see #TwGOD 1.15 & 3.13). Just like today, music played an important role in the life of people in David's time. It was used to worship God, but also in places of ill repute like pubs and brothels. Nothing new there.

O God, David found you in music. May I be able to make conscious and conscientious choices in my life, choosing you over everything else, also in music. Saint David, pray for us!

SINNER

David is not a typical saint: he was chosen by God to become a king of his people but did a lot of wrong as well. He cheated on his family, had sex with Bathsheba, the wife of his army chief, and then tricked him into death trying to cover up his sin (2 Sam 2). When David realised what he had done he felt extremely bad and wrote a song about it (see box). But in spite of all this, he also was a great lover of God. At one point he leaped and danced before the ark, the sign of God's presence on earth (2 Sam 6:16). He sang and danced with all his body at the very lively and rousing music (see Saint 1.27). Being such a great artist, David must have written songs for many occasions, not only for the worship of God, but also when enjoying the pleasures of wine, good food, and female company. It is interesting that none of the latter songs have survived; only his worship songs did. So, should we listen only to psalms and Gregorian Latin chant? Obviously not. There are many forms of music that are pleasing to God's ear (see Saint 1.23).

SAINTS AND SINNERS

Have you ever been to a church event and sat through it, cringing because the music was so awful? Also in worship music there is good and bad, and very bad! The same applies to the lyrics. It does not mean that as long as they are about Jesus it is automatically good music! Good lyrics are not necessarily about God. In fact, the psalms speak of every human experience and emotion, for example in the long Psalm 118 (119). And that is the Bible, the very Word of God! The American artist Matt Maher has sung about sinners and saints: that seems to sum up the possible content of lyrics. Like in the psalms, in modern lyrics every human emotion and experience can be helpful in finding God.

VALUES

The answer to the question of what makes for good and suitable lyrics is more about values than about words. Psychologists agree that positive music can help you feel better, while violent or dark

---

A SONG WRITTEN IN GUILT

'Have mercy on me, O God,
according to your steadfast love...
Wash me thoroughly from my iniquity,
and cleanse me from my sin.
For I know my transgressions,
and my sin is ever before me.
Against you, you alone, have I sinned,
and done what is evil in your sight...
Indeed, I was born guilty,
a sinner when my mother conceived me...
Create in me a clean heart, O God,
and put a new and right spirit within me...
O Lord, open my lips,
and my mouth will declare your praise.' [Psalm 50 (51)]

---

lyrics and melody can increase negative emotions and thoughts, leading to aggression or depression. So, the question is important if you wish to live conscientiously and choose what you listen to. The keywords here are vices and values (see #TwGOD 4.10). Vices: Do these lyrics draw me into myself, making me exclude others? Does this raise negative or violent thoughts? Does this draw me away from God? Values: Does the text help me in my life? Does it uplift me? Does it open me towards others? Does it support me in my faith? On the basis of these questions, you can discern what is good for you and what not. Ultimately, the question is what helps you and others in your relationship with God. What music will you choose?

It takes effort and skill to compose good music and write lyrics. All music and lyrics that bring you closer to God — even without mentioning him — help you as a Christian.

SAINT
NICHOLAS OWEN

 CA. 1562 – 1606   ENGLAND   22 MARCH

SCAN

Q: CAN I BE A FAITHFUL CATHOLIC AND LOVE VIDEO-GAMING?

Nicholas often went about unnoticed because of his very small stature. He lived in Oxford, England, at a time of great persecution of Catholics, and among other things, was the servant of the later martyr and priest, Edmund Campion. Nicholas was a carpenter and builder during the day, and constructed 'priest holes' during the night. He helped many a priest to find safety from persecution in ingenuously constructed hiding places in staircases, cupboards, and libraries, for example. He used aliases like 'Little John', and 'Little Michael' to hide himself from his persecutors. One day he even helped two Jesuit priests to escape from the Tower of London. You may see why he is the patron saint of escape artists like Houdini!

O God, Nicholas was always connected to the real world. Help me to discern between good and bad ways to relax, and always remain connected to you. Saint Nicholas Owen, pray for us!

RELAX

Gaming can be a great way to relax. You escape temporarily from the real world and immerse yourself in another, virtual life as it were. Some people do this by reading books, others by watching films, and again others find this relaxation in gaming. This can be fun, precisely because your virtual self can do things you could not or would not do in 'real life'. Everyone can be a hero — temporarily. Still, you do not simply read, watch or play everything: you make conscious choices about what you like and what is appropriate. It is important to realise the impact of the game on you. Some games have an inappropriate content, or your character has to do really violent, gross or immoral actions. Then it is no longer fun and relaxing in a proper way. To quote saint Paul: 'Keep your minds on whatever is true, noble, right, pure, holy, friendly, and proper' *(Phil 4:8)*.

SPIRITUAL CAST OF MIND

'The unity existing between [Nicholas Owen and the other martyrs] depends from the deeply spiritual cast of mind which they had in common. In so many other respects they were completely different - as different as any large group usually is: in age and sex, in culture and education, in social status and occupation, in character and temperament, in their qualities, natural and supernatural, in the external circumstances of their lives. So we find among these 40 Holy Martyrs priests, secular and regular, religious of different orders and grades; and we have, amongst the laity, men of the highest nobility, and people who rank as ordinary, married women and mothers of families. What unites them all is that interior quality of unshakable loyalty to the vocation given them by God - the sacrifice of their lives as a loving response to that call.'

[Pope Paul VI, Homily at the canonisation, 25 October 1970]

REALITY

While it can be very healthy to forget reality temporarily, the danger exists that the world you escape into becomes more important than the real one. Nicholas helped others to escape, not into a virtual world, but into safety. Although his history reads like a novel, his end was very real and cruel. After a number of narrow escapes, he was arrested and imprisoned in the Tower of London. He was tortured in order to find out the names and hiding places of the many priests he had helped, but he died on the torturing rack without revealing anything. He was canonised as one of the forty martyrs of England and Wales.

CAUTION

There are various potential problems connected to gaming. Gaming can be very addictive, often without you noticing immediately, and you can spend far too much time on it. A further problem is that the world of the game can become a hiding place from the 'real world'. Life as a hero with great skills in the game can feel so much better than life in this world where it is easy to feel you are a loser. And then there is the temptation to join in a new rage, even though the game is really too violent or immoral for a Christian to play. If you are aware of these potential problems and overcome them by making adult choices, you can be a good Catholic and love gaming too. Avoid any form of misbehaviour, and instead behave in the game with the same patience, attention and love you would apply in the real world. Would you like gaming in this way?

Gaming can be a fine way to relax. Some games are less appropriate for Catholics who always search for what is true, noble, right, pure, holy, friendly, and proper.

SAINT **NORBERT** OF XANTEN

📅 CA. 1080 – 1134   🕯 6 JUNE

🌍 GERMANY, FRANCE, BELGIUM, NETHERLANDS

.SCAN

Q: IS THERE SOMETHING BAD ABOUT HORROR MOVIES OR BOOKS ON MAGIC AND TELEPATHY?

Norbert grew up in a noble family in Xanten, Germany. He was ordained a lower cleric to sing daily prayers in Xanten's parish church, but he engaged someone to take his place and sit in choir for him for a nominal fee. Meanwhile, he accepted a position as almoner of the emperor in Cologne, where his task was to organise aid to the poor. Thus he got double pay for a minimum amount of work. Norbert was happy to remain a lower cleric with more freedom to do as he pleased, for his interest was not in piety, nor in a Church career. Rather, he used his generous income to live a life of pleasure, parties, and luxury. Only God's grace through a life-changing event made Norbert realise that he had lived outside reality, and that he needed to change his ways *(see box)*.

O God, Norbert discovered that reality with you is much better than living a dream. Help me to discern what is good and helps me in my relationship with you. Saint Norbert, pray for us!

TWO WORLDS

Norbert escaped from the real world into a life of entertainment and pleasure. Most of us need to escape reality now and then. Some do this through long nature walks, dinner with friends, a visit to an abbey, by reading novels or watching films. Norbert's problem was that he believed his world of entertainment to be the real world, and it took a lightning bolt to bring him to his senses (see box). As with gaming, films and novels help you immerse yourself temporarily in another, virtual world (see Saint 1.25). The important thing is to know your measure, and retain the difference between the world of fantasy and the real world in which we live with God and our fellow people.

STORYTELLERS

Jesus himself was a storyteller who used many parables to explain how God is with us in various ways. Over the ages, many great books and films have been created by people of very different background. Also Catholic minds dedicated themselves to literature, with authors like Jules Verne, JRR Tolkien and CS Lewis. Among great Catholic directors are Alfred Hitchcock, Krzysztof Kieślowski, and Martin Scorsese. Scary stories are considered entertainment precisely because they are not real, and can be enjoyed in physical safety. No need to say that killing, bloodthirstiness, and fear are the opposite of Christian values. Similarly, in real life, sorcery, magic and paranormal appearances are bad for us, and they can weaken our relationship with God — even without us noticing (see #TwGOD 4.18; Deut 18,10-11).

CHOOSE

Films and books are fiction, and for entertainment other rules can apply. Tolkien and Lewis, for example, wrote stories in which magic plays an important part. The films of Hitchcock can be scary, and blood flows. Still, their works are examples of good and constructive entertainment. This does not mean that every film or book with horror or witchcraft is good for you.

STRUCK BY LIGHTNING

One day, on his way to a party in another city, Norbert was overtaken by a thunderstorm. A flash of lightning split the ground just in front of his horse, and he was thrown off violently. As he regained consciousness, he realised how close to death he had been. Reconsidering his life and what he had achieved, he realised that he was not truly happy. After a time of prayer and penance, he discerned that his vocation was to become a priest. His turnaround was complete and he had found inner peace. His former friends called him a hypocrite, for now Father Norbert was denouncing their life style which he had enjoyed before. He gave away his possessions, and asked the pope permission to become an itinerant preacher in the area around today's Belgium. Soon he founded the Premonstratensians or Norbertines, at the request of the pope.

[cf. Life of Saint Norbert, 12th c. - summarised by the author]

Discernment is needed. For example, the courage, friendship and sacrifice of Harry Potter are great examples, while, for example, his unnecessary lying is less so. Does this make these books and films unsuitable? The key question for your discernment is whether you can distinguish clearly between fantasy and reality, evil and good, wrong and right. The bottom line is that your entertainment should not lead you away from God, make you hesitant about your faith, or change your relation to other people. What is good entertainment for you?

Entertainment can be very good, as long as you maintain a clear distinction between reality and fantasy: nothing should take you away from your relationship with God.

SAINT
VITUS

📅 CA. 290 – CA. 304 🌍 ITALY

🕯 15 JUNE; 16 MAY (EAST)

SCAN

Q: IS DANCING APPROPRIATE FOR CHRISTIANS?

Vitus was a teenager in southern Italy, who died because of his faith. It was only in the middle ages that he became really famous as a saint. Many fabulous stories are told about him, so that it is not easy to distinguish fact from fiction. It is said he was a Christian against the will of his father. He had learned the faith from his nurse Crescentia and his father's servant Modestus. Ironically, although he is the patron saint of dancers, Vitus refused to dance when his father brought in attractive girls and beautiful music. Some accounts tell how he danced with angels to honour God *(see box)*.

DANCING PROCESSION

Especially in northern Europe, it became popular to celebrate the feast of Vitus by dancing in front of his statue. Probably it was a Christianisation of an old Germanic elven dance. The term 'Saint Vitus's dance' was used to indicate a muscular illness (chorea). Especially underfed people were struck by this disease and could not stop moving because of muscular convulsions.

O God, Vitus was steadfast in his faith. Help me to praise you also through my body, so that my dancing may be passionate and modest at the same time. Saint Vitus, pray for us!

The origin of Saint Vitus's procession may well have been a collective prayer to ask God to be freed from muscular disease. Also other saints are honoured through religious processions with dancing. Have you ever visited the dancing procession in honour of Saint Willibrord in Echternach, Luxembourg, on Whit Tuesday, two days after Pentecost?

DANCING IN THE BIBLE

The Bible generally speaks positively about dancing. There are various occasions where people dance for God *(see Saint 1.24)*. The great and wise Solomon said that there is a time for everything, also for dancing *(Eccl 3:4)*. Jesus spoke of festive dancing when the prodigal son returned home, an image of the joy and celebration in heaven for someone who turns away from sin *(Lk 15:25)*. So, dancing can be very Christian! At the same time it is good to realise that the aim of Christian life is dedication in love and purity to God, and service to your neighbour. Saint Peter warned against 'living in licentiousness, passions, lust, drunkenness, orgies, carousing, and lawless idolatry' *(1 Pet 4:3)*. When one or more of these elements are connected with dancing, it is no longer Christian to join in. You are called to keep your dancing chaste and beautiful, and beware of immoral dancing.

DANCING SAINTS

When you are dancing as a Christian, you are in the good company of the saints. Possibly you can imagine the 'people's fool' Saint Francis dancing *(see Saint 1.35)*, but did you know that also the serious Saint Teresa of Avila jumped on a table and danced for her sisters in the monastery while clicking a pair of castanets? She allegedly said: 'When you dance, dance, when you pray, pray' *(see Saint 2.4)*. And the dignified Saint Ignatius once danced a Basque dance on the roof terrace to cheer up a depressed brother from Flanders *(see Saint 1.34)*. So, the message of the saints is that there is no objection at all against chaste and joyful dancing. Do you like to dance in this way?

Dancing is a great way to express your joy. As long as it is chaste it can greatly enhance the celebration of life and of God

BLESSED
MARIJE TUCI

 1928 – 1950   ALBANIA    5 NOVEMBER

BLESSED JERZY
POPIEŁUSZKO

 1947 – 1984   POLAND   19 OCTOBER

Q: IF WE CANNOT LIVE IN PEACE AMONG RELIGIONS, ISN'T IT BETTER TO HAVE NO RELIGION AT ALL?

Marije was born into a farming family in Ndërfushaz, Albania. She felt called to join the Franciscan sisters who ran her school, but in 1946 the Communist regime suppressed all religious activity and the convent was closed. The church became a government courthouse. Over the years, the regime would impose increasingly severe measures in order to promote a fully atheistic state. Marije became a teacher. In 1949 she was arrested, probably because she spoke of the faith at school. She was treated most barbarously, and tortured in terrible and humiliating ways that left her totally disfigured. But she remained faithful to Jesus, and did not renounce her faith. In the end, she was brought to hospital, where she died at the age of 22. She was beatified in 2016 together with 37 other blessed martyrs of Albania.

O God, Marije and Jerzy suffered great injustice. Help me to bring peace wherever I can, while being truthful to you and myself. Blessed Marije Tuci and Jerzy Popiełuszko, pray for us!

.SCAN

SILENCED BY FORCE

Jerzy was a charismatic young priest from Okopy, Poland. He was born when his country was under communist occupation. During his seminary training he was forced to join the army, in the hope that he would lose his vocation. This only made him more determined. As a priest, he warned his parishioners against the dangers of communism. His homilies were often transmitted via radio, and many people were strengthened in their faith and hope. He was considered a danger to communism because of his peaceful opposition. Jerzy escaped several of the government's attempts to silence him by threats and by force. One day, his car was stopped by three security police officers. He was violently beaten and locked in the trunk of their car, after which they threw him in a reservoir with a heavy stone attached to his feet. News of the murder enraged many people, and his funeral was attended by hundreds of thousands of people. Five years later his country was freed from communism (see Saint 1.9).

NO RELIGION, NO WAR?

Superficially considered, it might seem that the world would be more peaceful without religion, given that over the centuries people have caused much suffering in the name of religion. Note, however, that the motive for war usually is not purely religious, as also political, economic and selfish arguments are involved. To fight a war in the name of your religion may sound better than when you do so to become more rich or powerful. True religion is founded on God, who is kind, loving, and caring. The horrors of war greatly sadden and hurt him. Any religion which says the contrary is distorting the truth about God (see #TwGOD 1.8). Even though the Old Testament may seem to promote violence, Jesus's message is one of love and peace only (see Saint 2.22).

ATHEISM

Communism was built on the ideas of Karl Marx, who called religion 'opium of the people'. He considered religion to be a kind of

---

THE TRUTH WILL SET YOU FREE

'Truth never changes. It cannot be destroyed by any decision or legal act... A man who tells the Truth is a free man despite external slavery, imprisonment or custody... Overcoming fear is a key element in the process of setting people free. Fear springs from threat. We fear suffering; we fear the loss of some goods, the loss of freedom, health or job. This fear makes us act against our conscience and it is by means of conscience that we measure Truth. We overcome fear the moment we agree to lose something for the sake of higher values. If Truth becomes a value worth suffering for, worth taking a risk, then we will overcome fear that keeps us in slavery.'

[Jerzy Popiełuszko, Homily on freedom, 31 October 1982]

---

drug by which the ruling classes kept the working classes sedated. Communism promotes atheism as the solution for equality of all. The horrors experienced by Marije and Jerzy are just an example of the many people who suffered and died, simply because they believed in a higher power than that of communism. Obviously, most atheists, like most believers, are living a life of peace. The terrible excesses of communism show that peace cannot be found by imposing atheism. Nor can it be found by imposing religion. One of our most important and inviolable freedoms is religious freedom (see Saint 1.15). Instead of fighting religion, we should fight for freedom and against every form of discrimination, injustice and violence. Do you want to join this fight?

> Both believers and atheists waged wars. No religion should preach violence, for God is love. Purging the world of religion would mean going against the truth that God wants to bring.

SAINT
FRANCIS XAVIER

📅 1506 – 1552   🕯 3 DECEMBER

🌍 SPAIN, INDIA, MADRAS (CHENNAI), JAPAN, CHINA

.SCAN

Q: CAN CHRISTIANS DO YOGA OR ZEN MEDITATION?

Francis was born in Xavier Castle in Navarra, Spain, and had very good prospects for his life. When he studied in Paris, he met Ignatius of Loyola *(see Saint 1.34)*. After much persuasion, Francis joined him as one of the first Jesuits. He became a very powerful missionary with one great desire: he wanted to tell everyone how much happiness they could find when they opened themselves to God in their lives and in their prayer *(see box)*. In this sense he is very much like the Apostle Paul *(see Saint 2.38)*.

MISSIONARY

Francis first went to Goa in India. With the help of interpreters he spoke to poor fishermen. Tirelessly, he went from village to village to explain the faith, using a small catechism in the Tamil language. Within a few years, thousands of people asked to be baptised. He deemed it important to ensure the continued pastoral care of these communities and encouraged the education of native clergy. Francis's only desire was to help people find the way to Jesus in their lives. With that in mind he continued to travel.

O God, I thank you for Francis's dedication to you. Help me to follow his example and speak with love and conviction about Jesus everywhere I go. Saint Francis Xavier, pray for us!

At one point he visited the tomb of the Apostle Thomas in Madras (Chennai). In Malacca he met a Japanese man who told him about the culture and beliefs in his home country. Francis wanted very much to go to Japan, to offer everyone the possibility to accept the Christian faith and be baptised. He managed to go to Japan, and even met the emperor. The great missionary finally died when he was on his way to China.

YOGA AND ZEN

On his travels, Francis encountered many different religions, in particular Hinduism and Buddhism. The word yoga is used for various Hindu schools of spiritual and ascetic discipline, supported by physical exercises. Hinduism, with its many gods and spiritual customs, is very different from the unique Christian God of love, who wishes to share our lives. Obviously, as Catholics we cannot pray to the many Hindu gods. In Japan, Francis encountered zen, which refers to various Japanese schools of Buddhism. While for Christians the individual is important because each of us is created by God himself, in zen the aim is to go beyond the individual existence towards a growing awareness. A second element is the search for enlightenment or awakening: one can wake up to see what life is really about. The greatest difference with Catholicism is that zen focuses on the self rather than on God. Catholics search to be ever more open to God's presence in their lives. Only then can they realise themselves fully.

EXERCISE ONLY

So, in many ways, yoga and zen are incompatible with the Catholic faith. Although Francis was convinced that missionaries must adapt to local customs and language, he was critical of other religions. He feared that Christians might lose their faith, and with it, their soul and future with God. Some claim that it is possible to separate Hindu or Buddhist spirituality from the physical exercises. If that separation is truly possible, some of these exercises can be used for the physical well-being of a person. In fact, breath

I WANT TO CRY OUT LIKE A MADMAN

'In these parts many people do not become Christian because…there is no one to tell them about Christ… I would want to cry out like a madman to…those students in Europe… They should not only study science and gain knowledge, but keep in mind with what intention God has given them their talents. Then they would surely dedicate more attention to their prayer life. They would get to know God more closely and give him a place in their lives. They would learn to listen to what God wants to say to them. They would be able to renounce their personal ambitions and desires, and choose only to live according to God's desire and choice for them. Then they would exclaim from the bottom of their hearts: "Lord, here I am. Tell me what you want me to do. Send me everywhere you want me to go, even to India."'

[Francis Xavier, Letter XIV, 1543]

control, mental focus, and bodily postures are widely practised for health and relaxation, and are also known in Catholic spirituality (see Saint 2.5). When this helps people in their Christian prayer, that is great! It is important, however, to avoid any mix of religions. Saint Francis would insist that Jesus Christ is the only sure path towards God. How can you best find him?

Yoga and zen are rooted in religions that do not know Jesus. As he is the only centre of our lives, we should ensure that our physical and spiritual exercises bring us closer to him.

VENERABLE
MATT TALBOT

📅 1856 – 1925   🌍 IRELAND   🕯 [†7 JUNE]

1.30

SCAN

Q: CAN FAITH HELP TO OVERCOME AN ADDICTION LIKE ALCOHOL, SMOKING, OR DRUGS?

Matt's father and brothers were drunks. At the age of 12 he started working for a wine merchant in Dublin, Ireland, and sometimes secretly sampled the merchandise. Soon he too was hopelessly addicted to alcohol. He later worked in the whisky stores at the docks. The work was hard and life in poverty was difficult. With his brothers and friends he sought temporary refuge in drinking. This is how he built up a debt, so that he had to pawn his clothes and borrow money. He even stole a fiddle from a blind beggar to buy alcohol. One day, when he was 28 years old, penniless and out of credit everywhere, he was waiting in front of the pub. He hoped that one of his friends would buy him a drink, but they passed him by one by one. Standing there, Matt began to realise how empty his life was, and how false the happiness he found in drink. Suddenly he despised himself.

O God, Matt overcame his addiction with your help. Help me believe that when you are with me, I can do the impossible, sustained by the Holy Spirit. Venerable Matt Talbot, pray for us!

GOD'S GRACE

Everyone thought he was a lost cause, but the grace of God was greater. As he came home, he announced to his mother that he would pledge not to drink for three months. His mother warned him not to take such a pledge without being very serious about it. But he was. After having realised the misery of his life, and having felt so much disgust for himself, he rediscovered his faith and the love of God. He confessed his sins, prayed, went to Mass daily and started reading about his faith. He repaid his debts and had Mass celebrated for the blind beggar whose fiddle he had stolen. After three months without a drop, he took a pledge for six months and eventually for life. The first years were especially very difficult, but he kept his promise. Matt had to take one day at a time, but with divine grace he overcame his addiction. So can you if you are in a similar situation!

ALCOHOL, SMOKING, AND DRUGS

Having a drink together can be very social and enjoyable. Jesus too had a cup of wine in good company from time to time. This is different from taking drugs, as drugs — even soft drugs — make us withdraw within ourselves, rather than being sociable, and destroy the body (see #TwGOD 4.46; see box). Smokers standing outside often have a pleasant chat, but they separate themselves from the others, and the addictive tobacco is very bad for your health. Smoking, drugs and too much alcohol are very harmful for your health and for your body, which God has entrusted into your care. When you are not addicted, give praise to God, and stay away from temptation. But when you are addicted, do not despair! Matt's experience shows that God can help you do the impossible (Mt 19:26).

FREE FROM ADDICTION

'Never be too hard on the man who can't give up drink,' Matt once said. 'It's as hard to give up the drink as it is to raise the dead to life again. But both are possible and even easy for

---

NEW FORM OF SLAVERY

'Drugs have inflicted a deep wound on our society and ensnared many people in their web... This is undoubtedly a "new form of slavery" alongside several others that afflict individuals and society in general today... It should come as no surprise that so many people fall into drug addiction because worldliness offers us a wide range of opportunities to enjoy passing pleasures, which in the end are nothing but poisons that corrode, corrupt and kill. Step-by-step, a person begins to destroy himself and to destroy everything around him... Even though drug prevention is a priority, it is also fundamental that we work for a full and certain rehabilitation of drug victims in our society; to give joy back to them so that they can regain the dignity that one day they lost.'

[Pope Francis, To the Pontifical Academy of Sciences, 24 November 2016]

---

our Lord. We have only to depend on him.' These words may encourage everyone who is struggling to break free from an addiction. God is on your side! Your spiritual director can be of great help (see Saint 1.10). You may pass through the same steps as Matt, recognising your misery, despising yourself, and especially embracing God's grace. Even if you fall, like Jesus under the cross, do like him and get up. Step-by-step you can grow in strength and your conviction to stay away from alcohol, smoking, or drugs. God is with you! Do you want to believe in his strength?

Addiction is often the result of false promises and hopes. When we place all our hope in Jesus, and try to be consistent in our relation with him, step-by-step we can find a way out.

SAINTS
PERPETUA & FELICITY

 CA. 203   TUNISIA

🕯 7 MARCH; 1 FEBRUARY (EAST)

Q: IS THERE A CATHOLIC WAY OF DRESSING?

WHAT ABOUT FASHION?

Perpetua was 22 years old when she was arrested in Carthage for the sole reason of being a Christian. She was married and had a small child. Felicity was pregnant when she was arrested, and gave birth in prison just before being put to death together with other Christians. The two women stood very firmly in their faith, knowing that losing their lives for God would mean being with him forever in heaven. They spoke of the day of their martyrdom as the day of their victory (see box). When that day came, the women were told to dress like pagan priestesses, but they refused valiantly. Even to save their own lives they did not want to offend God by dressing improperly. The two women were stripped naked, but the crowds were shocked to see them so vulnerable, and insisted that they be dressed before being thrown to the wild animals. After being tossed by a mad heifer, Perpetua was in pain, but the first thing she did was to arrange her tunic over her thighs and re-pin her hair for the glory of God. The two girls died with great love for God.

O God, Perpetua and Felicity were modest to the end. Help me to dress with a good balance between modesty and Christian pride. Saints Perpetua and Felicity, pray for us!

SCAN

APPEARANCES MATTER

The experience of these two young women shows that clothing and appearance are important — as a sign of more essential things. You may wonder how one can think about such matters when faced with death. At the same time, you too will probably think frequently about what you look like and how you appear in the eyes of others. The crowds understood this perfectly when they asked that the girls be dressed. Clothing is important for our dignity and helps us express our personality. There is no need to be ashamed of your body: you are created by God, right? To show your beauty at its best is giving glory to God for having created you! Look at Perpetua: in the face of death she re-pinned her hair, in order to face her fate gracefully, in full knowledge of her beauty. This is a good example of correct and right Christian pride.

SEXY OR BEAUTIFUL

Often, we confuse sexy and beautiful. Obviously, it depends how you use these words. "Sexy" is often related to a desire for sex, which is good and proper in the right context, but not always and everywhere *(see Saint 2.40)*. When you get dressed and do your hair, do you do this to radiate the beauty God has given you, and thus to give glory to him like Perpetua? Or do you have more personal reasons? Showing too much of your body may give the impression that you are simply looking for a partner in sex. Also, it may distract people from your real beauty, which goes far beyond your looks and includes your entire being. Modesty in the right sense of the word can help.

MODESTY AND FASHION

Apart from protecting us against the weather, clothes are a way of disclosing only certain parts of our body. Which parts depends on culture and era. Perpetua covered her thighs, 'out of modesty' *(see box)*. Today in many cultures, showing your thighs is not considered immodest. Still, beauty is not

---

> ## LOVE ONE ANOTHER
>
> *'The day of their victory dawned, and they marched from the prison to the amphitheatre joyfully as though they were going to heaven, with calm faces, trembling, if at all, with joy rather than fear. Perpetua went along with shining countenance and calm step, as the beloved of God, as a wife of Christ, putting down everyone's stare by her own intense gaze. With them also was Felicity... Then Perpetua called for her brother and spoke to him together with the catechumens and said: "You must all stand fast in the faith and love one another, and do not be weakened by what we have gone through."'*
>
> [Acts of the Christian Martyrs, Oxford 1972]

---

simply in nakedness. Someone who dresses modestly can still look very beautiful. Modesty is not old-fashioned, but a way to show yourself to the best advantage. It is important when looking for a Christian way to dress. Fashion can help, but not at all costs: here too we need to discern between spending on ourselves or helping others. Perpetua cared for her appearance, for she wanted to give glory to God. How can you do the same in your life?

> *Your body and your beauty are gifts of God. Modesty is a keyword when searching for the best way to show your body in a Christian manner. This also applies to fashion.*

SAINT **TERESA DE LOS ANDES**

 1900 – 1920   CHILE   12 APRIL

.SCAN

Q: HOW SHOULD I DRESS FOR CHURCH?

Juanita was a girl like many others, and came from a farming family in Santiago, Chile. She had many friends, laughed a lot, and loved various sports like horse riding, swimming, and tennis. Juanita also had a great interest in music and dancing. She could play the guitar, piano and harmonium. At times she could be stubborn and vain, and sometimes she was very temperamental and fought with her sister. On Sundays, Juanita would dress up with her five siblings to go to church. This was not just a custom, it was part of the reverence she wanted to show God. She loved him above everything and everyone else.

PROMISE TO GOD

When she was 14 years old, she promised him her life, and decided to become a Carmelite sister. An important inspiration for her was the autobiography of Saint Thérèse of Lisieux *(see Saint 2.42)*. However, she first had to finish school. When she was 18 years old, she entered the convent of the discalced Carmelite sisters in Los Andes. Her new religious name was Teresa of Jesus.

O God, Juanita loved you above all else. Help me to understand the importance of dedicating myself to you in everything, also by my way of dressing. Saint Teresa de los Andes, pray for us!

Her habit of dressing up for church continued, for she would now don a white cape over her brown religious dress whenever she entered the church for prayer with her community. Within a year she contracted a fatal form of typhus, and made her final vows as a religious on her deathbed. She was 19 when she died. You may wonder about what she ever accomplished. She did what was most important: she believed in Jesus as sent by God, and loved him with all her heart. That is ultimately all our lives are about (*Jn 6:28-30; see box*).

GETTING READY

Juanita dressed up for church. When you enter a mosque or Buddhist temple, you take off your shoes. In a mosque, girls cover their hair, and in a synagogue, men cover their heads. So, what to do when you go to church? You could argue that God is more interested in your soul than your outward appearance (*1 Pet 3:3-4*), and that therefore you do not need any specific dress to go to church. Essentially that is true, and you are still very welcome in church when you are casually dressed. But is it fair that you make a great effort to get dressed for a party, while to meet God at Mass is the greatest party of all? It is therefore a good habit to dress up and get ready to meet the Lord. How to dress depends on your customs and background. Maybe the clothing guidelines at the Vatican might give a general idea (*see picture*).

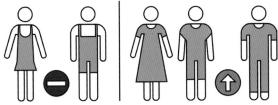

DO'S AND DON'TS

Possibly the most helpful guideline is: 'Don't dress to impress'. This is about God and not about you. Sometimes you may see women wearing a hat or chapel veil (mantilla) during Mass.

Saint Paul wrote that in his time it was improper for women not to cover their head (*1 Cor 11:5-6*). Today we see this differently, and no one can impose such customs on others. However, in certain formal circumstances it is considered a sign of respect, like for a man to wear a tie, and thus an expression of honouring God. The custom that women keep their hats on, and that men uncover their head when entering a church still stands, so gentlemen, take off that cap please! Also, your chewing gum is not needed in church... How would you dress for church?

Meeting God in church is a great feast! There is no specific dress code, but if you realise that this is a party, you may wish to adapt your clothing accordingly.

SAINT
MARCELLA
OF ROME

📅 325 – 410   🌍 ITALY   🕯 31 JANUARY

SCAN

Q: IS IT OKAY FOR A CATHOLIC TO USE MAKEUP, PERFUME, AND JEWELLERY?

Marcella 'was young, wealthy, highborn and distinguished for her beauty', wrote Saint Jerome (see #TwGOD 1.13 & 2.24). Her mother brought her up as a Catholic. Marcella was well appreciated in the fashionable society of Rome. Like other women of her standing she loved to wear makeup, new robes of shining silk, careful hairdressing, and beautiful jewellery. She married a wealthy aristocrat, but sadly he died seven months after their marriage (see box). At that moment she decided to live the rest of her life for God alone in chastity (see Saint 2.37).

A NEW LOOK

Marcella changed her life style drastically. She no longer wore makeup or jewellery, and chose a life of charity, prayer and fasting. Soon, other women followed her lead. They dressed in plain brown dresses, without makeup or gold. These religious women prayed together, studied the Bible, and cared for the neediest.

O God, Marcella dedicated herself to you. Help me choose carefully to honour you even in my choice of makeup, perfume, and jewellery. Saint Marcella, pray for us!

Marcella's house became a refuge for pilgrims. The great Bible scholar Saint Jerome called it her 'house church', and stayed there for three years. Marcella asked him many questions about the faith, and Jerome wrote her many letters full of wisdom. When Rome was sacked by the Goths in 410, Marcella was treated very brutally. She was tortured and dragged to a church, where she died the next day.

ADORNING YOURSELF

Today, the use of makeup, perfume, and jewellery is very common, regardless of background or wealth. In many respects, Marcella was a good Christian even before turning around drastically. Thus she shows that caring for your appearance and wearing makeup, perfume, or jewellery is possible for Christians (see Saint 1.31). Still, when she dedicated her life drastically to God alone, she decided not to need any of that, and almost tried to hide her beauty in brown sackcloth. If you do an internet search on Catholics and makeup, you find pages that totally condemn the use of makeup, and others that condone or even encourage it. So what is the right answer?

INTENTION

The key is in your intention. Christian life is about placing God at the centre of your life, not yourself. There is no objection to well-applied makeup, delicate perfume, or elegant jewellery, which enhance your natural beauty, and thus help you to give glory to God, especially when applied intentionally with moderation and modesty. However, are you trying to hide your natural appearance? Do you wish to appear different from who you are? Are you trying to seduce others for pleasure? Do you seek to be the centre of attention? If the answer to any of such questions is yes, you should stop for a moment and consider what it means to live your life with Jesus. Ultimately, it is not about you, but about him! As long as you are aware of that, you will be able to choose your makeup, perfume, and

INSIDE RATHER THAN OUTSIDE

'Marcella...had been married less than seven months when her husband was taken from her. There she was, young and highborn, as well as distinguished for her beauty – always an attraction to men – with her self-control. An illustrious consul named Cerealis paid court to her with great assiduity. Being an old man he offered to make over to her his fortune. But Marcella answered: 'If I wished to marry... I should look for a husband and not for an inheritance'... She put non-Catholics to confusion by her choice to live as a Christian widow in line with her conscience. For women of the world are wont to paint their faces with rouge and white-lead, to wear robes of shining silk, to adorn themselves with jewels...and to scent themselves with musk. While they mourn for the husbands they have lost they rejoice at their own deliverance and freedom to choose fresh partners...to rule over them... As a widow, Marcella's clothing was meant to keep out the cold and not to hide her figure. Of gold she would not wear so much as a seal-ring, choosing to store her money in the stomachs of the poor rather than to keep it at her own disposal.' [Jerome, Letter CXVII to Principia]

jewellery carefully. Obviously, there are differences between cultures and generations. While it is good to be careful not to offend anyone with your choices, there is nothing wrong with expressing yourself in your own way, especially when you seek to please God in everything. What choices would you make?

The answer lies in your intention: as long as it helps you to show the beauty received from God with modesty and appropriate pride this is fine.

SAINT **IGNATIUS OF LOYOLA**

📅 1491 – 1556   🌐 SPAIN, ITALY   🕯 31 JULY

SCAN

AD MAJOREM DEI GLORIAM

IHS

Q: CAN A CATHOLIC HAVE TATTOOS OR PIERCINGS?

Ignatius was born in Loyola Castle, in Spain. He had a romantic view of knighthood and military action, which he saw as a way to personal success and fame. Still, he was a good though short-tempered soldier, who survived many a duel, and boasted of his skills. Ignatius was a womaniser: he loved fancy dress and dancing. His vocation story reads like a novel *(see #TwGOD 4.5)*. He used to bear his family shield just as some wear a tattoo of dedication on their body. After over a decade of battles without injury, one day he was gravely wounded. Confined to his bed for months, he discovered how he could discern God's Will by listening to his deepest feelings. It was not easy to discern these feelings. For example, he loved thinking of the way he could conquer a beautiful woman, or lead an army to victory in battle.

O God, Ignatius learned to discern your will in everything. Help me to make my decisions only for your greater glory, and discern my deepest desire. Saint Ignatius of Loyola, pray for us!

DISCERNMENT

To his great surprise, Ignatius discovered that such thoughts gave him a sense of pleasure, but when he left that thought, he would feel a little empty and unfulfilled. On the contrary, when he began thinking about the great things he could do in the service of Christ the King, a feeling of quiet and peace would remain with him. Thus he discovered how to discern between what he liked on a superficial level (women, battles), and what he truly desired from the bottom of his heart (serving God). Eventually he became the founder of the influential order of the Jesuits (see Saint 1.10; #TwGOD 2.40). Like Ignatius, Christians in Albania wanted to dedicate themselves totally to Jesus. Amidst persecutions, it became a custom to tattoo a small cross on their hand. Similarly, Coptic Christians have a small cross tattooed on their wrist. Among other things this serves as an admission sign at the church door. Many Pacific Island cultures encourage tattoos as a cultural expression, so in that context they are clearly acceptable, even now that they have adopted Christianity.

FORBIDDEN?

So, did saint Ignatius wear a tattoo or piercing? Not as far as we know. He is, however, a master of discernment, which is needed here, for a tattoo will accompany you for life, and a piercing may change your appearance. The Bible seems to be opposed: 'You shall not cut your flesh for the dead or tattoo any marks on yourselves' (Lev 19:28). As always, the context is important. This prohibition is related to the old custom to cut oneself as an expression of grief, and to tattoo oneself with the mark of a deity of choice. Our Christian God of love invites us to dedicate ourselves to him — without constraint and without obligatory tattoos. Consequently, as long as your piercing or tattoo does not bind you to a pagan god or an ideology, there is no problem. Moderation is a virtue, though: is your tattooed sleeve or series of heavy piercings a genuine expression of yourself, or does it disguise a discontentment with your body?

> ### PRAISE, REVERENCE, AND SERVE GOD
>
> *"Human beings are created to praise, reverence, and serve God our Lord, and by doing this, to save their souls. All other things on the face of the earth are created for human beings to help them pursue the end for which they are created. Therefore, we are to use the things of this world only to the extent that they help us to this end, and we ought to free ourselves from them in so far as they get in the way of this end."*
>
> [Ignatius, Spiritual exercises, The first principle and foundation, 23]

(see #TwGOD 4.31). In the second case, a tattoo or piercing will not solve your problem! Also, be careful with more sensual areas of your body, as chastity remains an important Christian virtue (see Saint 2.40).

MARKED FOR GOD

As we have seen, discernment is important. Are you acting on a superficial desire, like the women or enemies Ignatius wanted to conquer? Or will your tattoo or piercing help you in your relationship with God? Take ample time to discern. Ask yourself why you want to mark your body in this way, and how you will look at your tattoo in 15 years time. Ignatius tried to do everything for the greater glory of God (Ad Maiorem Dei Gloriam, AMDG). If you try to do the same, you will be able to make the right decision. Do you feel like marking your body for God?

> Tattoos or piercings can go together with Christianity. Discernment is important. Be careful with certain sensual areas, and consider that you will be marked for life.

SAINT
FRANCIS
OF ASSISI

📅 CA. 1181 – 1226   🌍 ITALY   🕯️ 4 OCTOBER

SCAN

Q: DOES LOVE FOR CREATION MEAN CARE FOR ANIMALS?

Francis was born into a cloth merchant family in Assisi, Italy. As a young man he lived an extravagant life with beautiful silk clothes and accessories, while partying, squandering money on drink and girls, and playing practical jokes on people. In a whimsical search for adventure he enlisted as a soldier, and was taken prisoner. He spent a year as a captive. After his liberation, he felt depressed at the thought of picking up his frivolous life once more. The only moments of consolation were those of secret prayer in a corner of the church. One day, he met a leper on the road. Without thinking, he descended from his horse and embraced the man with the contagious disease, giving him what money he had on him. In a deserted chapel, dedicated to San Damiano, he knelt before the icon of Jesus on the Cross. Here, he heard a voice telling him to repair God's house. First, he thought that he was to restore the chapel, which was crumbling down. Then he realised that the entire Church community was crumbling down, and that preaching the faith was of the utmost importance. This discovery changed his life completely.

O God, you gave Francis a great love for all creatures. Help me to care for creation wherever possible, recognising the great gifts you placed at our disposal. Saint Francis of Assisi, pray for us!

COMPASSION AND LOVE

To his family's shame, Francis began to live like a beggar, asking for alms and counting on God's providence alone. He did not want to have any earthly possessions, and spoke with great joy to anyone he met about the love of God for every creature. So great was his love for God, that he even preached when no one was present, addressing his enthusiastic words to the animals he encountered in nature.

He saw God's splendour in people, animals, and nature alike (see box). Soon, his example attracted followers, the first Franciscan friars. They lived by a simple Rule written by Francis, which focuses on poverty and preaching. Francis undertook various attempts to preach the gospel outside of Italy. He even tried to convert the Sultan of Egypt, and received permission to go to the Holy Land, where to this day the Franciscans are in charge of the holy places as 'Custodians of the Holy Land.' Francis's closeness to Jesus was clear in everything. Probably he is so universally loved precisely because he so closely resembled Jesus in his own life.

LOVE FOR CREATION

Francis was profoundly in love with God, and had great care for both people and animals. In everything he demonstrated a love for God's creation. For example, he 'invented' the nativity scene — with a real ox and donkey — so that people could use all their senses in recognising the mystery of Jesus's birth. He cared for these animals by giving them a manger with straw.

Francis even called animals his sisters and brothers. He knew that God has given human beings stewardship over creation, which includes care for animals. In some places, on Saint Francis's feast day people bring animals to church, where these are blessed. World Animal Day is dedicated to him.

> **CANTICLE OF THE CREATURES**
>
> *'Praised be you, my Lord, with all your creatures,*
> *especially Sir brother Sun...*
> *Praised be you, my Lord,*
> *through sister Moon and the stars...*
> *Praised be you, my Lord, through our sister Mother Earth,*
> *who sustains and governs us,*
> *and who produces various fruit*
> *with coloured flowers and herbs...*
> *Praised be you, my Lord, through our sister Bodily Death,*
> *from whom no one living can escape...*
> *Praise and bless my Lord and give him thanks*
> *and serve him with great humility.'*
>
> [Francis, Canticle of the Creatures, 1224]

DIVINE COMMANDMENT

It is very Catholic to care for creation. God entrusted us with stewardship over nature, including animals (Gen 1:28-30; see #TwGOD 1.3, 1.48 & 4.48). Animals can serve for our well-being, for example as food or for transportation. At the same time, animals have the right to be protected and cared for. Pope Francis said that every act of cruelty towards animals is contrary to human dignity (Laudato si, 92). God himself ordered us to care for creation. In line with Saint Francis, we can see all creatures and creation as our brothers and sisters. Do you want to praise God for all creation?

> God entrusted the care for animals and all creation into our hands. It is very Christian to care for animals and protect them against harm, while using them in a just manner.

SAINT **KATERI TEKAKWITHA**

CA. 1656 – 1680   USA   14 JULY

SCAN

Q: IS IT CATHOLIC TO CARE ABOUT THE ENVIRONMENT AND CLIMATE CHANGE?

Tekakwitha was a native American girl, born in a Mohawk village to the west of today's New York, USA. Her father was a Mohawk chief and her mother a Catholic Algonquin. Tekakwitha and her brother were not baptised. When she was four years old, her family was killed because of a smallpox epidemic. Tekakwitha survived the illness, but all her life she carried the scars on her body. For a long time she hid her face because she felt humiliated by her disfigurement. She was taken in by her uncle, a chief like her father, who had a great dislike for the Jesuit missionaries that came to the village. However, their words touched the heart of Tekakwitha. To the great dismay of her uncle, she refused to marry the man who was chosen for her. From now on she was treated as a slave by her family, having to labour very hard in the household.

O God, Kateri Tekakwitha was close to you through nature. Help me to show just care for nature created by you, and given to all people. Saint Kateri Tekakwitha, pray for us!

KATERI

At the age of 19, Tekakwitha gathered all her courage and asked a visiting priest to baptise her. She received the baptismal name of Kateri, after saint Catherine *(see Saint 1.48)*. During her walks through the woods she would leave small crosses behind as a sign of her dedication to Christ. Some neighbours started rumours about sorcery, so that her life was in danger. Kateri secretly decided to leave her native village and moved to a Christian community near Montreal, Canada. Here, she became known for her holy lifestyle. She was a Christian through and through. In everything she did, she placed God at the centre, not herself. She prayed, fasted a lot, and lived a life of penance. Kateri prayed especially for the conversion of her fellow Mohawks. She did not know everything about the faith, but had a great Christian intuition. At 23 years of age she took a vow of celibacy. A year later she died of tuberculosis. Her dedication to Jesus in chastity gained her the title Lily of the Mohawks.

SEEDS AND FRUITS

'The best known witness of Christian holiness among the native people of North America is Kateri Tekakwitha... She always remained what she was, a true daughter of her people, following her tribe in the hunting seasons and continuing her devotions in the environment most suited to her way of life, before a rough cross carved by herself in the forest. The Gospel of Jesus Christ, which is the great gift of God's love, is never in contrast with what is noble and pure in the life of any tribe or nation, since all good things are his gifts... I wish to urge the local churches to be truly 'Catholic' in their outreach to native peoples, and to show respect and honour for their culture and all their worthy traditions.'

[Pope John Paul II, Meeting with native peoples of the Americas, 14 September 1987]

NATURE AND CLIMATE

As a Mohawk, Kateri was very close to nature. She regularly went to the woods for private time with God, listening to him in her heart and in nature *(see box)*. Catholics are pro-life in every sense, for life has been given to us by God. He also entrusted the care of creation to us, ordering the first people to be stewards of the earth *(Gen 1:28)*. Climate change is one of the challenges humanity faces. To the extent that this is due to human intervention, we need to do what we can to reduce the effects. Here too, the manner of responding should be just, with great attention given to basic human rights. For example, reducing the emission of carbon dioxide is important, but less-developed countries should not be limited in their chances to survive and develop as a result of these reduction measures.

STEWARDSHIP

God created the earth and all it contains for one reason: to offer a good home for the people he loved. For all of them. Therefore, care for creation goes much further than planting trees, however important that is. All people need nature for a dignified life. That means, for example, the need to introduce green spaces in all our cities, but equally, the just division of the fruits of the earth *(see Saint 1.37)*. Too often, poor countries cannot profit from the rich resources offered by nature in their territory because the income goes to foreign companies. Water, air, land, nature, are not infinite resources and need to be shared equally among all people. Hence it is a divine directive to care for the environment and to be just stewards of God's creation. How can you contribute to this?

Care for people and care for creation go together. We are all responsible for caring for each other, sharing, and being good stewards. This includes a just response to climate change.

SAINT
MARTIN OF TOURS

 CA. 325 – 397   🌐 HUNGARY, ITALY, FRANCE

🕯 11 NOVEMBER (WEST); 12 NOVEMBER (EAST)

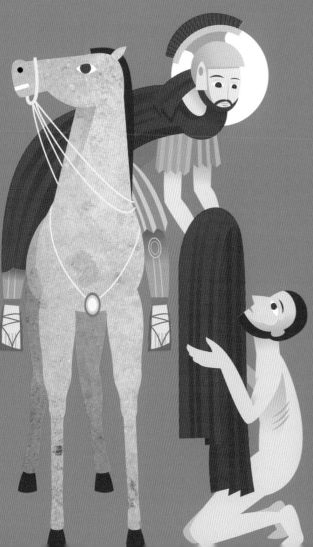

Q: HOW IS GLOBAL SHARING RELATED TO WASTE?

IS WASTING FOOD OR WATER REALLY SO BAD?

Martin came from Savaria, Hungary. He grew up in northern Italy. His father was a high-ranking officer in the Imperial Guard, and when he was 15, Martin had to follow his father and join the army. His parents were pagans, but Martin was touched by the new religion in the empire, and converted to Christianity. He was baptised when he was about 18 years old. The remainder of his life is only known from legend. A famous story is that as a young soldier, he met a beggar during a cold night. Sitting on his horse, Martin took off his cloak, cut it in half, and gave this half to the beggar. That night, he dreamt of Jesus telling him: 'Martin, in preparing to be baptised, you have clothed Jesus himself.'

O God, in his desire to follow you, Martin shared both his food and his faith. Help me to be open to the needs of others, and adapt my life accordingly. Saint Martin of Tours, pray for us!

CACKLING GEESE

A few years later, Martin petitioned the emperor to let him leave the army to dedicate himself to God alone. He followed Saint Hilary of Poitiers, became a monk, and preached against the Arians, who denied that Jesus was God *(see #TwGOD 2.22-2.23)*. When the people of Tours were in search of a new bishop, they lured Martin into the city under the pretext of ministering to a sick person. When he realised their scheme, he tried to hide — allegedly in a goose barn — but the geese gave him away by their cackling. When he had given in and was ordained a bishop, he started to reform his diocese, visited the parishes, and preached against heresies and paganism. However, he also pleaded to be merciful to heretics, as they too were created by God. As a bishop, he missed his monastic prayer life, and founded an abbey where he could withdraw from time to time. He was a tireless missionary who preached the faith with great enthusiasm, calling his people to share their possessions and faith with those in need. He is among the first publicly venerated saints not to have died as a martyr.

GLOBAL SHARING

Martin shared both his own cloak and his faith. We are called to do the same — in our own way. The first Christians 'were of one heart and soul, and no one claimed private ownership of any possessions, but everything they owned was held in common' *(Acts 4:32)*. God gave the resources of the earth to all people in common use. Only by working together on a global level can we get to a fairer division of goods and respond to ecological threats *(see Saint 1.36)*. This does not take away your personal responsibility, though. One concrete way of contributing to a just sharing is to be careful with waste. It may seem easier and cheaper to throw something away and buy a new version. This may be true locally, but the global effects are often forgotten. Waste causes not only serious environmental questions, but also the use of even more resources that could have helped other people.

> ## CULTURE OF WASTE
>
> '[The] "culture of waste" tends to become a common mentality that infects everyone. Human life, the person, are no longer seen as a primary value to be respected and safeguarded, especially if they are poor or disabled, if they are not yet useful - like the unborn child - or are no longer of any use - like the elderly person. This culture of waste has also made us insensitive to wasting and throwing out excess foodstuffs, which is especially condemnable when, in every part of the world, unfortunately, many people and families suffer hunger and malnutrition.'   [Pope Francis, General Audience, 5 June 2013]

WASTE

This becomes most visible in the waste of food and drinking water. Pope Francis said: 'whenever food is thrown out, it is as if it were stolen from the table of the poor, from the hungry!' *(see box)*. The right to food and clean water are among the most basic human rights. How can we claim to be Christians when we throw away food or spill water while for somewhere else these are lacking? At least a third of the food produced in the world is never eaten. With that food, we throw away the resources that were needed to produce it. Now this is something we can easily help to counter on an individual level. Not so much by shipping our leftovers to other places, but first of all by consuming and wasting less ourselves. How can you contribute?

> All together we inherited the earth with everything in it. Wasting is the opposite of sharing, which becomes especially clear when we throw out food while others are starving.

SAINT **GIANNA BERETTA MOLLA**

 1922 – 1962 🌐 ITALY 🕯 28 APRIL

SCAN

Q: WHY ALL THIS FUSS ABOUT UNBORN LIFE?

WHAT ABOUT ABORTION?

Gianna was from Magenta, Italy, and loved skiing and mountaineering. She was a youth leader in Catholic Action, while she also actively worked for the poor and less fortunate. She studied medicine and surgery in Pavia, and decided to specialise in paediatrics, the medical care of children and pregnant mothers. In her own clinic she helped mothers and children but also elderly and poor people. For a while she considered becoming a nun, but then realised that God had another vocation in mind for her. Gianna met her future husband, Pietro Molla, at the first Mass of a mutual priest friend. Pietro was an engineer. He worked as a manager in a match factory. Their marriage was very happy, and soon they had three children. Gianna had a great faith and regularly went to pray in the nearby church of Our Lady of Good Counsel.

O God, Gianna loved life. May I too have the greatest love for life as a gift from you, doing everything I can to protect and nurture that life. Saint Gianna Molla, pray for us!

CHOICE FOR LIFE

When she was pregnant with her fourth child, Gianna was diagnosed with a fibroma, a tumour in her uterus. This is a dangerous condition, and the tumour needed to be removed for Gianna to survive. She was presented with three options (see #TwGOD 4.30). The safest would be to remove her uterus together with the tumour and the unborn child. The second possibility was to remove the tumour and the child, leaving the uterus in place. The third and for the mother most risky option would be to try to remove the tumour while preserving the child. As a doctor, Gianna was well aware of the risks, but chose the third option with conviction. She believed with all her heart that the baby was a gift from God and she wanted to preserve that life even at the risk of losing her own. She said: 'One cannot love without suffering, nor suffer without loving.'

SAVE THE BABY

Gianna knew that the delivery would be very painful and dangerous. She prayed to God that she would give birth to a healthy child, while also surviving herself so that she could care for the baby and the other children. Still, she was ready to sacrifice her life if necessary. A few days before giving birth she told her husband Pietro: 'If you have to decide between me and the child, do not hesitate. Choose the child, I insist on it. Save the baby!' Gianna was brought to hospital on Good Friday, and the next day she gave birth to her healthy daughter, Gianna Emanuela. The mother's condition deteriorated quickly, and she suffered a lot of pain. She wanted to receive the Eucharist, to be close to Jesus. She died seven days later. Her daughter Gianna Emanuela became a doctor herself and gave a moving testimony: 'Dear Mum, thank you for having given me life two times: when you conceived me and when you permitted me to be born' (World Meeting of Families 1997).

ALIVE BEFORE BIRTH

Gianna's message is not only her heroic self-sacrifice. Maybe another mother would make a different choice

> ## INVIOLABLE DIGNITY
>
> 'Gianna...received the grace of a united family, rich in faith and love. She was a happy mother, but a great trial awaited her during her fourth pregnancy. In the dramatic choice between saving her life and that of the creature she carried in her womb, she did not hesitate to sacrifice herself. Her testimony is heroic, a true hymn to life, in violent contrast with a certain widespread mentality today! May her sacrifice inspire courage in those who participate, through personal and community commitment, in the Movement for Life and in other similar movements, so that the inviolable dignity of every human being is recognised, from the moment of conception until natural death, as a foremost and fundamental value in respect to every other human and social right.'
>
> [Pope John Paul II, Thanksgiving for the beatification, 25 April 1994]

(see #TwGOD 4.30). But the deliberate abortion of human life is always gravely wrong (see #TwGOD 4.28-4.29). Gianna realised that an unborn child, however young, is already a human person and thus has the right to be protected, nurtured, and loved. A baby does not come to life at the moment of birth, but is alive since the very beginning, the fusion of two cells at conception. After conception a continuous development takes place (see #TwGOD 4.26). Gianna showed that this life deserves all the love it can get! Whether a child is born or not yet born, it is a human being. And the first human right is the right to life. What can you do to promote life?

> Human life is a gift from God. Even an unborn foetus is a child of God with its own personality and human rights. The first right is the right to life itself, so abortion is a great wrong.

SAINT **LIDWINA OF SCHIEDAM**

 1380 - 1433　　 NETHERLANDS　　 14 JUNE

SCAN

Q: CAN THERE BE A MEANING TO MY SUFFERING?

IS EUTHANASIA A SOLUTION?

Lidwina was a beautiful young girl from a poor family in Schiedam, the Netherlands. One day, when she was 14 years old, she went ice-skating on the frozen canals in her city. When one of her companions accidentally bumped into her, Lidwina fell and broke a rib on her right side. The wound did not heal well, and she was confined to her bed. This was the beginning of a long path of suffering which would last 38 years. Various famous doctors visited her without being able to offer her relief. Slowly, her body decayed with wounds that would not heal, while she suffered headaches, toothaches, fever, tumours, and later also kidney stones.

SUFFERING

At the beginning, Lidwina was rebellious and had difficulty in accepting her fate. How could God allow this to happen? She had always tried to live as a good Christian! However, as time went by, she began to realise how close she could be to Jesus, precisely in her suffering. Did he not suffer even more than her when he was nailed to the cross?

Lord, Lidwina abandoned herself and offered you all her suffering. Help me to see life as your precious gift and stay with you, even in my suffering. Saint Lidwina of Schiedam, pray for us!

The only goal of Jesus's suffering was to save people and bring them to God (see #TwGOD 1.37). As her love for Jesus increased, Lidwina began to desire to join Jesus in his mission of saving people through his suffering (see box). Thus her faith gave meaning to her suffering. You can do as she did, and offer the unavoidable pain and suffering you have to face to Jesus. This can help you grow in faith and your relationship with him.

FOOL OR SAINT?

Although Lidwina faced criticism and was depicted as a fool and a fraud by some, great numbers of people considered her a saint and were inspired by her example. During her life, the local government drew up a declaration, which testified among other things that Lidwina lived for years without eating anything else but holy Communion, brought to her every two weeks by the priest to whom she also confessed her sins. She was not focused on herself and her suffering, but on Jesus, and on the people who cared for her. This is the quiet strength that kept her alive for many years, and through which she was able to inspire many people.

UNBEARABLE?

Today, we often hear that people should be able to end their lives when suffering becomes unbearable. It is indeed terrible when someone has to suffer, and we should do everything we can to help alleviate their pain (see #TwGOD 4.39). But when are pain and suffering really unbearable? Before Lidwina was able to accept her suffering with a smile, she passed through many tough experiences. And she was able to help many people as a result. She shows that even in great suffering life is meaningful. And that our faith can even bring meaning to senseless suffering. Still, just the thought that we will possibly have to suffer pain paralyses many of us in advance. Maybe we should not try to look forward too much. Living in the present moment can be of great help for living our lives to the best, and

---

SUFFERING WITH JESUS

'When Lidwina sensed an attack of fever coming up, she decided to consider the suffering of the Lord. She then commanded herself and her own suffering to the Passion of Jesus, for in him all the bitter is sweet... She confided from time to time to some of her regular caretakers that she would endure her daily ailments for 40 years, or rather better until the end of time, if she could convert a sinner with it or save the soul of a faithful from purgatory... She could help the many visitors who came to her from far and wide to ask her advice, with consolation in their spiritual and with healing in their physical distress.'

[Thomas à Kempis, Vita Lidewigis, Ch. VIII]

---

even for bearing our suffering — today. Thankfully, God 'will not let you be tested beyond your strength' (1 Cor 10:13) and helps you with his grace (2 Cor 12:9-10). Euthanasia is never a solution. If life is a gift from God (see #TwGOD 4.38), who are we to take it away when things get difficult? Obviously, to be able to endure suffering with a holy joy like Lidwina is another gift from God, for which we can only pray. Even so, her example and prayer can help everyone to find a certain sense in suffering, accept the unavoidable and fend off being defeated by the evil which caused it. How can you deal with the suffering in your life?

Suffering is terrible. Faith can help you to see a certain sense in suffering, and endure it in abandonment to God. Euthanasia means rejecting God's gift of life, and is very wrong.

SAINT
HOMOBONUS OF CREMONA

 † 1197   ITALY   13 NOVEMBER

Q: CAN I BE A CATHOLIC AND A SUCCESSFUL BUSINESSWOMAN OR BUSINESSMAN?

Homobonus was a successful businessman from Cremona, Italy. He was happily married and already during his life he was considered an example of a virtuous Christian by his fellow-citizens. His parents must have foreseen something when they gave him his name, for Homobonus literally means "good man." His father was a merchant too, and had left his son enough capital to start a large commercial business, which Homobonus ran with great diligence and success. For him, his professional life only made sense in the light of his service to God. He prayed and attended Mass every day. Charity was an essential part of his ideal for successfully running a business. He died in church during the singing of the Gloria.

O God, Homobonus was a good man, also in the way he ran his business; may I too be Catholic in the way I lead my professional life. Saint Homobonus, pray for us!

 SCAN

WORK ETHIC

Homobonus saw it as his task as a Christian to take great care in the way he ran his business. Honesty and consistency were very important elements of his work ethic. He was often worried that he would inadvertently cheat or wrong someone. While his business continued to grow, he was very generous to the less fortunate, and he supported the poor wherever he could. His wife was sometimes afraid that they would not have enough left to live comfortably, but he did not share her fears. Homobonus's example can help us analyse what makes a businessman Catholic. Basically it means applying your Christian conviction to every aspect of your life, including your business decisions.

THREE PRINCIPLES

At least the following principles seem to apply to everyone working in business or service.

- First, a Christian business will give evidence of a clear commitment to people. This does not only involve the way it deals with clients, but also those working there. This includes possibilities of personal and professional growth, a just flexibility allowing workers to care for their families, and obviously fair remuneration.

- A second key concept is integrity in the broadest sense. Basically this means walking the walk. A Catholic business will comply with all the moral laws and ethics in every business decision.

- A third concept is to strive for excellence in everything. Excellent products and service do not only make clients return, but are also a disguised image of the future life we expect with God, who is perfect (Mt 5:48).

JUSTICE AND CHARITY

'Although distant in time, Homobonus does in fact figure as a saint for the Church and society of our time... In pursuing the path of the Gospel Beatitudes, in the time of the Communes when money and market trends constituted the centre of city life, Homobonus combined justice and charity and made almsgiving a sign of sharing, with the spontaneity of one who from the assiduous contemplation of the Crucifix learned to testify to the value of life as a gift... Thus Homobonus' image emerges as that of a businessman engaged in the cloth trade and, while involved in the market dynamics of Italian and European cities, conferred spiritual dignity on his work: that spirituality which was the hallmark of all his activity.' [Pope John Paul II, Letter to Bishop Nicolini, 24 June 1997]

EVANGELISATION?

Homobonus applied these principles in his professional life. He added to this his commitment to charity. For him it was only natural to share his wealth with others less fortunate than he. Both at a personal and business level, charity is a very important principle. One could ask whether another principle for a Catholic businessman should be evangelisation. The answer is yes, but this does not mean that one needs to speak overtly about God at every moment. Your first task is to run your business in a way expected of a Christian. That in itself is a great testimony to today's world. How can you apply these principles in your life?

Catholic businesspeople will show commitment to clients and personnel, are people of integrity in everything, strive for excellence and charity, while personally living holy lives.

SAINT
CUNEGUNDE

📅 CA. 975 – 1040   🕯 3 MARCH

🌍 LUXEMBOURG, GERMANY, FRANCE

SAINT **HENRY II**

📅 973 – 1024   🕯 13 JULY

🌍 LUXEMBOURG, GERMANY, FRANCE

Q: IS IT POSSIBLE TO BE A GREAT LEADER AND A DEVOUT CHRISTIAN AT THE SAME TIME?

Cunegunde's father, Siegfried, was the first ruler of Luxembourg. She loved God so much that she took a vow of virginity. This was rather awkward, as she was destined to bear children for one or other noble household. When she married Henry, Duke of Bavaria, Germany, their marriage remained childless. Henry had wanted to become a priest. However, his vocation was to take over the crown of Bavaria. The bond between Cunegunde and Henry was very strong, with her being his closest political adviser. When the pope crowned Henry II Emperor of the Holy Roman Empire, she became Empress. The couple gave much of their wealth away to charity. In thanksgiving for his beloved wife's recovery after a serious illness, Henry founded a Benedictine convent in Hesse, Germany.

O God, Cunegunde and Henry lived completely for the task that you had given them. Help me to do the same and lead as a good Christian. Saints Cunegunde and Henry II, pray for us!

SCAN

REFORM AND SERVICE

Henry realised that not only his empire, but also the Church needed to be reformed in order to continue to be effective in its mission of spreading the gospel. In all his efforts to make this happen, he respected the Church's independence. Together with his wife, he dedicated time to prayer and devotions, but also founded schools, worked for peace in Europe, and quelled rebellions. His desire for religious life never left him, but his vocation was to be a world leader. As emperor, Henry ordered the abbot of Verdun to accept him as a Benedictine monk. After his vows, the abbot — now his superior — ordered Henry to continue to rule the empire. At the death of her husband, Cunegunde briefly took over as ruler of the Empire. A year later she entered the convent in Hesse. She is buried at Bamberg Cathedral beside her husband. The two of them show that it is possible to be wealthy and powerful, and still live as devout Christians.

CHRISTIAN LEADERS

The best example for a Christian leader is Jesus: the Good Shepherd who was ready to lay down his own life for his sheep (Jn 10:11). Henry had many of the qualities of such a leader: he was humble but not timid, generous and pious, supporter of justice and a merciful leader. Unlike many leaders, he did not abuse his power for his own good and enrichment. He was also a loving husband and a devout Christian who supported the Church where he could, together with his wife Cunegunde. Both are a great example of different ways in which to put Jesus's commandments into practice. As second in command, Cunegunde always supported Henry with great commitment and without any jealousy or envy. Precisely because of their dedication and selflessness, they are recognised as great leaders even today.

> ## HEAVENLY BLISS BEFORE EARTHLY GOODS
>
> *'Even while it lasts, our great glory is fleeting and empty unless at the same time we give thought to the eternity of heaven. But in his mercy God has given man a useful remedy: he has made a share in heavenly fatherland the reward for our earthly wealth... Turning a ready ear to our Lord's commands and eager to obey God's prompting, we wish from the riches he has so generously given us to lay up for ourselves treasures in heaven where thieves do not break in and steal, neither does moth nor rust consume (Mt 6:20). There too as we consider all that is now gathered here, our heart often turns in desire and love.'*
>
> [Henry II, Letter of confirmation of Bamberg diocese, 1007]

RESPONSIBILITY AND GOD

In retrospect, people may easily recognise mistakes in the decisions they have taken. That is the case for every leader. You have to decide here and now, often without complete information. Henry was not afraid to make mistakes: he wholeheartedly embraced his task as a leader, and took his decisions one by one in prayer to God and dialogue with his wife and advisors. Had the choice been entirely up to them, they might have chosen a different path in life. However, instead of complaining they accepted the great responsibilities that were entrusted to them and tried to be the best leaders they could be. That is all God asks of everyone, whatever their responsibility! Are you prepared to do the same?

> *With Jesus as example and chief, Christian leaders will be responsible, humble, generous, attentive, just, and merciful in their dealings with those entrusted to their care.*

BLESSED
CHARLES
OF AUSTRIA

📅 1887 – 1922   🌍 AUSTRIA   🕯 21 OCTOBER

SCAN

Q: WHY SHOULD CHRISTIANS CARE ABOUT POLITICS?

CAN POLITICIANS LIVE HOLY LIVES?

Charles was born into the influential Habsburg family in Austria. His great uncle Franz Joseph was emperor of the Austro-Hungarian empire, but Charles was not in direct line for succession. He married princess Zita of Bourbon-Parma. It was a marriage born of love. They were directly involved in important events in Europe. In 1914 Charles's uncle Franz Ferdinand was assassinated in Sarajevo, which marked the beginning of the First World War. Unexpectedly, now Charles had become the crown prince, destined to succeed his uncle Franz Joseph. Two years later he became ruler, in a time of war and great social turbulence. Charles received a tremendously difficult task for one man to carry out, to look after the enormous territory of the Austrian-Hungarian empire. After the war he was forced to retire in exile to the island of Madeira, where he died at the age of 33.

O God, Charles carried great political responsibility but never forgot that he depended on you. Help me to have a similar attitude in my involvement with politics. Blessed Charles of Austria, pray for us!

DIVINE MISSION

Charles was a modest and gentle man, quiet and introspective. For him, it was God who had entrusted him with the task of being emperor. He saw it as his first duty to follow Jesus in everything he did. He prayed before each important decision and frequently withdrew into the chapel to spend time with Jesus present in the Blessed Sacrament. Another in his place might have decided to abdicate and choose an easier life of wealth and prosperity. Not so Charles. He accepted the hardships and difficulties of his task, and continued to serve God as a politician and statesman. This does not mean that all his decisions were right. But he made them in deep faith, and with the sole desire to do good. Thankfully, holiness does not depend on human imperfection.

TRUST IN GOD

In their loving marriage, Charles and Zita complemented each other. Prayer and home devotions helped them to educate their eight children in the faith, and live their lives in mutual love and appreciation. Their marriage was so important for Charles, that his wedding anniversary, 21 October, is also his liturgical feast. With all his many responsibilities during the war, Charles made sure to keep very frequent contact with his wife and children. He is a great example to all those carrying heavy responsibility. He took his duty very seriously, but never forgot his first duty as a Christian husband and father. He realised that he could only co-operate with the grace of God, but that the outcome was beyond his grasp.

POLITICIAN AND CHRISTIAN

Charles did not succeed in all his political attempts. Still, he did everything he could to halt the war and bring peace to Europe. Important for us is Charles's attitude as a politician and a social leader. Today too we need politicians who are ready to dedicate themselves to the service of the common good on the

OFFICE AS A HOLY SERVICE

'The decisive task of Christians consists in seeking, recognising and following God's Will in all things. The Christian statesman, Charles of Austria, confronted this challenge every day. To his eyes, war appeared as 'something appalling'. Amid the tumult of the First World War, he strove to promote the peace initiative of my Predecessor, Benedict XV. From the beginning, the Emperor Charles conceived of his office as a holy service to his people. His chief concern was to follow the Christian vocation to holiness also in his political actions. For this reason, his thoughts turned to social assistance. May he be an example for all of us, especially for those who have political responsibilities in Europe today!'

[Pope John Paul II, Homily at the beatification, 3 October 2004]

basis of their Christian faith. Politicians who are ready to risk making mistakes, while working not for themselves but for the service to their fellow human beings. In brief, politicians who take their task seriously, while abandoning themselves to God in everything. At any rate, we are part of society, and as Christians each of us should be involved by voting for the best possible candidates. Do you want to be one of them?

Politicians can become saints! We need good Christian politicians who dedicate themselves to the service of the common good, efface themselves and abandon themselves to God.

SAINT
PATRICK

 CA. 5TH C. SCOTLAND, IRELAND 17 MARCH

SAINT **ANDREW KIM TAEGŎN** AND 102 MARTYRS

 1821 – 1846 KOREA

 16 SEPT. (ANDREW), 20 SEPT. (KOREAN MARTYRS)

SCAN

Q: HOW CAN YOU BE PATRIOTIC WITHOUT IDOLISING YOUR COUNTRY?

WHAT IS THE DIFFERENCE BETWEEN RADICALISM AND FUNDAMENTALISM?

Patrick was born in Roman Britain and raised as a Christian. Information on his life is intermingled with legend, from which a general picture of a strong Christian missionary emerges. When he was about 15, he did something terrible, for which he felt ashamed and sorry all his life, although we do not know what this was. A year later, he was abducted by pirates and sold as a slave in Ireland. Years later he managed to escape, and started studying to become a priest. He was sent to preach the gospel to the Irish Celts and their druids tried to duel with him. He is the national patron saint of Ireland, and with reason, for thanks to him the entire Irish island was won over to Christ. Irish folklore recounts many stories about his life, and he has become synonymous with the Irish national identity. The same is true for the shamrock that he allegedly used to explain the holy Trinity, which is three and one in itself *(see #TwGOD 1.33)*.

O God, help me to love my country, but love you above all else like your saints did. Saints Patrick, Andrew Kim Taegŏn and companions, pray for us!

103 MARTYRS

The Korean Church is founded on the missionary work of lay people. In the 18th century, some Catholic books were imported from China and studied by Korean scholars. Some were struck by what they discovered. In 1784 one of them went to Beijing to study the faith and was baptised as Peter. He went back to Korea and his faith was so inspiring that many followed his lead and asked to be baptised. When, many years later, a Catholic priest arrived, he met thousands of Catholics. They had never seen a priest, and were thrilled with his arrival. The local rulers did not like Christianity and considered it a foreign influence *(see box; Saint 1.15)*. Many Christians were martyred in horrid persecutions. But their number kept growing. The first Korean to be ordained a priest was Andrew Kim Taegon. He was executed a year later, just as thousands of others were in the course of that century. 103 of them were officially declared martyrs for the faith.

RADICAL PATRIOTS

The 103 Korean martyrs remind us that faith makes us strong and steadfast in love. They were radical in their choice for Jesus, and died cruel deaths as a consequence. At first sight, these martyrs do not seem to have much in common with Patrick, nor with us. But they do! Each of them served their country with great love, trying to bring their people what was most needed, namely the truth and love of Jesus. They all faced persecution as a consequence of their stance for the truth.

FUNDAMENTALISM

What they also have in common is that in spite of their patriotism, they placed their love for Jesus and the Church above everything else. Patriotism is love for one's country or origin, which can be very good. That is different from

---

MY LAST HOUR

'This is my last hour of life, listen to me attentively: if I have held communication with foreigners, it has been for my religion and for my God. It is for him that I die. My immortal life is on the point of beginning. Become Christians if you wish to be happy after death, because God has eternal chastisements in store for those who have refused to know him.'

[A. Kim Taegon, in: The New Glories of the Catholic Church, London 1859, 118]

---

ideologised nationalism, which is often based on a sense of superiority and in extreme cases even hatred of the other. Such dangerous ideas can lead to religious fundamentalism among other things. The Korean Martyrs, and saints like Patrick, Joan of Arc, and Thomas More *(see Saint 1.11 & 1.44)* show that this behaviour is completely opposite to the view of Christianity. Jesus calls us to be radical in love alone, and to bring the truth about him to all people wherever they are and whatever their origin or nationality. Do you love and pray for your country?

Patriotism is fine as long as you realise the precedence of God's commandments. Extreme fundamentalism in any form is opposite to Christianity, which wants to be radical only in love.

SAINT
THOMAS MORE

📅 1478 – 1535 🌐 ENGLAND 🕯 22 JUNE

Q: SHOULD CHRISTIANS ALWAYS FOLLOW THE LAWS OF THEIR COUNTRIES?

Thomas had great prospects: he went to the best schools, studied in Oxford, England, and trained to be a lawyer in London. At one point he seriously contemplated entering monastic life, but discerned that God had another plan for him. He was happily married and had four children. He was elected to parliament, where he was known as honest and effective. His book *Utopia*, about an idealistic society on a fictional island is still read today and considered a social-political satire. King Henry VIII recognised Thomas's skills and gradually gave him more important duties, until he was made Lord Chancellor. One of his roles was to work to uphold the civil law and defend the Catholic faith in England against the ideas of the Reformation, which he did with fervour and justice. He served the king with loyalty, efficiency and precision. Thomas was a man of great faith. Although he could have had anything he desired, his personal life was simple, with penitence and prayer at the centre (see Saint 2.9).

O God, Thomas chose to serve you above everything else; help me choose carefully and stand up for my convictions and faith, listening to my conscience. Saint Thomas More, pray for us!

DISAGREEMENT

All went well until King Henry tried to obtain an annulment for his marriage to Catherine of Aragon, in order to marry another woman, because he wanted a male child (see #TwGOD 2.39). Thomas refused to support the king in this, for at the time he had married Catherine with a special permission from the pope himself. The pope could do nothing but reject the request for the annulment. This is when Henry started to prepare the separation from the Catholic Church. Thomas felt that he could no longer serve his king, as his loyalty to God came first. When he refused to recognise Henry as head of the Church in England, he was imprisoned in the Tower of London. In spite of his brilliant defence speech, Thomas was found guilty by the less than impartial court. Just before his execution, he asked the crowd to pray for the king, and proclaimed himself the king's good servant but God's first. Allegedly he pulled his beard aside when he laid his head on the chopping block, joking: 'I pray you let me lay my beard over the block lest ye should cut it.'

GOD FIRST

With his total integrity and dedication, first to God and then to the civil ruler, Thomas is an example for each of us. He did not compromise his moral values and belief to please the king. At the same time, he was a very faithful servant as long as his conscience permitted. When they are not against a higher commandment of God, we are supposed to follow the civil laws, whether we like them or not. This is a gesture of humility, even abandonment to God. However, no secular ruler has jurisdiction over the Church of Christ. And no ruler can order us to go against the commandments of God! For example, even if local law considers abortion or euthanasia to be legal, for Christians this directly violates the law of God, so that we can never collaborate with this way of taking people's lives (see Saint 1.38-1.39).

PRAYER IN IMPRISONMENT

'Give me the grace, good Lord to set the world at naught. To set the mind firmly on you and not to hang upon the words of men's mouths. To be content to be solitary. Not to long for worldly pleasures. Little by little utterly to cast off the world and rid my mind of all its business... To be joyful in tribulations. To walk the narrow way that leads to life... To have continually in mind the passion that Christ suffered for me. For his benefits unceasingly to give him thanks. To buy the time again that I have lost. To abstain from vain conversations. To shun foolish mirth and gladness. To cut off unnecessary recreations. Of worldly substance, friends, liberty, life and all, to set the loss at naught, for the winning of Christ. Amen.'

[Thomas More, Prayer in the Tower of London, 1534-1535]

CONSCIENCE

Each of us is personally responsible for choosing the right thing in our lives. So we cannot justify ourselves for doing something morally wrong by saying that the civil law or government allows or even decrees this. Many of us will, at some point, be confronted with the choice between our faith and conscience on the one hand, and regulations or customs on the other. The example of Saint Thomas, and his prayer, may be of great importance at such a moment! What will you do when your friends maintain a different view than you do? Or when your employer issues a rule of conduct which forces you to choose between work and your convictions?

Civil law cannot make us go against our conscience and faith. If necessary, it is better to face hardships and ridicule than to violate the laws of God. He will be at your side.

SAINT
LOUIS IX

📅 1214 - 1270   🌍 FRANCE   🕯 25 AUGUST

Q: DO MONEY AND POWER CORRUPT?

CAN A RICH PERSON GO TO HEAVEN?

Louis was destined to be king of France from birth, and was crowned in Reims at the age of twelve. His mother governed in his name until he came of age. His loving marriage with Margaret was founded on their shared fondness of God. He was skilled in diplomacy as well as armed defence, and ruled his kingdom with dedication, fairness and charity. His daily life was regulated by prayer, and he attended at least one Mass every day. In spite of his reforms towards a fairer tax system, he was a truly rich man. He never renounced his enormous wealth, but used part of it to care for the poor and sick and set up hospitals and institutions. He personally visited them, and knelt down to care for them with love. He supported sacred arts throughout his kingdom, and built a splendid chapel in Paris to hold the relics of Jesus he had brought from the Holy Land. His desire for the crusades was to defend Christianity against attacks *(see #TwGOD 2.31)*. His true care for his subjects was expressed in many ways and he shows that money and power do not necessarily lead to corruption.

O God, King Louis knew that money and power are not everything. Help me recognise that my relationship with you is my most precious 'possession.' Saint Louis of France, pray for us!

SCAN

THE EYE OF THE NEEDLE

Jesus seems to pick on the rich especially: 'It is easier for a camel to go through the eye of a needle than for someone who is rich to enter the kingdom of God' (Mt 19:24). However, when the disciples asked who then can be saved, Jesus said that for God all things are possible. So, wealth does not exclude you from salvation, as is also proved by various wealthy saints: Pier Giorgio Frassati, Cunegunde, Henry II, Thomas More, Homobonus, Nicholas, Louis and Zelie Martin, for example. They were generous, but many of them held on to their fortune of which they considered themselves stewards. So if wealth in itself is not the stumbling block, what is?

GOD AT THE CENTRE

What these saints all have in common is that they placed God at the centre of their lives. Their wealth was secondary. Jesus warned against the danger of money becoming an idol: 'No one can serve two masters... You cannot serve God and wealth' (Mt 6:24). There is a true danger that money and the power which comes with it corrupts a person. Whenever the gospel exalts poverty, it is not because it is so nice to be poor. On the contrary, Jesus calls on the rich to help the poor to get out of their condition. The poverty of the gospel means having nothing that holds you back from embracing God's love wholeheartedly: not wealth, not power, no disordered affections... This goes for all of us: as soon as you can, get rid of whatever hinders you from following Jesus in your life. But if your possessions are less important than loving God and doing his will, you may hold on to them, and use them wisely according to your vocation.

CHALLENGE OR OPPORTUNITY?

Every possession comes with the responsibility to use it well: 'From everyone to whom much has been given, much will be required' (Lk 12:48). This is a challenge we all have to face. Obviously it is your responsibility to use your bike or car without

---

INSTRUCTIONS TO MY SON

'My dearest son, my first instruction is that you should love the Lord your God with all your heart and all your strength. Without this there is no salvation... If the Lord has permitted you to have some trial, bear it willingly and with gratitude, considering that it has happened for your good and that perhaps you well deserved it... If the Lord bestows upon you any kind of prosperity, thank him humbly and see that you become no worse for it, either through vain pride or anything else, because you ought not to oppose God or offend him in the matter of his gifts... Be kind-hearted to the poor, the unfortunate and the afflicted. Give them as much help and consolation as you can... Be devout and obedient to our mother the Church of Rome... Thank God for all the benefits he has bestowed upon you, that you may be worthy to receive greater.' [Louis of France, Instructions to his son, ca. 1267]

---

hurting anyone. But whoever owns a means of transportation can also use it to help others, like doing the shopping for your neighbour or driving her to church. The same applies to your other possessions. Not everyone is called to give all of their possessions away. Just imagine the unlikely scenario that we would all act like Saint Francis, giving everything away to start begging: there would be no one left to give us something then! It can be all right to live a comfortable life, as long as God comes first and you are ready to help those in need. Or, in the words of Saint Augustine: 'Love, and do what you will.' What does this mean for you?

> As long as God, not money or power, is the centre of your life, wealth and responsibility are not wrong. You do not have to give every penny away, although charity is an important virtue.

SAINT
JOHN VIANNEY
– CURÉ OF ARS

 1786 – 1859 FRANCE 4 AUGUST

Q: WHY SHOULD I GIVE MONEY TO THE CHURCH?

IS GOD INTERESTED IN MONEY?

John came from a Catholic family in Dardilly, France. He grew up at the time of the French Revolution, which led to the persecution of priests and faithful. John saw the priests who continued their ministry in these dangerous times as heroes and wanted to be one of them. He was not the best of students and struggled, especially with Latin. Thanks more to his devotion to God than to his knowledge, he was eventually ordained to the priesthood. Three years later he was appointed parish priest of Ars, which had little over 200 inhabitants. This would not seem to be the best place for a bright career in the Church…*(see Saint 1.50)*. But John immediately devoted himself to the care of his parishioners, who — as a result of the Revolution — spent their Sundays partying and drinking rather than praying and serving others.

O God, John wanted to give honour to God by building up the Church and giving material aid to the poor. Help me to support the Church as much as I can. Saint John Vianney, pray for us!

SCAN

CONFESSIONAL

John reminded his little flock that service to God and fellow human beings was the only way to find true and lasting happiness. He taught them devotion to the Blessed Sacrament and spent hours of prayer in front of the tabernacle (see Saint 2.13). This is where he found inspiration for his sermons against blasphemy, self-indulgence, indifference, and about the love for God and the duty of the faithful. His great dedication to the souls of his flock gained him a growing fame and people came from far away to see him. John spent 12 or even more hours every day in the confessional listening to them, forgiving them in God's name, and giving them his spiritual advice. Tens of thousands of pilgrims flocked to Ars over the years. Somewhere in his heart he desired to become a monk, and even ran away several times to a monastery. Each time, he came back, because he felt that it was in the confessional in Ars that he had to live his vocation.

MONEY FOR THE CHURCH

John led a very poor life, with an extremely simple diet. Like most priests today, he lived from what the people gave him for his ministry and happily shared the best parts with those in need. He lived a strict life of penance and fasting (see Saint 2.9), but he was gentle to those who confessed their sins, saying: 'I give them a light penance and perform the rest myself.' He did not mind spending his small revenue on the poor or on the decoration of his church. Nothing was too good for God, and over the years the faithful decorated the parish church of Ars with beautiful works of art. John wanted to show people what was most important in life: the presence of God, to whom we should give all the honour we can both in the liturgy and in the service to our neighbour. Many of his penitents wanted to bring a little sacrifice, and entrusted John with the money he needed for his good works.

LOVE IS THE SOURCE OF PRAYER

'I love you, O my God, and my only desire is to love you until the last breath of my life. I love you, O my infinitely lovable God, and I would rather die loving you, than live without loving you. I love you, Lord, and the only grace I ask is to love you eternally... My God, if my tongue cannot say in every moment that I love you, I want my heart to repeat it to you as often as I draw breath.'

[John Vianney, Prayer, in: Catechism of the Catholic Church 2658]

GIVING

God is not interested in money as such, but it is a means to an end. Jesus was able to travel and preach thanks to the financial support of his followers (Lk 8:3). 'It is more blessed to give than to receive' (Acts 20:35). Giving is a little sacrifice through which you can bring honour to God. By giving money to the Church you help support her important ministry. The answer to what the Church can do with your money is manifold: help poor people, educate children, decorate and maintain the church building, feed ministers, publish books or work with new media, proclaim the gospel, and much more. So, there is good reason and a great need to support the Church. Do you sometimes give money to the Church?

God is interested in the sharing of his love, which can be helped by money. Jesus was also supported financially, and also today the Church can do much good with your money.

SAINT **MARY MAGDALENE**

📅 1ST C.   🌐 HOLY LAND   🕯 22 JULY

SCAN

Q: ARE WOMEN CONSIDERED INFERIOR TO MEN IN CHRISTIANITY?

Mary Magdalene was one of Jesus's most faithful followers, together with some other women who supported him financially (Lk 8:2-3). She is mentioned over 12 times in the Gospels, which is much more than many of the Apostles. Jesus had cast seven demons out of her (Mk 16:9; Lk 8:2). Because of this, later generations saw her as a penitent sinner, possibly a prostitute, who came to Jesus for forgiveness, and washed his feet with holy oil (Lk 7:36-50). However, there is no proof that this is the same Mary.

FEMALE PRESENCE

Unlike the great majority of the male Apostles, Mary Magdalene stood firmly at the feet of Jesus's cross at the moment of his greatest agony. She was accompanied by two other women called Mary, one of them surely the mother of Jesus (see #TwGOD 1.30).

O God, Mary Magdalene followed Jesus closely. Help me to appreciate the contribution of every member of your community and find my personal vocation. Saint Mary Magdalene, pray for us!

Jesus was 'born of a woman', Scripture says (*Gal 4:4*). And he died in their comforting and prayerful presence. After his resurrection, he did not show himself first to the Apostles, but instead turned to the women who came to care for him even in his death. The scene of Jesus meeting with Mary Magdalene in the garden of the tomb is very beautiful and powerful (*Jn 20:1-18; see box*). Jesus made her a key Apostle, who was chosen to bring the news of his resurrection to the eleven Apostles!

MARY'S POWER

God clearly gave a great responsibility to women like Jesus's mother (*see Saint 2.50*)and Mary Magdalene. Unfortunately, in the history of the Church this has not always been acknowledged. Thankfully, today the awareness is growing that we need to rebalance responsibility within the Church. Both women and men are part of God's creation, and of the Church community. Each of the sexes have their strengths and weaknesses. All of these are needed in our community. We need to recognise both the absolute equality of value, and pay attention to the natural differences as created by God (*see #TwGOD 2.16*). In the end it is about God calling people for specific tasks in the Church. And these tasks are different for every individual.

GREAT CONTRIBUTION

Pope John Paul II called Mary Magdalene the 'first witness of the resurrection' (*21 May 1997*). Pope Francis referred to her as the 'Apostle of the new and greatest hope' (*17 May 2017*). Her role as an apostle is different from that of the male Apostles, but surely not less important. The testimony of someone who was as close to Jesus as she must have been very powerful. Throughout the ages there have been many female missionaries who have done great work for the proclamation of the gospel, precisely because of their passion and love for him (*see e.g. Saint 1.07, 1.11, 1.16 & 1.48-1.49*). And think of the women scientists, teachers, world leaders, sisters, heroic mothers,

> ### I HAVE COME TO FREE YOU
>
> *'Jesus calls her: "Mary!": the revolution of her life, the revolution destined to transform the life of every man and every woman begins with a name which echoes in the garden of the empty sepulchre. The Gospels describe Mary's happiness. Jesus's resurrection is not a joy which is measured with a dropper, but a waterfall that cascades over life. Christian life is not woven of soft joys, but of waves which engulf everything. You too, try to imagine, right now, with the baggage of disappointments and failures that each of us carries in our heart, that there is a God close to us who calls us by name and says to us: "Rise, stop weeping, for I have come to free you!"'*
>
> [Pope Francis, General Audience, 17 May 2017]

politicians... The role of women can definitely not be considered inferior to that of men (*see #TwGOD 2.16*). Not in any way! Not in society and not in the Church! Much can still be improved, though. May Mary Magdalene's example inspire our Church structures to uphold the equality of women and men, while taking advantage in the positive sense of the great contribution of women, with respect for their mutual difference. What contribution can you give?

Women and men have equal importance in the eyes of God and the Church, and are called to be great apostles. Equal treatment is imperative, while recognising their different qualities.

SAINT
CATHERINE
OF SIENA

 1347 – 1380   ITALY   🕯 29 APRIL

.SCAN

Q: WHY IS THE CHURCH SUCH A MAN'S WORLD?

Catherine was born in Siena, Italy, in a Catholic family of cloth dyers. She was a wilful teenager and once cut off her beautiful long hair in protest at her mother trying to make her attract a husband. She was similarly adverse to life as a cloistered nun. Thus, she opted for an active and prayerful life in the lay branch or third order of the Dominicans. She promised God that she would not marry, but continued to live at home (see Saint 2.3). She donned the Dominican habit, spent much time in prayer and solitude, and cared for the sick and poor. Soon she attracted a group of followers. She started to travel with them through parts of Italy, and called for the reform of the clergy. She also called people to change their lives by abandoning themselves to the love of God.

DIPLOMAT AND MYSTIC

Catherine became very influential because of her deep knowledge of philosophy and theology, combined with her total dedication to God. She exchanged letters with influential friends, and even with Pope Gregory XI. She begged for peace and for the reform of the clergy.

O God, Catherine did a lot of good for the Church. Help me to find my own vocation and by living it to the full, contribute to our Church community. Saint Catherine of Siena, pray for us!

At the time, the popes lived in Avignon, France (see #TwGOD 2.33). In 1376, Catherine was sent to Avignon as ambassador of the Republic of Florence. Her attempts to establish a peace treaty with the Papal States were unsuccessful, but she also used the opportunity to try to convince the pope to return to Rome. A year later the pope indeed changed his residence to Rome. He sent Catherine to Florence to bring about peace, which she eventually was able to do. During all her diplomatic activity she spent much time in prayer, and she had various mystical experiences. She wrote hundreds of letters, prayers, and her profoundly spiritual book *The Dialogue of Divine Providence*. She died when she was 33 years old.

ROOM FOR CHANGE

Since the time of Catherine, much has changed: most prelates are living in accordance with their vows, and women are more valued. At the same time, much still needs to be improved. However, the question of why the Church is such a man's world starts from a wrong perspective. The Church consists of all the baptised faithful, laity and clergy together. Each of them is called to join in 'running' the Church, each according to the vocation to which God calls him or her. Every individual is like a brick in the wall of the single church building (see Saint 1.50). Ordination is just one of the vocations, and the clergy amounts to approximately 0.03% of the faithful (see #TwGOD 2.1). Looked at from an organisational point of view, it seems rather strange to concentrate all power for decision-making in this small group. Appointing women in key positions would indeed be a great improvement, but the reflection needs to go deeper. We need to grow in our understanding of the vocation of the lay faithful, which goes beyond just performing a role in a specific position.

CLERICALISM

Pope Francis was aware of the importance of involving women at the level of decision-making. Just as his

THE FEMININE GENIUS

'When they tell me... "In the Church women must be dicastery heads, for example!" Yes, they can, in certain dicasteries they can; but what you are asking is simple functionalism. That is not rediscovering woman's role in the Church... This is a great thing, it is a functional thing; but what is essential to the woman's role is – speaking in theological terms – to acting in a manner which expresses the feminine genius. When we face a problem among men we come to a conclusion, but when we face that same problem with women the outcome will be different. It will follow the same path, but it will be richer, stronger, more intuitive. For this reason women in the Church should have this role...to clarify the feminine genius in so many ways.'

[Pope Francis, Address to the religious of Rome, 16 May 2015]

predecessor, Gregory XI, listened to Catherine, he wanted to listen to the 'feminine genius' (see box). At the same time, he warned strongly against every form of clericalism. Clericalism is closely related to careerism and looks at position or importance rather than vocation. Clericalism is wrong for both clergy and laity. The pope said: 'Women in the Church must be valued, not "clericalised."' The challenge for the future is to find new ways to truly include women and lay faithful in decision-making in the Church, with respect for their personal vocations. Will you join in this honest search?

The Church consists of all faithful, laity and clergy together: each individual should live their personal vocation. We need to search for just ways to involve women at the highest levels.

SAINT
HILDEGARD
OF BINGEN

 CA. 1098 – 1179   GERMANY   17 SEPTEMBER

.SCAN

Q: IS THE CHURCH AGAINST FEMINISM?

WHAT ABOUT "GENDER THEORY"?

Hildegard was educated by Benedictine sisters in the Rhineland, Germany. At the age of 42, she was chosen to succeed her holy teacher Jutta as abbess. This is when Hildegard's 'public' life started. This truly remarkable woman had great skills in mathematics, pharmacy, medicine, philosophy, and theology, but also in music, poetry, writing, preaching, and composing, for example. Above all, she was a woman of God who dedicated herself fully to him in her religious life as a Benedictine nun. She was so close to him that she had regular visions which helped her to see daily reality in the light of God's love. This prompted her to call on all faithful, including the clergy, to reconvert to him, and to change their lives. In spite of her poor health, she went on several preaching tours through Germany. She exchanged letters with the popes of her time. Pope Eugenius III was especially impressed by her work, and a great supporter of her writings. Because of her wisdom and knowledge, many people turned to Hildegard for advice.

O God, Hildegard was a woman after your own heart. Help me to fight any form of discrimination, while upholding the truth about you. Saint Hildegard of Bingen, pray for us!

FEMINIST?

Generally, feminism advocates women's rights on the basis of the equality of the sexes, while recognising that man and woman are not exactly the same. The Church can only be in favour of such striving for equal rights *(see Saint 1.47)*. Things become more difficult when feminism is connected to other themes like gender theory *(see below)*, same-sex relations *(see Saint 2.38)*, or claiming a "right" to specific vocations *(see Saint 1.48)*. Hildegard took on many tasks that were considered "male" in her time, and she did not hesitate to confront world leaders, including Emperor Barbarossa, about their rule and political choices. She upheld the view that both men and women are created in the image of God, and that the sexes are complementary. Both men and women have something different to contribute *(see Saint 1.47)*. In Hildegard's time, God was often depicted with almost exclusively male traits. Her theology helped to get a more just view of God, who in his being encompasses both female and male qualities.

GENDER THEORY

In general, gender theories maintain that female or male identity is not the result of being born as a girl or a boy, but of the social and cultural context in which a child grows up. One of the consequences is that one would be free to discover one's own gender identity. Hildegard, with her view of the complementarity of the sexes, would strongly oppose such gender theories. Nature itself contradicts this view: people are born in a male or female body. Our body is part of our identity as created by God. It is true that a small percentage of all women and men struggle with the gender in which they were born, and these people deserve understanding and help *(see #TwGOD 4.31)*. But it would be wrong to confuse the many children that do not have this problem.

RECIPROCITY AND EQUALITY

'The human being exists in both the male and female form. Hildegard recognised that a relationship of reciprocity and a substantial equality between man and woman is rooted in this ontological structure of the human condition... In Hildegard are expressed the most noble values of womanhood: hence the presence of women in the Church and in society is also illumined by her presence, both from the perspective of scientific research and that of pastoral activity. Her ability to speak to those who were far from the faith and from the Church make Hildegard a credible witness of the new evangelisation.'

[Pope Benedict XVI, Hildegard of Bingen Doctor of the Church, 7 October 2012]

DISCRIMINATION

Discrimination against transgender people is very wrong, and these people should be helped and accompanied, also by the Church. At the same time, the result of gender discussions can easily lead to discrimination in the other direction. Freedom of religion is a fundamental freedom *(see Saint 1.15)*, and should apply to everyone. The Catholic view that gender is given at birth, and that God created our bodies with our entire being, does not intend to discriminate against anyone. Rather, it upholds the truth God wants to share with us. Catholics upholding this truth should be free to do so, and not be discriminated against. How can you contribute?

Both women and men have equal rights; their complementarity should be recognised. 'Gender theories' can lead to confusion and must be approached carefully.

SAINT **ANDREW THE APOSTLE**

 CA. 69   30 NOVEMBER

 HOLY LAND, GREECE, BULGARIA, RUSSIA

SCAN

Q: IS IT POSSIBLE TO MAKE A CAREER IN THE CHURCH?

Andrew was the brother of Peter the Apostle (see Saint 1.4). Both were fishermen, just like the Apostles John and James. In the Gospels, Jesus's disciples are often mentioned in groups of four, and Andrew is always in the first group. So, he was very close to Jesus. However, if you read the Gospels carefully, Andrew is simply a steady presence in the background. He seems to be the least of his group. He is always mentioned after his brother. Still, it was Andrew who met Jesus first, and then brought Peter to him *(Jn 1:40-42)*. That gives a good idea of his entire career: like most of us he is not the first, not the most important, but he is a very faithful follower of Jesus. And he does not have a problem with this! Rather, he is happy to be with Jesus.

SERVICE

Andrew is a good example for all who sometimes desire to advance in the community, to become more important or famous than others. Andrew did become famous, yes, and also important, but he never looked for it, and he did not grasp for himself what was not meant for him.

O God, Andrew followed Jesus closely, while being humble and simple. Help me not to be overtaken by wrong ambition, but to live only for Jesus. Saint Andrew the Apostle, pray for us!

Rather, he simply lived his life as a Christian and accepted the mission given to him as a service to Jesus and the community of the faithful. An ancient tradition tells us that after Jesus's death, Andrew became the Apostle of the Greek-speaking world: he went to Greece, Bulgaria and even to Russia. His 'career' seemed to end with the anti-climax of his death as a martyr: he was crucified like a criminal on a cross shaped like an X, which henceforth was called Saint Andrew's Cross. But for him it was the highpoint in his spiritual career!

NO CAREERISM

Whenever people speak of 'making a career in the Church' something goes completely wrong! The only career a Christian should wish for is to be close to Jesus. This does not mean that ambition is always wrong *(see Saint 1.13)*. However, in our society, we think in terms of the important, the famous... We consider it normal that kings, rock stars, or bishops receive the best places and are served by others. But no one in the Church should claim such treatment for their own. Therefore, Pope Francis often warned against the dangers of careerism in the Church *(6 June 2013)*. Obviously, we need to distinguish between role and person. A bishop who visits one of his communities is bound to sit in the middle, and get all the attention. This is natural and good, for he is their leader and shepherd. Also, he cannot carry out his great responsibility alone: he needs every help and support he can get! But a leader is first of all a member of the community. Jesus said that a real leader is appointed to serve the others, not to be served *(Lk 22:24-27)*.

JUST A STONE

Andrew realised that in the end every Christian, regardless of their function, is just one single stone in the great brick building which is the Church *(see #TwGOD 3.20-3.21)*. And each of these stones can be taken out without the entire building collapsing immediately. That danger exists only when many

> ## *WE HAVE FOUND CHRIST*
>
> *'When Andrew had been with Jesus, and had learned so much from him, he did not keep this treasure to himself. He made haste and ran to his brother, to share with him what he had learned... This action of sharing his spiritual gains with others was born of brotherly love, family ties, and genuine affection... But notice also the eager and obedient spirit of Peter. The moment he heard the news he hurried at once to Jesus with his brother... Andrew brought him to Jesus. He put Peter into his hands so that he could learn everything from Jesus himself... Andrew, who was not capable of giving a full explanation...brought his brother to the source of light itself, in so much haste and joy that he would not brook the slightest delay.'*
>
> [John Chrysostom, Homily on Saint John's Gospel, 19,1]

stones are corrupted. The lady who waters the flowers in church, the treasurer, the woman leading the parish council, the priest or the bishop: each of them has a specific role to fulfil. Each of them is one single stone in the building of the Church. Depending on their role they are placed at a certain position in the stone wall. But they are all stone bricks that look exactly the same, and have the same value in God's eyes. So why aspire to be more than you are?

The only career to desire is to be close to Jesus. Selfish desire to grow in importance is wrong. Everyone is called to live their own vocation to the full.

BLESSED
PETER TO ROT

1.51

 CA. 1912-1945 🌐 PAPUA NEW GUINEA 🕯 7 JULY

VENERABLE
SUZANNE AUBERT

 1835-1926 🌐 AUCKLAND, WELLINGTON

🕯 30 NOVEMBER [†1 OCTOBER]

SCAN

Q: DO I NEED TO BECOME A PRIEST OR NUN TO BECOME A SAINT?

Peter was born in the village of Rakunai, in today's Papua New Guinea. At the age of 18, he started to train as a catechist with the Missionaries of the Sacred Heart (msc). He excelled in his studies, and developed a particular love for the Bible. As a catechist, he was known for his clear teaching and openness to the needs of others. He married Paula Ia Varpit, and they had three children. They prayed together every day, and Paula supported her husband in his intense tasks as a catechist. Together they lived what he taught. In 1942 the Japanese invaded the island. They imprisoned the missionaries and destroyed the churches. Peter did what he could to help the people in his district maintain their faith. He prayed with them, baptised children, married couples, distributed the Eucharist to the sick, presided over funerals, and even built a church out of branches. When the Japanese occupiers tried to reintroduce the practice of polygamy, Peter protested and called his people to remain faithful to God's commands. At the end of 1944 he was arrested and imprisoned in a concentration camp. The Japanese, seeing his influence, killed him secretly. The crowd of faithful at his funeral recognised him as 'A martir ure ra Lotu': a martyr for the faith.

O God, Peter and Suzanne embraced their vocation with great passion. Help me to do the same and give you all my love. Blessed Peter To Rot and Venerable Suzanne Aubert, pray for us!

LIVING FOR OTHERS

Suzanne was born in a village near Lyon, France. Her parents arranged her marriage, but with the help of the Curé of Ars she found her true calling (see Saint 1.46). She secretly studied medicine and chemistry before becoming a missionary sister in Auckland, New Zealand. Unhappy with her initial task of teaching wealthy girls, Sister Mary Joseph co-founded the community of the Holy Family in Freeman's Bay to educate Māori children. She placed much emphasis on the study of the local language and culture. In 1871 she moved to Hawke's Bay to support the mission there. Together with old Māori she searched for medicinal herbs and treatments of new diseases. In her desire to stimulate communication, she revised a Māori prayer book and compiled several phrase books. In the area of the Whanganui River, she set up a dispensary, a church, a school, and everything else that was needed. In 1892 Mother Aubert founded the Congregation of the Sisters of Compassion. To make a living, she sold her medicines with great success. In 1899 she arrived in Wellington, where she got busy immediately by setting up a soup kitchen, creche, orphanage, hospitals, and much more. In Rome she obtained the official recognition of her congregation from the pope. She was the first woman in New Zealand to be buried with national honours.

A MARRIED SAINT

Not much needs to be added to find an answer to the question at hand. Peter and Paula's vocation to married life did not keep them from leading a holy life. In fact, they show how teaching and witnessing the faith is a task of all faithful, and that this call is fully compatible with married life. Paula even supported Peter when he risked his life for teaching the

---

THE SURE PATH TO SAINTHOOD

'Let us love God alone. Let him be really ours and let us be really his. Let him reign in us, and let us live in him. He is ever near us with his kindness and mercy, which he desires to pour on souls. Let us respond to his designs by the practice of charity.'

[Suzanne Aubert, in: Directory 2, p 195]

---

faith. Suzanne was restless in her desire to help people in their difficulties, and to teach them the faith. She could not have done all she did had she been married, so that her way of becoming a saint fits perfectly with her vocation to the religious life.

VOCATION TO SAINTHOOD

Everyone has their own vocation — but we all are called to become saints. There is no need for you to copy the lives of Peter or Suzanne in everything. You have your own calling. Husbands, sisters, priests, wives, nuns, catechists, we are all called to live our personal vocation to the full. That is the best and only way to become a saint. What is your vocation?

Everyone is called to become a saint, not only priests and religious. When you abandon your own desires, you can find your personal path to God. This will lead you to sainthood!

'If you are
what you should be,
you will set the
whole world on fire!'

Saint Catherine
of Siena

Online
with
Saints

PART 2

SAINTS ON OUR RELATIONSHIP
WITH GOD AND OTHERS

SAINT
BENEDICT
OF NURSIA

📅 CA. 480 – CA. 545   🌐 ITALY

🕯 11 JULY; 14 MARCH (EAST)

.SCAN

Q: HOW DID THE SAINTS PRAY?

HOW CAN I LEARN TO PRAY LIKE THEM?

Benedict was born in Nursia, Italy, where he grew up with his sister Scholastica. The little we know about his life comes from the writings of Saint Gregory. Benedict studied in Rome, but felt himself drawn to silence, so that he could contemplate the love of God quietly. He became a hermit, living alone in a cave near Subiaco for several years. He was asked to be abbot of a nearby monastery, but his governance was considered too strict, and apparently someone even tried to poison him, so he returned to his cave. As disciples gathered around him, he decided to found the monastery of Monte Cassino in a deserted place in Italy. He wrote a monastic Rule, containing a set of rules to help his monks live a life of prayer, study, manual work, and community life. This Rule of Saint Benedict shows him as a fatherly figure, firm but loving, and above all a man with great love for Jesus. It presents a balanced way of life, alternating between prayer and work, duty and rest, private study and community life. This is summarised in the motto *ora et labora*, pray and work. Benedict's Rule inspired the foundation of many monasteries throughout Europe and the entire world *(see #TwGOD 2.9 & 2.25)*.

O God, Benedict dedicated his entire life to work and prayer, in his search to be with you. Help me to search for you in my life and learn to pray better. Saint Benedict of Nursia, pray for us!

BENEDICTINE READING

The most visible part of Benedictine prayer is the liturgy of the hours: seven times a day the bell rings, and the monks stop whatever they are doing to gather in the church to pray together (see #TwGOD 3.13). And they also take time for personal prayer. In his Rule, Saint Benedict spoke of the importance of spiritual reading of the Bible, also called Lectio Divina (see Appendix 4). This existed already before Benedict, and consists of four basic steps to help you pray. Read — take a Bible text, read it slowly, and see what it says in itself. Meditate — take time to absorb what you read and ponder on the meaning of the text. Pray — speak to God on the basis of what you read, praising, asking, thanking... Contemplate — basically just be with God, surrendering yourself to him, trying to see things from his perspective. As a final point, bring your faith into action by learning more about God and helping your neighbour.

CARMELITE MYSTICISM

Love much, do not think much, Saint Teresa of Avila said about prayer (see Saint 2.4). She refrained from giving a specific method, and saw prayer as a friendly conversation with God. 'We need no wings to go in search of God, but have only to find a place where we can be alone and look upon him present within us.' First, prayer is not in abstract thinking, but in realising the love of God for you — and his presence in your soul. Second, be willing to spend time alone with God, surrendering yourself to him, letting go of your personal desires. Third, try to look at God present in your soul. Teresa's advice: 'Do not tire your brain by trying to work it during meditation.' Contemplative prayer is about contemplating God, about looking at him, like you could look at a sleeping person whom you love, without any words or action.

IGNATIAN SEARCHING

Saint Ignatius gave a very specific description of how to go about praying in his Spiritual Exercises, which helped many

---

> ## ASKING GOD
>
> 'Whenever we want to ask some favour of a powerful man, we do it humbly and respectfully, for fear of presumption. How much more important, then, to lay our petitions before the Lord God of all things with the utmost humility and sincere devotion. We must know that God regards our purity of heart and tears of compunction, not our many words. Prayer should therefore be short and pure, unless perhaps it is prolonged under the inspiration of divine grace. In community, however, prayer should always be brief; and when the superior gives the signal, all should rise together.'
>
> [Benedict of Nursia, Rule, Ch. 20]

people to learn to pray and to find God's Will (see Saint 1.34). His step-by-step approach is easy to apply, and has been added as an example (see #TwGOD Appendix 4). Ignatius wanted to find God in everything, which is why he placed much emphasis on a brief evening prayer (see #TwGOD Appendix 5). Look back over your day to see how God was present, and what he might have wished to say to you.

Each of these three approaches to prayer may help you at some point, but note that what works for your neighbour may not work for you. Speak about your prayer method with your spiritual director (see Saint 1.10) and find which approach suits you best. Do you dare to try all three ways of prayer?

> The saints used different forms of prayer: reading the Bible in various steps, contemplating the love of God, or doing "spiritual exercises" so as to recognise the will of God for them.

SAINT
TERESA OF CALCUTTA

 1910 – 1997   ALBANIA, INDIA   5 SEPTEMBER

Q: IS PRAYER A WASTE OF TIME?

HOW CAN I FIND TIME FOR GOD WHEN LIFE WON'T SLOW DOWN?

Mother Teresa was an Albanian missionary in Calcutta (now called Kolkata), India. She had given up everything she had for a life of poverty. With her sisters, the Missionaries of Charity, she cared daily for many poor, sick, and dying people. Precisely because of her humble service to the poorest among the poor, she came to speak with leaders of nations, converse with popes, and receive the Nobel Peace Prize. Her great love for Jesus made her dedicate much time to prayer, in spite of her very active life.

WASTED?

Prayer is a gift to God of something very precious: your time and attention. This is the best way to answer to his love for you! For many years, Mother Teresa experienced total dryness in her prayer: nothing happened when she prayed; she felt empty and lonely (see #TwGOD 3.6 & 4.12). Still, she continued to make time for prayer every day. She knew deep down that she did not pray for her own well-being in the first place, but to spend time with God (see box).

SCAN

O God, Mother Teresa placed prayer before everything else. Help me to make time for prayer every day and be faithful in honouring it. Saint Teresa of Calcutta, pray for us!

Their daily hour of prayer in front of the Blessed Sacrament gave her and the sisters strength and inspiration to know, love and serve Jesus also in their brothers and sisters in need (see Saint 2.13). Far from being wasted, their prayer time was the source of everything else they did. The same is true for you: every minute spent in true and selfless prayer is very well spent, and will help you move forward in your life.

TOO BUSY TO PRAY

Sometimes many sick people were carried into the convent at the same time and all needed attention immediately. When stress was building up among the sisters, they might cry out: 'How on earth are we going to help all these people, there is too much to do!' You will probably sometimes feel the same. One evening, two young sisters asked Mother Teresa to be freed from their daily hour of adoration because of all the work. Her remarkable reply was: 'Tonight, you shall pray two hours instead of one. In order to pray well, you sometimes have to pray more.' And at another time she said: 'If you are too busy to pray, you are too busy!'

MAKING TIME

The best way to grow in your relationship with God is to pray every day (see Saint 1.5 & 1.9). You can only find time for prayer if you make time! Your prayer can be very short in the beginning, the most important thing is that you pray (see #TwGOD 3.7). The following tips may help.

- Try to find a daily moment, dedicating your best time to God. Book your daily prayer time in your calendar, and honour it like you would any appointment.

- For example, calculate your prayer time as being part of your morning routine, sitting down for a moment amidst showering and brushing your teeth. You may have to get up a little earlier, but all your day will be brightened because of your prayer.

- Before you fall asleep, thank God briefly for the day, say sorry for what was not in accordance with his love, and you'll have prayed almost without noticing!

- Be inventive: try praying during your commute, or take a moment for prayer in the car before entering your house. Throw in little prayers of thanksgiving or intercession during the day. And maybe book a weekly 'lunch date with God'.

- Finally, don't get stressed when you miss your prayer time: God knows your honest desire to make time for him. Just tell him how much you love him, ask your favourite saint to pray for you, and get on with the emergency you are dealing with. Do you want to make time for prayer?

Even a short prayer changes your day: you're not alone but with God. You'll find time only when you make it, just as you make time for whatever is most important for you.

SAINT
ROSE OF LIMA

📅 1586 – 1617   🌐 PERU   🕯 23 AUGUST

Q: WHAT IF I DO NOT KNOW HOW TO PRAY?

WHAT IS THE BEST WAY TO PRAY?

Rose was born as Isabella in Lima, Peru, in a family of small landowners. She was so beautiful that she received the nickname Rose, which she officially took as her name at confirmation. Already as a child she wanted to become a religious sister. Rose's family wanted her to marry, but she remained true to the desire of her childhood. She became an external member (tertiary) of the Dominican order. Thus she was not officially a religious, but closely connected to the spirituality of Saint Dominic while continuing to live at home. At the age of 21 she formally vowed to live a life of virginity and prayer for the sake of Jesus and started to wear a religious habit.

O God, Rose dedicated her life totally to Jesus in prayer and service. Help me to learn to pray better and be faithful to my prayer time. Saint Rose of Lima, pray for us!

PRAYER AND PENANCE

Rose regularly withdrew to a small cabin behind her house to contemplate and pray. She wanted to be with Jesus at every moment, especially in his ultimate suffering on the cross. Therefore she chose a life of prayer, poverty, penance, and charity to those who needed her help. At a young age, when she started to attract suitors because of her great beauty, she marred her face with pepper and caused it to blister. You could say that this is self-harm, but her reasons were different. She wanted to place not herself, but God at the centre of her life. Be aware, however, that the great penance she chose to inflict on herself is not for everyone. There is no need for you to do the same. In today's world there is so much suffering that there is little need to add more! By accepting with faith the unavoidable suffering we encounter in our life and that of others, we can share in the saving suffering of Jesus *(see Saint 1.39)*.

COMMUNICATING WITH GOD

Prayer is communicating with God. There is no set way in which you should do this, and no need for complicated phrases. Keep it simple *(Mt 6:7-8)*. Basically, every form of prayer consists of opening your heart to God as Rose did. You can talk, shout, ask, tweet... Do not worry when you do not know what to say: God also understands you without words. Alternatively, you can always use the prayer that Jesus taught his disciples, the Our Father *(Lk 11:2-4)*. Do not give up too soon, and persevere in telling God your deepest desire *(Lk 11:5-13)*. The most important thing is to dedicate time to him in silence and prayer *(Mt 6:6)*. You can pray alone, or with others *(Mt 18:20)*. Also, you can ask the saints and Mary our Mother to join you in your prayer, for example by praying the rosary *(see Tweeting with GOD app)*. Whichever way of praying you choose, always ask the Holy Spirit to help you pray in such a way that not you but God is at the centre of your prayer *(Rom 8:26-27)*.

> ## AFTER SUFFERING FOLLOWS GRACE
>
> *'Let all know that after sorrow follows grace... I felt as if my soul could not be detained in the prison house of the body, but that it must burst its chains, and free and impeded, rush through the whole world calling out: "If only mortal people would know how wonderful divine grace is, how beautiful, how precious. How many riches it hides within itself, how many joys and delights!"'*
>
> *[Rose of Lima, Letter to Dr Castillo]*

Even when you ask God to help you with his grace *(see box)*, for example to pray better, you do not do this in the first place for your own good, but to become a better follower of Jesus.

FROM PRAYER TO ACTION

A life of prayer does not mean being sterile or detached from the pain and suffering of this world. Rose was successful in her vocation, precisely because it was based on her prayer life and her friendship with Jesus. She was always ready to help others and her neighbours never called on her for help in vain. The same applies to you: if you learn to pray better and abandon yourself completely to God in prayer, you will gradually discover how to discern his will for your life and live as a Christian. The important thing is to keep trying and reach out to God in your prayer every day. What would you like to pray for at this moment?

> *There are many ways to pray. The most important thing is to set apart time for God, and to open yourself to his presence: you can tell him anything you like!*

SAINT
TERESA OF AVILA

📅 1515 – 1582   🌍 SPAIN   🕯 15 OCTOBER

.SCAN

Q: CAN I EVER LEARN TO PRAY?

DO I PRAY TO GET A GOOD FEELING?

Teresa was born into a Spanish noble family in Avila, Spain, and grew up to be a beautiful and proud woman. She loved romance stories, nice clothes, flirting and rebelling. When she was 16, her strict father sent her to a convent to be controlled and educated. After an initial rebellion, Teresa started to like the convent, partly because the discipline was less strict than her father's. When she reached a good age for marriage, she had difficulty in making up her mind. A nun's life did not seem much fun, but marriage had not made her mother perfectly happy either. Teresa was convinced that she was a very sinful girl. She decided to enter a convent of Carmelite sisters so that she would be better protected against sin. Monastic life proved not to be very strict: her sisters, who had promised to leave their worldly lives behind and live only for Jesus, were leading a worldly life with jewellery, vanity, and many visitors. In fact, life in the convent led Teresa to pray less and less.

O God, Teresa knew the world, but chose to live only for Jesus. May I too be able to open myself for your love and start praying persistently. Saint Teresa of Avila, pray for us!

PERSISTENCE

Some 20 years into monastic life, at the insistence of a kind priest, Teresa decided to start praying again. This was very difficult, as she encountered many distractions in her prayer, and it required great persistence. You may recognise her experience: "My mind is so wild that it seems to be like a frantic madman no one can tie down" (see Saint 2.5). But eventually her persistence was rewarded. She received many graces and even visions of Jesus in her prayers. She loved him more and more and spoke very openly to him. One day she realised in prayer that she was too attached to friendships. This discovery gave her a lot of interior freedom, and while she dedicated less time to them, for her real friends she became even a better friend, without false attachments. She was a lovable person who enjoyed life and a good laugh (see #TwGOD 2.14). She loved Jesus above all.

REFORM

One day, she was travelling in bad weather along a muddy stream. Her carriage got stuck and she tumbled into the water with her belongings. As she complained to Jesus, he said: 'That's how I treat my friends', and she replied promptly: 'No wonder you have so few friends.' This made her think. Precisely because Jesus had so few friends, Teresa felt they had to be good friends. So she decided to do what she could to reform her own life, and the Carmelite order. A simple life of prayer and poverty was what she envisioned. She encountered a lot of opposition, and even inquiries by the Spanish Inquisition (see #TwGOD 2.32). But her faith was strong, and she was convinced of the power of prayer. Part of the opposition was because other sisters did not wish to change their lavish lifestyles. But she succeeded and founded many new convents.

THE SOUL AS A CASTLE

Teresa's story shows how you can grow into prayer step-by-step by growing in your relationship with Jesus, and achieve a lot

> ## SHARING BETWEEN FRIENDS
>
> 'When you start to pray, never stop again, even if your life is bad. For prayer is the way to change your life, and without prayer such change will be much more difficult… And for those who do not pray yet, I implore them by the love of the Lord not to deprive themselves from such a great good… If you persevere in prayer, I have good hope that you will receive the mercy of God, for no one ever became his friend without being rewarded amply. Mental prayer in my opinion is nothing else than an intimate sharing between friends; it means taking time frequently to be alone with him who we know loves us.'
>
> [Teresa of Avila, Life, 8,6-7]

when you abandon yourself completely to God. Prayer is not just to make you feel good: it helps you grow in your relationship with God, and ultimately leads to action! But you have to wait for God to speak… Teresa gave a simple but powerful image of the soul as a castle in which you move around. Every step in prayer life is like a room in the castle. Eventually you arrive in the centre where God lives and where he welcomes you. It will take a lot of effort to get there, but is worth every hardship (see box). Listen to her: 'Let nothing trouble you, let nothing frighten you. All things are passing; God never changes. Patience obtains all things. He who possesses God lacks nothing: God alone suffices.' Could that ever be enough for you too?

> Prayer is the result of a growing bond with Jesus. It is about much more than getting a good feeling: this is about your relationship with God. He alone suffices.

SAINT
JEROME

 CA. 347 – 420   SOUTHERN EUROPE, ASIA MINOR

 30 SEPTEMBER; 15 JUNE (EAST)

SCAN

Q: ARE THERE CATHOLIC TECHNIQUES FOR MEDITATION, BREATHING, CALMING MY MIND, BECOMING QUIET, AND DEALING WITH DISTRACTIONS?

Jerome was infamous for his bad temper. His acid pen for those who insulted God or taught error was caused by his intense love of God. He had not always been such a devout man: in his youth in Rome he joined his friends in sensual parties, for which he repented bitterly in later life. Above all he was a mystic who spent hours in silent prayer in his refuge in the desert of Chalcis, Syria. His prayer life was the basis for his extensive studies, which led him to translating the entire Bible into Latin. His translation is called the Vulgate, after the Latin word for 'common', because the common people of his time did not read Greek *(see #TwGOD 1.13)*. He said that praying is speaking with God, and reading the Bible is like God speaking to you *(Letter 22, 25)*.

O God, Jerome withdrew regularly into the silence of his heart. Help me to find the best way to do the same without being disturbed by distractions. Saint Jerome, pray for us!

CATHOLIC MEDITATION

When people hear the word 'meditation' they often think immediately of religious exercises linked to religions like Buddhism with mindfulness, yoga, zen... *(see Saint 1.29)*. As these religions do not intend to connect with God, most of the exercises do not correspond to what we need as Christians. Our prayer is more than mental or physical exercises. Thankfully, there is a long tradition of Christian meditation or contemplation, which was practised by many saints *(see Saint 2.1)*. The aim of Christian prayer is to open ourselves to the presence of God. We do not just want to speak to God and bring our petitions to him, but to speak with him *(see #TwGOD 3.2)*, and spend time with him. In the end, what happens in your prayer is a gift of God, and you can only do so much to get ready for that.

JESUS PRAYER

One of the problems you may face is that your mind keeps running, that you cannot focus and become quiet *(see Saint 2.4)*. Saint Jerome went to the desert to find peace, but that is not a solution for each of us. You could pray the rosary, of course *(see #TwGOD 3.12)*. Or maybe the 'Jesus prayer' can help you. This form of prayer is used in Eastern Catholicism and can help to reach a deep inner silence: *hesychia*, from the Greek 'calm' or 'peace'. You can pray the Jesus prayer on the rhythm of your breathing. Calmly inhale, while you pray: 'Lord Jesus, Son of God...', and as you exhale continue: '...have mercy on me, a sinner.' Repeat this prayer with every breath, at least for a few minutes. Optionally, you can use rosary beads to keep count of the prayers.

DEALING WITH DISTRACTIONS

Saint Thérèse of Lisieux admitted having many distractions in her prayer, when her thoughts drifted away from God *(see Saint 2.42)*. Here are a few tips to deal with such distractions.

> ## ON DISTRACTIONS
>
> "'I will sing praise. I will persevere in the way of integrity,' that I may understand what I am singing and meditate upon the meaning of the psalm; that my mind may not wander off in distraction; my body seems to be praying, but my soul without fruition.'
>
> [Jerome, Homily 27 on Psalm 100(101), in: The Homilies of St. Jerome, Vol. I, 1964, 213]

- Minimise external distractions by turning off your telephone and other means of communication. Do not check your mail or social media just before praying.

- It can help to briefly prepare your prayer so that you get into the 'mood'. For example, you can use the introduction to praying with the Bible *(see Tweeting with GOD Appendix 4)*.

- Accept that distractions are part of you. Ask God to help you stay focused. It is okay not to be perfect, to have difficulty focusing and not to succeed always.

- When you think of something you must do, place it in an imaginary folder somewhere next to you, and forget about it. If it is important, God will help you remember after your prayer.

- Do like Thérèse, and pray for the people, tasks or situations to which your thoughts divert. That way, your distraction gains some sense, and it helps you refocus on God. What tip do you want to try first?

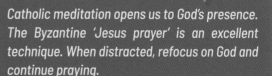

Catholic meditation opens us to God's presence. The Byzantine 'Jesus prayer' is an excellent technique. When distracted, refocus on God and continue praying.

SAINT
CHARBEL

 1828 – 1898 LEBANON

 24 JULY; 3RD SUNDAY OF JULY (MARONITES)

2.6

Q: IS IT REALLY POSSIBLE TO WITHDRAW FROM THE WORLD FOR A LIFE WITH GOD IN PRAYER AND HUMILITY?

Youssef was born into a Christian family in Bekaa Kafra, a Maronite mountain village in Lebanon. Already in his youth, he loved to pray and felt very close to God. The desire for prayer would mark his entire life. He entered the Order of Lebanese Maronite monks (OLM) and received the monastic name Charbel, after a Christian martyr from the second century. In the monastery it became clear that Charbel was very intelligent and he became a great scholar of ancient texts. His homilies showed his strong faith, and were very helpful to the faithful on their path towards God.

O God, the monk Charbel was always very close to Jesus. May I be a little like him in my thirst for prayer and humble service of God. Saint Charbel, pray for us!

.SCAN

FOR GOD ALONE

After 16 years in the monastery, Charbel felt that God was calling him to live a life of even greater silence and seclusion, in order to truly devote himself to God alone. He withdrew to a hermitage, a lonely place where he lived a life of quiet prayer close to Jesus present in the Eucharist with his own body, and hard work in the fields. Having dedicated his life entirely to God, he did not want to have anything for himself. Instead of donning a new religious habit from time to time, he would rather choose habits that were discarded by his brothers in the monastery, and wore these until they were completely in rags. He was careful in avoiding any boasting or display of his intelligence. He always chose the worst pieces of bread for himself, with some wasted fruits and vegetables, leaving the better ones for his brother monks.

HUMILITY

Some of his brothers laughed at him, considering their brother naïve and simple. They failed to see that this great mind was hiding his virtues in order to let the poverty of Jesus be seen to all. Charbel was a perfect example of Christian humility. He was always joyful, in spite of cold, heat, hunger or ailments. The last days of his life he kept praising God, asking for his mercy. Soon after Charbel's death, the faithful started to venerate his tomb, and many were strengthened in faith and body by the prayers of the saint. When he was exhumed in the 1950s in view of the process of his beatification, his body had not perished, but was complete and flexible as if he had just died. All this testifies to the graces he received because of his dedication to God alone.

TOTAL DEDICATION

You may not have a similar deep desire for prayer and closeness to God as he did. Most of us won't! Charbel is a great example of what is possible for those who dedicate themselves totally to God. He shows that with God's grace it is possible to withdraw completely from daily life and live only with God in prayer and humility. Charbel is a great saint to pray to if you wish to grow in sanctity. His is a very hopeful message to us, that a simple human being like us was able to achieve such intimacy with God: we too should be able to move at least a little closer to him. Do you want this?

PATHS OF HOLINESS IN SILENCE

"It is good that [Charbel] comes to remind us of the indispensable role of prayer, hidden virtues, and mortification. Next to apostolic works, the Church needs centres of contemplative life, from which praise and intercession rise to God in a fragrance of pleasant odour... May Blessed Charbel lead us along on paths of holiness where there is a place for silent life in the presence of God. May he make us understand, in a world too often fascinated by wealth and comfort, the irreplaceable value of poverty, penance, and asceticism, to free the soul in its ascent to God. Certainly, the practice of these virtues is different according to the state of life and the responsibilities of each, but no Christian can do without it if he wants to walk in the footsteps of Our Lord."

[Pope Paul VI, Speech at the beatification, 3 December 1965]

Some people are called by God to withdraw from everything else and live alone with God. They are a great example of dedication to God and spend their time praying for us!

SAINT
JUDE THADDEUS

📅 CA. 70　🌐 HOLY LAND

🕯 28 OCTOBER; 19 JUNE (EAST)

.SCAN

Q: WHAT ABOUT PRAYER FORMULAS THAT GUARANTEE A REQUEST WILL BE GRANTED?

Jude Thaddeus is often confused with Judas Iscariot who betrayed Jesus. But they are not the same person! *(Jn 14:22)*. Apart from his being an Apostle and therefore very close to Jesus, we know little of him. He was a brother of James the Lesser *(Mk 15:40; Jude 1)*. An old tradition says that Jude went to preach in Persia and possibly even in Armenia. He is considered the author of the brief letter of Saint Jude in the New Testament. He warned us to remain faithful in difficult times, when it seems impossible to find a way out, and to persevere in love for God and continue to hope in the mercy of Jesus *(Jude 17–24)*. Maybe this is why he gained his reputation as the patron saint of desperate and hopeless cases! He shares this reputation with Saint Rita of Cascia *(see #TwGOD 4.16)*. You can call on them in any situation that is particularly difficult.

O God, Jude was a man of great faith; may I have similar faith, and only ask you to give me what is good for me and in accordance with your will. Saint Jude Thaddeus, pray for us!

GUARANTEED OUTCOME?

Poor Jude is sometimes abused. Certain people claim guaranteed results when you repost a prayer to Saint Jude on your timeline, for example. Or when you pray a specific novena, nine days of prayer, asking for his intercession. Usually there is a meticulous description of how to go about this prayer day by day to get your guaranteed result. We hate to disappoint you, but this is just not the way prayer works. Prayer is not about saying magic formulas *(see Saint 1.30)*. It is not simply heavenly shopping. If we were sure of the outcome, it would not be prayer. The key to getting results in your prayer is to open yourself to God and his will *(Ps 37:4)* and to pray with great faith and persistence *(Lk 18:1-8)*.

GOD'S WILL

Sometimes, there seems to be a difference between what we want and what God wants. A good example is the prayer of Jesus when he expressed his human fear just before he was to suffer greatly: 'My Father, if it is possible, let this cup pass from me; yet not what I want but what you want' *(Mt 26:39)*. Contrary to us in many situations, Jesus knew very well the will of God. Still, he expressed his desire to his Father. We can do the same. You can ask anything of God, however impossible it may seem. However, like Jesus, always add the words 'Thy will be done' as we pray daily in the Our Father *(Mt 6:10)*. Jesus promised that God grants any prayer that is in accordance with his will *(Jn 15:7; I Jn 5:14)*. Prayer can indeed change situations, heal the sick, help you pass your exams, bring back what you have lost. But just as with miracles, it is essential to leave the outcome in the hands of God *(see Saint 2.23)*. And you will need to do all you can to collaborate with his help.

GRATITUDE

Prayer is first of all about a relationship *(see Saint 1.6)*. As you get to know God better and communicate with him in

---

DO NOT BELIEVE THEM

'In the last time there will be… worldly people, devoid of the Spirit, who are causing divisions. But you, beloved, build yourselves up on your most holy faith; pray in the Holy Spirit; keep yourselves in the love of God; look forward to the mercy of our Lord Jesus Christ that leads to eternal life. And have mercy on some who are wavering; save others by snatching them out of the fire; and have mercy on still others with fear.'

[Jude, Letter 18-23]

---

prayer, you are better able to recognise his will for us people in general, and for yourself in particular *(see #TwGOD 4.6)*. Secondly, be grateful for what you have in the first place, and only then ask whatever you would like more for others or for yourself. Truly selfish prayers are not answered, for example when you ask for pleasure at the expense of others *(Jas 4:3)*, but God 'hears the prayers of the righteous' *(Prov 15:29)*. Thirdly, you need faith. Believe that you will receive whatever is good for you *(Mt 21:22)*, even if you cannot see the outcome, for 'we walk by faith, not by sight' *(2 Cor 5:7)*. You may be sure that God hears your prayer, and that of the saints. 'Whatever you ask for in prayer with faith, you will receive' *(Mt 21:22)*. The tricky part is to have this great faith! Can you pray like this?

The outcome of your prayer is in God's hands, not in yours! When you pray with faith, God surely hears you, and you can also be sure that he will give you what is good for you.

BLESSED
PETRUS DONDERS

 1809 – 1887   THE NETHERLANDS, SURINAME

 14 JANUARY

2.8

.SCAN

Q: WHY DOES GOD NOT ANSWER OUR PRAYERS AND HELP THE SICK?

Petrus was lovingly called Peerke and was born into a poor family in Tilburg, the Netherlands. Already at a young age he felt that God was calling him to become a priest. After his priestly ordination he volunteered to go to Suriname to help spread the gospel there. He was moved deeply by the living conditions of people who had contracted the contagious and incurable disease of leprosy. They were excluded from the community and were banished far into the jungle where no one else wanted to live. In a place called Batavia, these sick people were left to their fate. They had to take care of themselves. 'Some had no toes, others no hands, again others terribly swollen legs', he wrote in an emotional letter. Father Peerke asked permission to go and live with these people, who were fighting amongst themselves in search of survival. He wanted to help them live in peace, and rediscover their humanity. He cared for the sick in Batavia for most of his life. Petrus never got infected with leprosy, which is a miracle in itself. He died of kidney failure after many years of service to the outcasts of society.

O God, Petrus Donders gave his life for the sick and suffering. Help me to pray for the sick, while leaving the outcome in your hands. Blessed Petrus Donders, pray for us!

SALVATION

Some Old Testament passages may give the impression that illness is a punishment from God for sin *(2 Chr 26:19-20)*. But Jesus strongly opposed this view *(Jn 9:1-3)*. He healed many sick people. However, just like God does not take away all disaster, Jesus did not heal all people. His overview of life, suffering and death is wider than what we can see. He wants us to live forever with God. Therefore, he wants to heal us first of all from the negative effects of our sins *(Mk 2:5)*. Sin, not illness, makes a person ugly! Jesus told those he healed: 'Do not sin any more' *(Jn 5:14)*. Peerke wrote about the sick people he cared for: 'Their illness is no disfavour. How good God is to them, and how fatherly is his providence! For the majority of them, their illness is the only means of salvation.' What Peerke meant is that thanks to their illness these people were able to open their hearts to the love of God and turn away from sin. 'Sin is worse than leprosy,' he used to say. Even if God did not take away their suffering here on earth, his promise of life eternal in heaven gave their lives a fully new perspective *(see Saint 1.39)*.

CLOSER TO GOD

The Bible encourages us to pray for the sick and to call a priest to anoint them with sacramental oil *(Jas 5:14-15; see #TwGOD 3.40)*. But in that same Bible, not everyone is healed when they pray. Look at the suffering of Job! *(see #TwGOD 1.25)*. Jesus only healed some people, and also today miracles of healing are very rare. So, why this encouragement to pray? Prayer brings us closer to God. And precisely when encountering difficulty, illness, and suffering we need his presence most. Especially then he is with us in various ways. Through our prayer and the sacraments, God wants to give his special grace to the sick, sometimes to find physical healing, and always to give spiritual strength to carry the heavy load of suffering. Thus he listens to our prayers after all.

PREACHING TO THE POOR

'Petrus Donders...is also an invitation and a stimulus to the renewal and re-flowering of the missionary impulse which, in the last century and in this century, has made an exceptional contribution to the realisation of the missionary task of the Church... He excellently practised what Saint Augustine proposed as the ideal for his religious: to imitate the virtues and examples of the Redeemer in preaching the divine Word to the poor. Through his life, he showed how the proclamation of the Good News of redemption, of liberation from sin, must find support and confirmation in an authentic evangelical life, of concrete love of neighbour, especially towards the little ones of brothers in Christ.'

[Pope John Paul II, Homily at the beatification, 23 May 1982]

GOD IS THERE

Peerke brought God's love and his sacraments *(see #TwGOD 3.35)* to people who were excluded from society without having committed any fault themselves. One may complain that God did not intervene, but he did! He sent Peerke to help those people who had been affected by a terrible disease. God did not leave them alone without help after all! Similarly, each of us is called to assist and help the sick in our own way: caring, visiting, praying... Do you dare to try?

Jesus's desire is our spiritual healing even before physical recovery. He is with the sick in the sacraments and in their prayer. You are called to join him in visiting and caring for the sick.

SAINT
ALPHONSUS LIGUORI

 1696 – 1787   ITALY   1 AUGUST

SCAN

Q: CAN I EVER DO ENOUGH PENANCE, FASTING AND MORTIFICATION?

WHAT IF I HAVE ANOREXIA OR TEND TO SELF-HARM?

Alphonsus was a successful young lawyer in Naples, Italy. As a result, he became proud and spoiled. He started to neglect his prayer life, and enjoyed his popularity in society with banquets and evenings at the theatre. One day, he made a huge mistake in a legal case and had to admit his faulty defence. The brilliant lawyer was devastated and did not eat for days. In his depressed state, he gradually came to realise that he had been counting too much on himself and not enough on God's grace. This made him decide to change his life. He started to pray daily and sought God at every moment. Eventually he came to realise that God wanted him to become a priest. Soon, he was popular because of his plain and simple preaching at missions around Naples. He also became known as a good confessor who gave valuable advice to the penitents. For him, nothing was as important as our personal relationship with God, our prayer, and the way we live with him.

O God, Alphonsus lived entirely for you. Help me to do like he did and endure pain and suffering as patiently as you did, while helping my neighbour. Saint Alphonsus Liguori, pray for us!

This led him to being quite austere with regard to himself. He lived a very simple life, and sold his possessions to feed the poor. He founded the order of the Redemptorists and later was made a bishop. Alphonsus was opposed to rigorism, and told his priests to treat penitents who asked for God's forgiveness as souls to be saved rather than as criminals to be punished.

INTERIOR GROWTH

Basically, penance is an act which shows that you are sorry about something you have done wrong. When Alphonsus came to realise ever more the great love of God for him, he also came to realise how much he wronged God by his sins. He wanted to make restitution, do penance, in order to grow closer to God. For him, mortification meant self-denial and self-sacrifice. He was often ill, but instead of complaining he said that we must mortify the body by enduring our bodily ailments patiently — if these cannot be taken away by medicine or care *(see Saint 1.39)*. Mortification also means undertaking penances like fasting, prayer vigils, and other holy activities. Each of these little sacrifices can help you grow in a conscious choice for God alone. You do not want to be a slave of your passions *(see box)*. However, Alphonsus considered it much more important to grow interiorly in holiness than to do outward penances.

NO ACHIEVEMENTS

If you want a healthy spiritual relationship with God, you will need to steer the middle road between two extreme tendencies. On the one hand, you can be too self-indulgent, think more of your comfort than of others and God, eat or drink too much, easily forget to pray or to collaborate with the graces that God wants to give you. On the other hand, you can be too rigorous in your mortification, be never satisfied with your 'spiritual achievements' or even find pride in these, forgetting that your life with God is based on freely given grace and not on your 'achievements' *(see #TwGOD 1.37)*.

NO SLAVE OF OUR PASSIONS

'What is the use of mortifying the body and performing exercises of devotion, while cherishing in our heart ambition, attachment to self-will and to self-esteem, or any other passion which brings ruin to the soul? ... Even works of piety must always be undertaken with a spirit of detachment; so that whenever our efforts are unsuccessful...we shall not be disturbed. Self-attachment hinders a perfect union with God. We must therefore seriously and firmly resolve to mortify our passions, and not to submit to be their slaves'.

[Alphonsus Liguori, The True Spouse of Jesus Christ, 7.1.4-7]

FASTING AND PRAYER

The biblical 'mortification of the flesh' *(Rom 8:13; Col 3:5)* does not mean that you have to hurt yourself physically. Beware of any form of self-harm! There is more than enough suffering in life, both physically and spiritually, and there is no need to add to this *(see Saint 1.39 & 2.3)*. Jesus suffered once and for all. Fasting can help your spiritual life if it means eating a little less or setting aside something you like in order to grow in your bond with Jesus. However, there too, moderation is important. For example, someone with anorexia should not even try to fast on food. You can do penance in other ways. Prayer and unselfish charitable acts are often the best choice when you desire to do something for God. What penance can you choose?

Acts of penance, charity, fasting or mortification can help you grow spiritually: you seek to live less for yourself, and more for Jesus. Moderation is important, and self-harm is wrong.

SAINT
MONICA

📅 CA. 332 – 387 🌍 ALGERIA, ITALY 🕯 27 AUGUST

SCAN

Q: CAN I PRAY MORE THAN ONCE FOR SOMETHING?

WHAT IS INTERCESSORY PRAYER? WHAT ARE WAYS TO PRAY FOR OTHER PEOPLE?

Monica came from Thagaste, Algeria. She was very young when she married Patricius. Her husband had a violent temper with regular outbursts. Unlike his wife, he was not a Christian. Monica loved her children and was especially worried about Augustine, who was leading a dissolute life (see Saint 2.41). Worse still was his interest in the Manichean sect, to the point where he tried to convert her. Monica shed many tears and prayed with all her heart for her son. Every day she visited church twice to implore heaven, for her one prayer intention was to bring about his conversion. One day, her ceaseless tears and prayers came to a happy end. After many years of wandering, Augustine converted and asked to be baptised as a Christian. Monica's persistent prayers were eventually answered.

O God, Monica was persistent in her prayers and in her faith. Help me to be like her and teach me to pray for all my intentions and for other people's needs. Saint Monica, pray for us!

PERSISTENT PRAYER

Monica shows that persistent prayer can be very powerful. Jesus invited us to pray in this way, for example in the parable of a widow who was treated unjustly: she continued to file her complaint with the local magistrate until he did her justice — if only to be delivered from her insistent visits *(Lk 18:1-8)*. Repeating your prayer does not mean you do not trust God to hear you the first time. Also, it is not presumptuous and rude to continue to bring your petitions to God. Rather, it is a sign of faith to ask and continue to do so, like praying every day: 'Give us today our daily bread', as Jesus taught us to do *(Mt 6:11)*. On the other hand, be aware that the answer can be different from what you think it will be. God will give us everything that is good for us, but in his own way and in his own time. Hence we also pray daily in the Our Father: 'Thy will be done' *(Mt 6:10)*.

INTERCESSION

To intercede for someone means to act as an intermediary, as a messenger if you like. So, intercessory prayer means praying for other people. You can do this in many ways. The basics are always that you bring to mind the person you wish to pray for, and ask God to help them. You can add every specific need you can think of. So, when someone is sick you can very well ask that the person be healed if God so wishes, but don't forget to ask also for strength to bear the pain (or face death). You can add a prayer that they will recognise how God is with them in their trial... Remember the importance of repetition in prayer. You could make a list of people you wish to pray for daily. If you like to be creative, you could maybe make a set of name cards, or a tree with their names on the leaves. Anything that will help you to intercede for these people.

I'LL PRAY FOR YOU

Have you ever told someone that you'd pray for them and later realised you never did? You are not alone. Thankfully, you saying so can be considered a (very) small form of prayer. However, the

---

WAIT ON THE LORD

"'Wait on the Lord; be strong, and let your heart take courage; yea wait on the Lord" (Ps 27(26):14). But when shall this be? It is hard for a mortal. It is slow for one who loves. But listen to the voice that never deceives, of him who says: "Wait on the Lord". Endure the burning of the reins bravely, and the burning of the heart valiantly. Do not think that what you do not receive has been denied to you. So that you do not give in to despair, see how it is said: "Wait on the Lord."'

[Augustine, Expositions on the Psalms, Ps 27(26):14)]

---

importance of insistent prayer still stands. Jesus said: 'Whatever you ask for in prayer with faith, you will receive' *(Mt 21:22)*. Even if your faith is not very strong, you can still make time for prayer *(see Saint 2.2)*. It may be a comforting thought that others are praying for you too! But they count on your prayers just as you count on theirs. So next time when you say 'I'll pray for you', you had better mean it. Remember: saying that you will pray does not take away your obligation to come into action in other ways as well to help the people around you. What would you like to pray for insistently?

Yes, praying persistently with faith can be very powerful. Intercession is to pray for other people. You can do so by asking God for what they need specifically at this moment.

BLESSED
LAURA VICUÑA

 1891 – 1904 🌎 CHILE 🕯 22 JANUARY

SAINT
NUNZIO SULPRIZIO

 1817 – 1836 🌎 ITALY 🕯 5 MAY

SCAN

Q: WHY SHOULD PARENTS BAPTISE THEIR CHILDREN?

IS IT NOT BETTER TO LET THEM DECIDE FOR THEMSELVES LATER?

Laura was born and baptised in Santiago, Chile. After the death of her father, her mother Mercedes took her daughters to Argentina, where she started to work as a servant. Mercedes entered into an irregular relationship with her boss, Mora, for he promised to pay for the education of her daughters. Laura was very happy at school with the Salesian Sisters (see Saint 1.5). She grew in faith and responded to Jesus's love by living in love with the people she met, helping where she could. The grace of her baptism was the basis for the preparation for her first holy communion and confirmation, which she experienced as a real spiritual strength. During the holidays, Mora made advances to Laura, and beat her when she refused him resolutely. She often said: 'Suffer silently and smile always.' Her great worry was that her mother was far from God and she prayed that Mercedes would leave Mora. In her prayer, Laura offered Jesus her life in exchange for the salvation of her mother. Laura fell ill a few months later.

O God, Nunzio and Laura loved you greatly. Help me to find a similar love, and place all my trust in you alone. Saint Nunzio Sulprizio and Blessed Laura Vicuña, pray for us!

One day, Mora assaulted her and beat her violently. Back in bed, Laura revealed her secret prayer to Mercedes, and asked her to repent and change her life. In tears, Mercedes promised to do so. Now the 12-year-old was at peace and exclaimed: 'Thank you, Jesus! Thank you, Mary! Goodbye, Mother! Now I die happy!'

NUNZIO SULPRIZIO

Nunzio was born and baptised in Pescara, Italy, to a poor family. His father died when he was three, and at the age of six, his mother passed away. His grandmother helped the young boy to grow in his faith, and often took him to church. But she too died. Unwillingly, his uncle took in the nine-year-old boy and made him work as an apprentice blacksmith. Nunzio was treated harshly and fed poorly. At the age of 14 he contracted gangrene in his leg. This was the beginning of five years of treatment and pain. His baptism and faith helped him to bear his suffering. In spite of everything, these were happy years, and he bore the sometimes excruciating pain calmly and with great faith. He was excited about the chance to receive his first holy communion. He often prayed with fervour: 'Mother Mary, let me do God's Will.' In his prayer he offered his suffering to God with great faith. Those who met him said he radiated peace and sanctity. Thanks to his closeness to Jesus, he was able to make sense of his unhappy youth and great suffering (see Saint 1.39). He died at the age of 19, looking at the crucifix.

BAPTISE CHILDREN?

Loving parents want to give their children everything they consider important and good. They make choices on behalf of their children for a good education, and want to pass on their faith which they profess on their behalf at baptism. Jesus asked us to baptise everyone (Mt 28:19). The supernatural second birth at baptism gives a child the grace and help of God to grow in faith, and to face life (see #TwGOD 3.36). Had

> ## THE MEANING OF LIFE
>
> 'At her young age, Laura Vicuña had understood perfectly that the meaning of life lies in knowing and loving Christ... That what counts is eternal life and that everything in the world and of the world passes inexorably. Thanks to her catechism classes, she understood her mother's dangerous situation... The gentle figure of the Blessed Laura...teaches everyone that, with the help of grace, one can triumph over evil; and that the ideal of innocence and love, however denigrated and offended against, in the end can only but shine on and enlighten hearts.'
>
> [Pope John Paul II, Homily at the beatification, 3 September 1988]

Nunzio and Laura not been baptised and educated in the faith, they would not have been able to live so serenely through their difficult youth and suffering.

A LIFE FOR A LIFE?

Did God indeed accept Laura's life in exchange for that of her mother? We will only know for sure in heaven. But the great faith with which she was able to offer herself to Jesus will certainly have amplified her prayers for the conversion of her mother. Without the baptism and education in the faith of her daughter, Mercedes would not have changed her ways. All this to say that when parents want to give their children a kick-start in life, baptism should be among the first gifts they confer on their child. Would you baptise your children?

Loving parents want to give their children all that is good. Baptism is the best gift, for this supernatural birth gives God's special grace, help and love to a child — needed also early in life.

SAINT
DOMINIC SAVIO

1842 – 1857   ITALY   6 MAY

2.12

Q: WHY DO I EVEN HAVE TO BE CONFIRMED?

Dominic was the son of a blacksmith and a seamstress from Riva di Chieri, Italy. His parents gave him a solid education in the faith. He had a great reverence and love for the Eucharist, which is why he was allowed to receive his first holy communion at an early age. Children can receive this sacrament when they are able to understand the importance of the Eucharist *(see Saint 2.13)*. Dominic was a dedicated altar server. Saints attract saints. When he met Don Bosco *(see Saint 1.5)*, he asked to be taken to Turin in order to study for the priesthood. Don Bosco quickly found that he was a good student. One day, Don Bosco said that everyone is called to be a saint, inviting the boys to diligently do the ordinary things of the day in an extraordinary way. When Dominic was a little too serious in his efforts to become a saint, Don Bosco told him to serve the Lord with joy, to dedicate himself to his studies and prayer, and to do good to others. Dominic tried to apply these counsels every day, with attention to that one companion who was alone, and praying for the ones he knew needed his prayers. Together with some other boys, he founded a group in honour of Our Lady with the aim of praying together, but also to help where they could.

O God, Dominic was fully aware that this life is but a preparation for heaven. Help me to live my life to the full while serving you and fellow human beings. Saint Dominic Savio, pray for us!

NO BIG THINGS

Dominic used to say: 'I cannot do big things. But I want all I do, even the smallest thing, to be for the greater glory of God.' He became great precisely because of this: he never complained and was always cheerful — even when the weather was bad, or tasks were annoying or difficult. He wanted to share the joy of knowing Jesus with others, and became an example to many. When he was 14, Dominic's health started to deteriorate, and he returned home to his parents to be cared for. With great faith he prepared himself for his death, confessed his sins, received communion and the sacrament of the sick. Shortly afterwards he said: 'Goodbye, Dad... Oh, what wonderful things I see...'

CONFIRMATION

Confirmation deepens your personal relationship with Jesus and the gift of God's grace which you received in baptism *(see #TwGOD 3.36-3.37)*. In fact, the sacraments of baptism, confirmation and the Eucharist are very closely interconnected, and together they complete your sacramental introduction into the faith *(see #TwGOD 3.35)*. This prepares you spiritually to share your faith with others and to be a witness of Jesus in your family, school, work, and the entire world (see Saint 1.19). Just like Dominic did in his own way. Pope Francis tweeted: 'Confirmation is important for Christians; it strengthens us to defend the faith and to spread the gospel courageously' *(21 February 2014)*. All Catholics are encouraged strongly to receive this sacrament, because of the great help God can give you through it.

COMPULSORY?

It is sometimes asked whether receiving confirmation is compulsory. Well, that is like asking whether it is compulsory to eat, sleep, or get your certificate at school. The short answer is no, for God created you with a free will. But if you say 'no', you have not understood well what this sacrament is about. It is a

---

DON BOSCO ON DOMINIC

'There is nothing extraordinary in what I have written about so far, although we might call extraordinary Dominic's exemplary and innocent life with his extraordinary spirit of faith and penance. The liveliness of his faith, his constant hope, his tireless zeal in doing good and helping others might also be called extraordinary. This went on until his last breath... His life was a continual preparation for death... Sometimes he would say: "I must hurry up or I will be overtaken by night, while I am on the way." By this he meant that he had not much longer to live and that he must do as much good as he could before death caught up with him.'

[Don Bosco, Life of Young Dominic Savio, Ch. XX-XXI]

---

good thing if you are obedient to your parents and therefore want to be confirmed. It is much, much better if you ask for this sacrament because you want to be fully introduced into your relationship with God. You do not have to follow Dominic in everything he did, for you have your own personal vocation. But as you search for and pursue your vocation, you will need all the help you can get! Confirmation is a very concrete way in which God wants to confer on you the necessary grace to become a better version of yourself. For like Dominic, you are also called to become holy in your life. Do you want to live your confirmation to the full?

Confirmation is — with baptism and eucharist — the conclusion of your introduction to the faith. You receive God's very special grace to live your faith and to share it with others.

SAINT **JOHN XXIII**

📅 1881 – 1963   🌍 ITALY, VATICAN   🕯 11 OCTOBER

SAINT **PAUL VI**

📅 1897 – 1978   🌍 ITALY, VATICAN   🕯 26 SEPTEMBER

SCAN

Q: MANY SAINTS PRAYED IN FRONT OF THE TABERNACLE: HOW IS THAT DIFFERENT FROM OTHER WAYS OF PRAYING?

John XXIII's name at his birth in Bergamo, Italy, was Angelo Roncalli. After some years as a priest, he became a diplomat of the pope, serving in Bulgaria, Turkey and France *(see #TwGOD 2.8)*. He then became Patriarch of Venice, and just before turning 77, he was elected Pope in 1958. He was nicknamed 'the good pope' for his sense of humour and good nature. His greatest contribution to the Church are his private prayer and his insistence on holding the Second Vatican Council, a world-wide Church consultation among all bishops *(see #TwGOD 2.48-2.49)*. To demonstrate this great achievement, the opening date of the Council, 11 October, is his feast day. He had a great love for Jesus in the Eucharist, and tried to promote devotion to the Blessed Sacrament among priests and faithful. He was sure that such prayer would bring them much closer to Jesus.

O God, your good popes recognised you in the Eucharist. Help me to recognise your love for me and often pray in front of the tabernacle. Saints John XXIII and Paul VI, pray for us!

PAUL VI

Paul VI was born as Giovanni Battista Montini in Concesio, Italy. He worked for 30 years in the Secretariat of State, the central Vatican ministry (see #TwGOD 2.5). Subsequently he was named Archbishop of Milan. He helped to prepare the Second Vatican Council and when he became pope in 1963, he concluded the work started by Pope John XXIII. He was the first pope to implement the teachings of the Council. Paul VI had a great devotion to Jesus present in the Eucharist, and wrote an important document about this (see box). He frequently withdrew to his private chapel to kneel down in front of the tabernacle to tell Jesus about his difficulties, and above all to simply spend time with him.

TABERNACLE

Jesus said: 'I am with you always, to the end of time' (Mt 28:20). The most concrete way in which Jesus is with us, is in the sacrament of the Eucharist. In the celebration of the Eucharist, he changes bread into his body, and wine into his blood (see #TwGOD 3.48). After the liturgy, the Eucharistic bread or the Host is conserved in a small and beautiful safe, the tabernacle. In the Old Testament, the tabernacle was the dwelling place of God (Ex 36:8-39:43). Every Catholic church contains a tabernacle, which we can call the ultimate dwelling place of God on earth (see #TwGOD 3.20-3.21). Next to the tabernacle a small light is placed, as a sign of the presence of Jesus. The tabernacle is typically located in the centre of the sanctuary or in a side chapel. Whenever we enter a church or pass the tabernacle, we genuflect on one knee as a sign of reverence and greeting to Jesus, who is present there.

PRAYER

As Jesus is so concretely present in the Eucharist which is reserved in the tabernacle, it is a great place to meet him and adore him (see #TwGOD 3.14). In the peace and quiet of the

> ## GOD WITH US
> 'The Eucharist is reserved in churches [in the tabernacle, for] Christ is truly Emmanuel, which means "God with us"... Anyone who has a special devotion to the sacred Eucharist and who tries to repay Christ's infinite love for us with an eager and unselfish love of his own, will experience and fully understand – and this will bring great delight and benefit to his soul – just how precious is a life hidden with Christ in God (Col 3:3) and just how worthwhile it is to carry on a conversation with Christ, for there is nothing more consoling here on earth, nothing more efficacious for progress along the paths of holiness.'
>
> [Pope Paul VI, Mysterium Fidei, 67]

church or chapel, the tabernacle helps to focus our prayers on Jesus himself. How vulnerable Jesus made himself when he gave his life on the cross. How vulnerable Jesus is, present in the Eucharist. It may seem to make little sense to sit down and just be there. However, you can think of it as visiting an old friend: you are happy to spend time together, without really being concerned about what you say or do. It is so with Jesus. As Mother Teresa said: I just listen, and he listens (see Saint 2.2). Such peaceful and silent dwelling in the presence of Jesus is what we all need from time to time, especially when life is busy. Feel free to make a short 'visit' to greet Jesus in the tabernacle, next time you are passing a church! How can the tabernacle help you in your prayers?

> The tabernacle contains Jesus's body as given to us in the Eucharist. Here, Jesus is present very concretely, desiring to share his love with you. You cannot come closer to him on earth.

SAINT
PHILIP NERI

 1515 – 1595   ITALY   🕯 26 MAY

2.14

Q: WHY ARE CHRISTIANS SO GLOOMY? AM I ALLOWED TO LAUGH IN CHURCH?

Philip was the son of a lawyer from Florence, Italy. When he was 18 years old, he felt strongly called to deepen his faith and moved to Rome, where he studied theology. He prayed a lot and led an ascetic life. Working for the poor and outcast of Roman society, including prostitutes and beggars, he realised the importance of bringing the gospel to everyone. The 'Apostle of Rome' as he was called, travelled through the city of Rome on home missions, speaking to people wherever he met them and helping them to discover the importance of the faith for themselves. Among other things, he introduced the devotion of taking turns in praying 40 hours in front of the Blessed Sacrament exposed *(see Saint 2.13)*.

ORATORY

Philip was ordained a priest at the age of 36, which is rather late for the time. For a moment he thought of volunteering for the missions in India, inspired by Francis Xavier, but his companions showed him how much work there was to be done in Rome.

O God, Philip had a profound relationship with you and a cheerful nature. Help me to work hard for my mission, while continuing to laugh at myself. Saint Philip Neri, pray for us!

SCAN

Together they set up the 'Oratory', named after the prayer room where they met for lectures and discussion on religious questions. Their mission developed quickly. They met in a different church every evening. Philip preached and heard confessions, while disciples like the famous composer Palestrina took care of the music. Trying to counter immoral scenes at the carnival, Philip organised pilgrimages on foot, praying in seven Roman churches in one day. Even today the Seven Churches Walk is popular among pilgrims and seminarians. In 1575 Philip officially founded the Congregation of the Oratory, a community of secular priests and brothers. This idea was followed quickly in other places, where independent oratories were set up.

HUMOUR

Philip was a man of profound personal prayer, who loved Jesus dearly. He often would get up early to spend private time with God. This did not make him a gloomy man, though. On the contrary, he was known for his gentle and playful sense of humour. He took his mission very seriously, but not himself. We too should laugh at ourselves a little more, and see how liberating this is! Philip could show up with half his beard shaven, read out loud from a joke book, or play a practical joke on an important person. He was heard saying: 'A heart filled with joy is more easily made perfect than one that is sad.' Thanks to his joyful and outgoing character, Philip made many friends, including Ignatius of Loyola, Charles Borromeo, and Pope Paul V.

GLOOMY CONGREGATION

The serious face many people make as soon as they enter a church shows that being earnest is a quality: life is not a laughing matter. Or is it? Philip was absolutely serious about his relationship with the Lord, and the earnest need to share

> ## CHRISTIAN JOY
>
> *'Interior Christian joy is a gift of God, flowing from good conscience, through the contempt of earthly things, united with the contemplation of the heavenly ones... Sin is opposed to our joy. On the contrary, one who is a servant of sin cannot even taste joy. Joy is also fully opposed to ambition, just as sensual things, vanity and distractions are its enemy. Our joy, my child, is in great danger and is often lost through the dealings with worldly things, by consorting with the ambitious, through the pleasure of secular entertainment.'*
>
> [A. Capecelatro, La Vita di S. Filippo Neri, book III, ch. XIII]

it with others. But precisely thanks to his sense of humour he managed to go where others might have been discouraged. Maybe we need to take his example more seriously! Faith is a laughing matter, in the sense that Jesus has freed us from chains that draw us down and instead wants to bring us upwards to our Father in heaven. So it is not necessary to treat that joke in the homily with a gloomy silence; you can laugh about a silly situation caused by a child running up the altar steps. As Saint Teresa of Avila said, 'God save us from gloomy saints' *(see Saint 2.4)*. Obviously, reverence for the sacred is important. But there can be something very holy in a sense of humour. We do not stop being human when entering a church. Jesus was human in everything but sin: it is sure that he must have laughed too! Do you laugh enough at yourself?

> *No gloomy faces, please! Joy and humour are important qualities that can help you to realise what is truly important in life (your relationship with God) and what is not (your self-dignity).*

SAINT
JOHN NEPOMUK

📅 1345 – 1393   🌍 CZECH REPUBLIC   🕯 16 MAY

.SCAN

Q: IS MY CONFESSION REALLY SECRET? DO PRIESTS ONLY WORK ON SUNDAYS? WHY ARE THEY CALLED FATHER AND DRESS IN BLACK?

John came from Pomuk, Bohemia, in today's Czech Republic. He studied in Prague and Padua, Italy, before he was ordained a priest and appointed parish priest in Prague. He was intelligent and wise, but above all a great believer in the love of God, and he was a humble man. Soon he started to rise in importance within the local Church, until he became vicar-general. People came from far away to listen to his passionate homilies in the cathedral. King Wenceslaus IV had become cruel and capricious in his reign, and was in constant battle with the Church. One day, the king ordered John to be tortured in a terrible way on the Charles bridge in Prague. He was then thrown into the river, dead or barely alive. This is why you can find John's statue on some bridges today. The exact reason for this atrocity is not known. Was it because John had signed the appointment of an abbot against the wishes of the king? Or did the king want to deprive the bishop of one of his most important assistants?

O God, John lived and died for his priesthood. Help me meet you regularly in the sacraments that you want to give me through the ministry of priests. Saint John Nepomuk, pray for us!

THE SEAL OF CONFESSION

Among the people of Prague the tale was shared that John had heard the confession of the queen, and had refused to tell the king anything. This would indeed have been a reason for John to keep silent even in the face of death. The 'seal of confession' is absolute, and revealing even a small part of this secret is among the greatest sins a priest can commit. The punishment is immediate: the priest would be automatically excommunicated. So, your confession is safe with the priest, who only acts as an intermediary *(see #TwGOD 3.38-3.39)*. Ultimately it is to God that you confess your sins, and it is God who forgives you — through the ministry of the priest.

FATHER

Jesus once said: 'Call no one Father' *(Mt 23:9)*. But obviously, he did not mean that sons could not say 'father' to their dads. The context of the text shows that he was speaking against the abuse of such 'title' for your own glory. Jesus himself called several people 'father' *(Lk 15:11-32; 16:19-31)*. Saint Paul called himself 'father', referring to his ministry *(1 Cor 4:14-15)*. Since the earliest times, bishops and priests were called 'father' for people considered them as their spiritual fathers. Rather than being a title of honour, this expresses a great responsibility, as they are called to be at the service of their flock. This service extends far beyond celebrating Sunday Mass. Although you find a few bureaucrats even among priests, most of them are working hard every day — often even more than is good for them.

MODEST DRESS

In the very beginning there was no distinctive daily dress for a priest. A long tunic reaching to the feet was seen as a sign of modesty, and so were dark colours (for they were cheap). The clergy probably retained this kind of dress when secular fashion developed new forms. The dark soutane or cassock

---

A GIFT OF GOD'S LOVE

'Like every priest, Saint John was chosen from among the people and was constituted as their representative in the things that concern God, to bring offerings and atone for the sins of the people *(Heb 2:17)*... He is first ordained to proclaim Christ, to celebrate his Mystery and to transmit his invisible grace to the faithful through visible and effective signs, such as the sacraments. Priests are a gift of God's love to the world.'

[Pope John Paul II,
Letter at the anniversary of John Nepomuk, 19 March 1993]

---

was considered appropriate for priests in the sixth century, also under influence of the monastic habit. In the Middle Ages, the use of the cassock became mandatory, and John Nepomuk is always depicted wearing one. The 18th century saw the introduction of shorter frock coats for travelling on horseback. Later came the clergyman suit which is often used today, although the attire for official occasions remains the cassock. Among other things, black is considered a symbol of the priest having died to himself and now living for the Lord alone. Higher clergy can use other colours *(see #TwGOD 2.10)*, while priests in warm countries often wear white. Do you ever pray for your priest?

> The seal of confession is absolute, and a priest would rather die than reveal what was said in confession. He wears black out of modesty, is a father to his flock, and available all week.

SAINTS **CYRIL** & **METHODIUS**

📅 CA. 827 – 869 (CYRIL), CA. 817 – 885 (METHODIUS)

🌍 GREECE, EASTERN EUROPE

🕯 14 FEBRUARY; 5 JULY (EAST)

SCAN

Q: IN THE BYZANTINE RITE, WHY DO YOU MAKE THE SIGN OF THE CROSS SO OFTEN? ARE YOU ORTHODOX OR CATHOLIC? DO YOUR PRIESTS REALLY MARRY?

Cyril and Methodius were brothers from Thessalonica, Greece. Cyril was the thinker and the scholar of the two: he was professor of philosophy in Constantinople. Methodius was a monk and abbot. Emperor Michael III and the Patriarch of Constantinople, Photius *(see #TwGOD 2.23)*, asked them to go and proclaim the gospel in the East of Europe. Cyril and Methodius were the first to use Slavonic in their explanations of the faith, for people in the East did not understand Latin or Greek. They translated the texts of the liturgy and the Bible into Slavonic (still used today as Old Church Slavonic). To do so properly, they invented a Slavic alphabet based on Greek letters, which was named after Cyril. The Cyrillic alphabet is still used for Russian, Ukrainian and several other Slavic languages. In Rome, Cyril and Methodius managed to convince Pope Adrian II to permit Slavic as the official liturgical language in the East of Europe.

O God, Cyril and Methodius were filled with your gospel, and proclaimed it in new ways. Help me to find proper ways to speak of you. Saints Cyril and Methodius, pray for us!

Cyril died during their stay in Rome. The pope sent Methodius back to the Slavs as archbishop. The two brothers have been of enormous importance for spreading Christianity in Eastern Europe, which is why they are celebrated as the 'Apostles to the Slavs.'

CROSSING YOURSELF

Cyril and Methodius celebrated the Byzantine liturgy, which is different from the Latin Rite used in the West (see #TwGOD 3.51-3.53). Not only is the language different, but also the form. One of the things people notice immediately is that the sign of the cross is made quite often. During a long liturgy, that may be more than 100 times. The sign of the cross reminds us of Jesus's sacrifice, which we accept and make our own by signing our bodies. In the Byzantine Rite you make the sign of the cross by placing the thumb, index and middle finger of the right hand together, moving from forehead to belly, from the right shoulder to the left (mirrored in the Latin Rite). Often it is followed by a bow. Sometimes the ground is touched before crossing yourself. The sign of the cross is made when entering or leaving the church, at the beginning and end of prayer, but also every time the Trinity is mentioned, at each petition in a litany, and when passing in front of the altar.

ORTHODOX OR CATHOLIC?

The Byzantine Rite is an official Catholic liturgical rite, just as the Latin Rite used in most Catholic churches around the world. After a sad schism in 1054, the Orthodox Churches came into existence, as they separated from the Church of Rome (see #TwGOD 2.30). The churches of the Byzantine Rite which returned to union with the Catholic Church, are called Eastern or Greek Catholics. They are fully Catholic and love the pope. It is the task of all Christians to work and especially pray for renewed unity in the Church of Jesus (see box).

SEARCH FOR UNITY

'Saints Cyril and Methodius [are] authentic precursors of ecumenism, inasmuch as they wished to eliminate effectively or to reduce any divisions, real or only apparent, between the individual communities belonging to the same Church... The fervent solicitude shown by both Brothers and especially by Methodius by reason of his episcopal responsibility, to preserve unity of faith and love between the Churches of which they were members, namely, between the Church of Constantinople and the Church of Rome on the one hand, and the Churches which arose in the lands of the Slavs on the other, was and will always remain their great merit.'

[Pope John Paul II, Slavorum Apostoli, n. 14, 2 June 1985]

MY FATHER IS A PRIEST

Another difference between Eastern Catholics and Latin Catholics is that in the East, priests can get married (see #TwGOD 3.41). So, you may find a seminarian presenting you with his girlfriend and telling you that his father is a priest. Still, he can also decide to consecrate himself to God in celibacy, just as priests in the Latin Church do, to be totally available for the service of God without the responsibility of a family. In both Churches, bishops always remain unmarried as a sign of their total offering to God and the Church — like Cyril and Methodius. Have you ever assisted in an Eastern Catholic liturgy?

Byzantine Catholics are fully Catholic. The sign of the cross is made often as a reminder of Jesus's sacrifice for us. Byzantine priests can choose to get married.

SAINT **TERESA BENEDICTA OF THE CROSS** – EDITH STEIN

📅 1891 – 1942   🌐 POLAND, GERMANY, NETHERLANDS

🕯 9 AUGUST

.SCAN

Q: WHAT IF I DOUBT?

HOW CAN I KNOW THAT GOD IS REAL?

Edith was born in Breslau, Poland, into a Jewish family, but she considered herself an atheist. She studied philosophy with the famous philosopher Husserl. During the First World War she served as a Red Cross nurse. She wrote a philosophical doctorate on empathy. She wanted to become a professor, but this was not allowed for women at the time. As she was reading the autobiography of Saint Teresa of Avila (*see Saint 2.4*) she discovered the truth of the Catholic faith and eventually asked to be baptised. This also began her interest in Catholic philosophy, with Saint Thomas Aquinas as a lead. Some ten years after her conversion, Edith entered the monastery of the discalced Carmelites in Cologne, Germany. Her religious name was Teresa Benedicta of the Cross. In the convent, she continued her studies of philosophy and published various important academic works.

O God, Edith found you after a long period of doubts and darkness. Help me, also when in doubt, to continue to ask your help and search for the truth. Saint Edith Stein, pray for us!

MARTYR

As the Nazi regime started to become a threat, her superior sent her to a monastery in Echt, the Netherlands. Here she studied the works of Saint John of the Cross, a spiritual friend of Teresa of Avila *(see Saint 2.4)*. This brought her closer to God. When the Dutch bishops publicly denounced Nazism *(see #TwGOD 2.47)*, Edith was sent to the extermination camp at Auschwitz, where she was probably killed in the gas chambers two days after arrival. She died as a direct consequence of the protest of the Dutch bishops against Nazism, and thus was killed for being a Catholic, which makes her a martyr of the faith.

DOUBTS

This strong woman is an example for every Christian. She dedicated her life to a frantic search for the truth, which she hoped to find in philosophy. But she was full of questions and doubts. She wrote: 'Whoever seeks the truth is seeking God, whether consciously or unconsciously.' You cannot see God, you have to believe in him, you may have heard. But that is easier said than done. You are not alone when you doubt. Pope Francis said: 'Of course, everyone has doubts at times! Doubts which touch the faith, in a positive way, are a sign that we want to know better and more fully God, Jesus, and the mystery of his love for us' *(23 November 2016)*.

FIVE STEPS WHEN IN DOUBT

- First, have faith! Or better put: trust that your doubts will eventually lead you somewhere. Even a great saint like Edith Stein passed through a dark period of doubts in her life.

- Second, check whether you are sad, depressed, or agitated. If so, wait a while until you are at peace again, and only then take your doubts seriously.

HER PERIOD OF DOUBT

'Catholicism is hardly a "religion of feeling". It concerns itself with questions of the truth, also with matters of life and the heart... When I look back...always in the foreground is the miserable inner state in which I found this unspeakable confusion... It was just a crisis long in coming. At the time it was for me like one who has a fear of drowning, but for a long time is sitting in a bright, warm room quite safe...only suddenly to have the image of the dark, cold, watery grave flash before her eyes. How could one not then feel a shiver and an eternal thankfulness for the strong arm that seized her and carried her along to a safe place?'   [Edith Stein, Letter to R. Ingarden, 13 December 1925]

- Third, read and study the theme by reading good Catholic authors. Do not only focus on online forums where people may hold very bold and equally unfounded opinions.

- Fourth, find a spiritual director who takes your doubts seriously and who can help you see beyond yourself. If there are obstacles between you and God, confess your sins.

- Five, do not stop praying. Tell God about your doubts. Ask him to help you. If you wish, you can formulate your prayer thus: 'If you are real....' Also, ask others including the saints to pray for you. Do you think you can find faith like Edith did?

Doubt is inherent to faith. Keep an open mind for the truth, continue to search and pray, alone and with others, and you will grow in love, hope and eventually also in faith.

SAINT **JOHN HENRY NEWMAN**

 1801 – 1890   ENGLAND 9 OCTOBER

.SCAN

Q: WHAT IF FAITH IS JUST A MYTH, INVENTED OUT OF FEAR OR DESIRE?

John Henry Newman was a prominent Anglican priest and scholar at Oxford University. At the beginning of his career he was strongly anti-Catholic. All his life he was an independent thinker. He was a leader in the Oxford Movement. Among others, this group of Anglican scholars *(see #TwGOD 2.39)* studied the teaching of the Church Fathers from the first centuries *(see #TwGOD 2.24)*. These great early thinkers were much closer to the time of Jesus than we are today. Therefore, Newman considered them to be an important source of information. To his surprise, he found that some ideas of the Anglican Church of his time came close to positions that were rejected as unorthodox by the Church Fathers. This made him study even more. Over time, he came to realise that he could only find the truth about God in the Catholic Church. He decided to become a Catholic, and some years later he was ordained a Catholic priest.

O God, John Henry searched all his life for the truth about you. Help me too to recognise this truth, and embrace your love with all my heart. Saint John Henry Newman, pray for us!

CONTINUITY

One of the questions that Newman studied in detail was the continuity of the faith. For him, history was very important. Very briefly put, the relation between human beings and God cannot have just come into existence at a certain point when people felt they needed him. If God is real, then there must be a continuous relationship with him throughout the ages. Otherwise, God would be the result of our desires, rather than exist in himself forever. Newman found the continuity of the faith among others in the fact that the Apostles — chosen and instituted by Jesus himself — handed over their ministry and teaching to their successors. We call this "apostolic succession" *(see #TwGOD 2.15)*. The discovery of the continuity of the teaching of the faith from the time of Jesus himself to our days was one of the main reasons for Newman's conversion to Catholicism.

EMOTION

'Faith is just an emotional experience,' you sometimes hear people say. If that were true, the faith would be completely subjective, depending on whom you talk to. God would always be different, and therefore he could not exist in himself. Newman came to realise that certitude about the faith cannot come from logical reasoning alone. It must come from God himself, through his revelation. All his life, Newman had been looking for the objective and undeniable truth about God. He came to realise that we should not confuse nature as created by God, including our emotions, and the supernatural existence of God in himself. For Newman, God's existence is an objective reality, which is true for everyone at all times, whether you believe it or not *(see #TwGOD 1.8)*. Therefore, God does not depend on our emotions or fears. He exists in himself and of himself.

JESUS

We know that our faith in God is not just a myth, because of what Jesus came to tell us. His coming had been announced

---

AN ENLIGHTENED AGE

'This is what we call an enlightened age: we are to have large views of things; everything is to be put on a philosophical basis; reason is to rule...enjoy them, but deign to recollect the while, that there have been views in the world before you...Catholicism, I say, had its First Principles before you were born: you say they are false; very well, prove them to be so: they are false, indeed, if yours are true; but not false merely because yours are yours. While yours are yours it is self-evident, indeed, to you, that ours are false; but it is not the common way of carrying on business in the world, to value English goods by French measures, or to pay a debt in paper which was contracted in gold. Catholicism has its First Principles, overthrow them, if you can; endure them, if you cannot. It is not enough to call them effete because they are old, or antiquated because they are ancient.'

[John Henry Newman, Lecture 7
on the Present Position of Catholics in England, 1851]

---

for many centuries *(see #TwGOD 1.27)*. During his life he told us the essential message that God loves each of us dearly. Jesus showed this love in particular when he was prepared to die on the cross, to make our relationship with God possible *(see #TwGOD 1.26 & 1.28)*. The greatest "proof" of God's love is that he made Jesus alive again, and promised that we too shall live forever. Since then, generation after generation have believed in God and passed on their faith. Thus handed on, the truth of the faith came to Newman, and now also to you! Do you want to believe?

We can give you some pretty convincing arguments for the existence of God. However, ultimately it comes down to faith in the love of God, as revealed to us by Jesus.

SAINT
VINCENT DE PAUL

2.19

 1581 – 1660   FRANCE   27 SEPTEMBER

SCAN

Q: IF GOD IS REAL, WHY DOESN'T HE HELP POOR, HUNGRY, AND THIRSTY PEOPLE?

Vincent came from a poor family in Pouy, France. Because of his intelligence, his father wanted him to study, and sold two oxen to pay for his seminary training. At the time Vincent was ashamed of his low origin. Once, he even refused to receive his father when he visited him at the seminary, as he was dirty and smelled of the farm. Later he recalled this painfully as a great sin. During a voyage overseas, Vincent was captured by pirates and sold as a slave in Tunis. He spent two years in captivity. One of his masters was an old doctor, from whom he learned a lot about medicine. After his death, Vincent was sold again, this time to a compatriot who had converted to Islam to escape servitude. Eventually the man had remorse and fled with his slave to France. Now, Vincent was free to work as a priest again. Among others he was appointed as a chaplain of galley slaves.

O God, Vincent greatly loved the poor like you do. Help me to reach out to those who struggle, and share with them my spiritual and material wealth. Saint Vincent de Paul, pray for us!

POVERTY

While working as a spiritual advisor to the highborn, Vincent also visited the countryside. There he met true poverty, both material and spiritual. He saw how many people tried to share from their poverty, but it happened that some sick people received too much and others nothing. Vincent started 'fraternities of love' to organise material aid to the very poor. This was the origin of the later Societies of Saint Vincent de Paul. For him, the service to the lowest and poorest went hand in hand with the proclamation of the gospel. He found great spiritual poverty among both the poor and the wealthy of society. Vincent founded the Congregation of the Lazarist fathers – or Vincentians – to preach to them. To complete this mission, together with Saint Louise de Marillac, he co-founded the Daughters of Charity to care for the sick, the poor, orphans and elderly. Vincent continued to beg the rich to share their wealth with the less fortunate. This also gave him the occasion to preach the gospel to them.

SELFLESS SHARING

In fact, there would not have to be poor, hungry and thirsty people at all if the resources and goods of our earth would be better distributed *(see Saint 1.36-1.37)*. But Jesus told us a hard truth: 'You always have the poor with you' *(Mk 14:7)*. He knew how much difficulty we have in sharing. Still, he invited each of us to do so in a selfless and disinterested way, especially with those who cannot repay us *(Lk 14:13-14)*. True, no individual can change all the misery of the world alone and it is not necessarily your vocation to give all your possessions away *(see Saint 1.45)*. Furthermore, a lot of organisation is needed to reach people who live far away from resources. But we have the example of Vincent de Paul: he simply started to help to poor people where he could reach them, and invited others to join him. If we all do this in our own little way, the world will soon be a better place to live for all!

GO INTO THE WHOLE WORLD

'Our vocation, is not to go to one parish, or even to one diocese, but throughout the whole world, and for what end? To inflame the hearts of men, to do what the Son of God did. He came to cast fire on the earth, to inflame it with his love. What else have we to desire save that it burns and consumes all?... It is not enough for me to love God if my neighbour does not love him. I ought to...act so that they may love each other for the love of God, who has so loved them as to deliver up his son to death for their sakes. That, then, is what I am obliged to...grant me the grace that your holy love may so fill my heart that it may be the life of my life, and the soul of my actions, so that in its overflow it may enter into and operate on those souls I am bound to help.'

[Vincent de Paul, Conference on charity, 30 May 1659]

CHARITY AND MISSION

God does indeed help poor, hungry, and thirsty people. He does so by calling you to share with others! Each of us is called to do so in our own way. Jesus did not condemn rich people, but avarice and selfishness. Nor are we to condemn others who have difficulty in sharing: we need to do our bit and at most can invite others to do so. Note that Jesus came in the first place for the spiritual well-being of the poor by preaching about the love of God. Vincent did the same. Real charity in the name of Jesus is to share both our possessions and our faith. Where can you start to share?

God helps the poor and needy by calling you to charity! If we all shared our possessions, there would be no poor. No one can do this alone: simply start to share where you are.

SAINT **MARY MACKILLOP**

 1842 – 1909   AUSTRALIA   🕯 8 AUGUST

Q: HOW CAN I TRUST IN GOD?

AND HOW CAN I TRUST THE CHURCH WITH ALL THOSE SCANDALS?

SCAN

Mary was born in Fitzroy, in the State of Victoria, Australia, of Scottish parents. She worked first as a clerk, then as a teacher, and later as a governess. Her skills came in handy when she started a school together with Father Julian Woods, and founded the Congregation of the Josephites. Soon the sisters became known as the 'Brown Joeys' because of their brown habits. Other schools followed all around Australia, plus institutions for orphans, endangered girls, elderly and dying people. One day, Mary discovered that a priest was abusing children, and she denounced him, so that he was sent back to his home country. A vindictive cleric considered her direct intervention a breach of his authority and influenced the bishop to excommunicate Mary on false grounds. Probably also the independent way in which the sisters were able to operate would have contributed to this decision. However, a year later she was absolved from all accusations and exonerated. Several difficulties followed, while the Josephite sisters continued to expand their good work also beyond Australia. The secret of Mary's success is that whatever happened, she continued to trust in God's grace, and did what she could to collaborate with him.

O God, Mary trusted you in spite of everything that happened. Help me to recognise your continuous love and presence in my life. Saint Mary MacKillop, pray for us!

CRIMINALS

It is the worst thing that can happen: someone you trust betrays you in secret. Some bishops, priests, and religious have misbehaved horribly. They literally abused the trust they received from their flock. What makes it even worse is that they received this trust precisely because of their supposed closeness to God! The abuse of children is among the worst crimes on earth, and Church people who commit such crimes must be punished severely, both by civil justice and Church courts. Church authorities should collaborate in every legal way to make this happen, and thankfully procedures to do so have improved greatly in recent years. But much is still to be done. You may wonder whether you can ever trust the Church again...

TRUST THE CHURCH

Mary was deeply disappointed and disgusted by the behaviour of certain Church authorities who committed crimes and treated her badly. Still, she never lost trust in the Church itself. She believed that the Church is the living body of Jesus, and as a whole it cannot go wrong (see #TwGOD 2.13). It is bad enough that some of the faithful — bishops and priests included — fall away from God's love and charity. At the same time, Mary also saw how the vast majority did everything they could to follow Jesus more closely and live a life worthy of a Christian.

IN GOD I TRUST

'Trust in God!' It is so easily said, but often so difficult to do. Still, you can trust indeed, in spite of certain crimes and terrible things happening (see Saint 2.24), in spite of suffering (see Saint 1.39), and in spite of your doubts (see Saint 2.17). These steps may help you to trust God better:

- Cry out to God: tell him of your pain, doubts and difficulties; continue to communicate with him. Get to know him better: it is difficult to trust what you do not know.

FORGIVE US!

'We ask forgiveness for... the abuse of power, the abuse of conscience and sexual abuse on the part of representatives of the Church. In a special way, we ask forgiveness for all those abuses that took place in different kinds of institutions directed by men and women religious and other members of the Church... We ask forgiveness for all those times when, as a Church, we did not offer to the survivors of any type of abuse compassion and the pursuit of justice and truth by concrete actions... We ask forgiveness for some members of the hierarchy who took no responsibility for these painful situations and kept silent... May the Lord preserve and increase this sense of shame and repentance, and grant us the strength to ensure that it never happens again and that justice is done. Amen.'

[Pope Francis, Penitential act in Phoenix Park, Dublin, 26 August 2018]

- Realise that God is worthy of your trust: contrary to people he does not lie, change his mind or commit crimes; he keeps his promises (Num 23:19). And above all: he loves you!

- Recognise how Jesus promised to be with his Church, how he cries and suffers when one single crime is committed by Church people, and that he is greater than any evil (see Saint 2.26).

- Realise that we live in an imperfect world, and that the best is still to come: life in perfect love with God in heaven.

- Do not be afraid or discouraged: God is with you at this very moment (Josh 1:9; Mt 28:20). Do you want to trust him?

Trusting God means crying out to him, and realising that he is present now. Jesus himself is the foundation of the Church, which is why people cannot bring it down.

SAINT
CHRISTOPHER

📅 CA. 250   🕯 25 JULY; 9 MAY (EAST)

2.21

SCAN

Q: IS SUPERSTITION REALLY THAT BAD?

Christopher was martyred by the Romans. Officially we do not know more than that. But his legend is so popular that he is one of the best-known saints! A tall man with broad shoulders, he was looking for Christ in his life but said he could not live like a monk nor fast or pray all day. So at the suggestion of a hermit he settled beside a river to carry over travellers, thus saving them from a possible death by drowning. One day, a child asked him to be carried over through the stream. But as he crossed the river with the child on his shoulders, the water rose, and the child became heavier with every step, so that Christopher started to fear for both their lives. When he finally reached the shore after great effort, the child said that he had not only carried the entire world, but also its Creator!

O God, Christopher protected travellers against the dangers of life's turbulent rivers. Help me to live only for your service and protect me on the road. Saint Christopher, pray for us!

CHRIST AT CENTRE

The child was the same Christ he had tried to serve faithfully through his service at the bank of the river. Christopher's story is confronting each of us with the question: how will I serve my Lord? There is no need to be extraordinary but just willing to serve him. You will serve him best when you do the things you excel in without any pride and with the intention to serve your neighbour. Even though such a life may seem a heavy burden at times, afterwards you may discover that you carried Christ himself, exactly when things were difficult! Christopher is the patron saint against a sudden death. Would that be the origin of the superstition that if you have a medal of this saint in your car, you will never be involved in an accident?

SAINTS AS LUCKY CHARMS?

There are other 'Catholic superstitions.' 'Touching wood' is not connected to the wood of the cross, but probably to the holy trees of the pagan Europeans before Christianity. Have you ever heard that if you bury a statue of Saint Joseph face down in your garden, you will sell your house for sure? You can even buy a 'St Joseph Home Seller Kit' on the internet! If this is done without faith, this is a pure superstition. It is normal to ask a friend to pray for you, but would you bury their image upside down in the garden? Saints are not lucky charms to be used for selfish benefits! So you can leave Saint Joseph on the side table and direct your prayers for help to God through his intercession. But why does it appear to work sometimes? Maybe heaven looks kindly on people making a fool of themselves... However, God especially loves those who remain close to him every step of their lives!

PRAYER, NOT SUPERSTITION

Obviously, real Catholic customs are no superstition. You may ask Saint Jude to pray for your favourite team to win (see Saint 2.7), or Saint Anthony to help you find your lost keys

---

> ## SUPERSTITION AND SCIENCE
>
> 'Science can purify religion from error and superstition; religion can purify science from idolatry and false absolutes. Each can draw the other into a wider world, a world in which both can flourish... Christians will inevitably assimilate the prevailing ideas about the world, and today these are deeply shaped by science. The only question is whether they will do this critically or unreflectively, with depth and nuance or with a shallowness that debases the Gospel and leaves us ashamed before history.'
>
> [Pope John Paul II, Letter to Fr G.V. Goyne sj, 1 June 1988]

(see Saint 2.30). There is nothing superstitious or magical here: you ask saints who are 'specialised' in certain subjects to pray for you. While they bring your petition to God, you leave him free to act or not. But whenever someone promises you a secured outcome if you pray in one or another way, be warned that they are conning you (see Saint 2.7). Still, there is nothing wrong with glueing a medal of Saint Christopher onto the dashboard of your car as a sign that you trust him to pray for your safety. But keep that wheel firmly in both hands when driving, for you need to collaborate with God's grace at every moment! Can you live without superstition?

> Superstition is the opposite to faith: it is not the act of touching wood or burying a statue that will save you, but only faith in God's saving works!

SAINT GEORGE

CA. 256 – CA. 285   🌍 TURKEY   🕯 23 APRIL

.SCAN

Q: WHY IS GOD SO VIOLENT IN THE OLD TESTAMENT?

George was a Christian soldier from Cappadocia, Turkey. He served in the Roman army as an imperial guard of Emperor Diocletian. When the emperor decreed his violent laws against Christians *(see #TwGOD 2.19)*, he proposed that George quietly convert to the Roman gods. George refused, and was beheaded because of his persistent adherence to Christ. This is as much as we know historically about Saint George, who is venerated by both Christians and Muslims. An important legend about his life gained him world-wide fame. A voracious dragon was living in a pond. To keep it from destroying their city, people offered it sheep and later also human sacrifices, chosen by lottery. One day, the lot fell to the princess. Dressed as a bride, she was to be fed to the dragon. This is when Saint George arrived. He fought the dragon and wounded it. He brought it to the city and said he was sent by God. He could only kill the dragon if the people would be ready to believe in Jesus. They all embraced the faith and asked to be baptised. Saint George killed the dragon and thus the people were saved twice: first by Saint George's lance, and then by God through baptism.

> O God, George was ready to stand for his faith and to fight evil. Help me to always fight evil, while remembering that love is the greatest gift of all. Saint George, pray for us!

VIOLENCE OR LOVE?

The violence used against the dragon by Saint George to save a damsel is usually considered appropriate, because he was fighting evil. Understandably we have much more difficulty with violent passages in the Old Testament. God drowns almost all humanity in the great Flood (*see #TwGOD 1.22*). Violence, homophobia, slavery, killing children and entire peoples, all of this seems to be either done by God or executed under his orders. How does this correspond with the God of love Jesus tells about?

NO HISTORY BOOK

The Bible consists of many different books, written by various authors in different times (*see #TwGOD 1.10 & 1.13*). What unites them is that each of these books is inspired by God (*see #TwGOD 1.12*). This ensures that the entire Bible speaks the truth. So, does this mean that violence is good? Absolutely not: if you say that, you are reading the Bible completely wrong. It is not a simple history book, and not everything is to be taken literally (*see #TwGOD 1.20*). The only way to read the Bible correctly is in its entirety. The starting point is always Jesus's preaching of the love of God, and his greatest gift of all when he died on the cross. The highest truth expressed in the Bible is God's love for all humanity.

POETRY

So, how to read those violent texts in the Old Testament? It is good to realise that the way God interacted with his people has developed over time, preparing for the coming of Jesus (*see #TwGOD 1.19*). Like other texts, for example the story of creation (*see #TwGOD 1.1-1.4*), you could try to read them in a symbolic way. You could see God's call for violence against enemies as a poetic description of his desire to eradicate evil in a drastic and definitive way. This is very similar to the story of Saint George saving an entire city — twice. His is also a poetic story, as we do not know much about George historically (nor about dragons). If the violent Bible texts were written today, then the authors would probably have chosen different examples. However, the central message still stands, and is in line with the New Testament: God fights for his people and asks us to do everything we can to eradicate evil and spread his love. Do you want to join him in doing so?

The Old Testament prepares for Jesus's ultimate sacrifice out of love. You can read the texts in a symbolic way as good battling evil: God is with his people!

SAINT
JUAN DIEGO

2.23

 1474 – 1548   MEXICO 🕯 9 DECEMBER

Q: WHAT TO THINK OF MIRACULOUS EVENTS IN THE BIBLE?

CAN A MODERN PERSON BELIEVE IN MIRACLES?

SCAN

Juan Diego was an indigenous native from Cuauhtitlan, Mexico. He was known for his deep devotion to Jesus and his mother Mary. He diligently cared for his sick uncle. One day, Juan had an experience that would change his life, and that of many others. As he was hurrying towards Mass, he saw a beautiful and radiant woman who told him she was Mary, the ever-virgin Mother of God. She informed Juan to tell the bishop to erect a chapel in her honour, where people could come and pray. The bishop did not believe him. On his way back, Juan met Mary again. She asked him to repeat her request to the bishop. As he did, the bishop asked for a sign. At his third encounter with Mary, she promised Juan to give him a sign the next day.

O God, Juan recognised your supernatural love when he met the Virgin Mary. Help me to be open to your love and recognise your presence in my life. Saint Juan Diego, pray for us!

OUR LADY OF GUADALUPE

However, he missed his appointment because his uncle was dying and Juan had to get a priest to administer the last rites. The next day, he took another route to avoid facing Mary. But she appeared on his new path and told him to pick the roses that suddenly blossomed between the rocks where only cactus could grow. He used his mantle to carry the flowers to the bishop as the promised sign. As soon as Juan opened his bundle, the bishop fell down on his knees in awe, because the mantle carried an imprint of the Virgin's image. Juan saw Mary once more, and his uncle fully recovered from his illness. Up to the present day, the image which appeared on Juan's mantle is venerated by millions of pilgrims every year in the shrine of Our Lady of Guadalupe in Mexico City. Many scientifically recorded and unexplainable miracles have happened since, at the intercession of Mary.

MIRACLES

The Bible is full of miracles where God temporarily sets aside the laws of nature and intervenes directly to heal people or to support them otherwise. Jesus walks on water *(Mt 14:25-27)*, turns water into wine *(Jn 2:6-10)*, heals people *(Mk 2:9-12)*, and raises the dead *(Lk 7:12-17)*. You may have difficulty in understanding these miraculous events. We all do. They cannot be proven scientifically, which is precisely why they are called miracles. Science can establish that they happened, but we do not know how. You may wonder why God sometimes decides to perform a miracle, but mostly seems to let events unfold as they do. Ultimately, God alone knows the answer to this question. However, in many cases it is a miracle in itself that people stand up to help others in a selfless and faithful way *(see Saint 2.26)*. Such miracles are much more frequent than you might think at first sight! Also today God is performing miracles through his people.

THE MIRACLE OF MERCY

'"The Lord is near", the Apostle Paul tells us, and nothing should perturb us. He is close by. He is not alone but is with his Mother. She said to Saint Juan Diego: "Why are you afraid? Am I not here who am your Mother?" He is near. He and his Mother. The greatest mercy lies in his being in our midst, in our being in his presence and company. He walks with us, he shows us the path of love, he lifts us up when we fall and with such tenderness he supports us in our labours, he accompanies us in every circumstance of life. He opens our eyes to see our wretchedness and that of the world, but at the same time he fills us with hope.'
[Pope Francis, Homily at the feast of O.L. of Guadalupe, 12 December 2015]

GOD'S LOVE

Many people have difficulty believing in miracles. Thankfully, not miracles but God's love for every human being is what is most important. At the same time, every miracle is an expression of this love. The greatest miracle God ever performed is the creation and the redemption of his people through the death and resurrection of Jesus. Miracles are part of God's supernatural intervention in our lives with the sole aim of bringing us to himself to live with him forever. Your existence is a miracle in itself for which you can thank God. In answer, you can collaborate with the supernatural grace and help that he wants to give to anyone who reaches out to him. You can ask the saints to intercede for you, so that you may grow in faith, hope, and love! Do you want to believe?

Miracles are the ultimate expression of God's love: he intervenes directly, often bypassing the laws of nature and science, to reach out to us with love and grace.

SAINT
JOSEPHINE BAKHITA

📅 CA. 1869 – 1947   🌍 SUDAN, ITALY   🕯 8 FEBRUARY

Q: WHY DO BAD THINGS HAPPEN TO GOOD PEOPLE?

WHERE IS GOD THEN?

Bakhita was born in Olgossa, a village in Sudan. She was happy and did not know suffering. When she was seven or eight years old, she was kidnapped by Arab slave traders, and sold. One of her first owners made her a maid for his daughters, who treated her well. But one day, when she allegedly offended their brother, she was beaten extremely hard. After weeks of recovery she was sold. A Turkish General made her serve his wife, by whom she was beaten daily and even tortured in a beastly way. She was then sold to the Italian Vice Consul, who was milder and did not beat her up. He took her to Italy, where she was given away to another family. When they had to leave the country, Bakhita was placed temporarily in the care of religious sisters in Venice. When the family came to pick her up, she refused to go with them. She first wanted to finish her introduction into the Catholic faith, which she had discovered living with the sisters. An Italian court ruled that she never had been legally a slave. She was free to go, for the first time of her life.

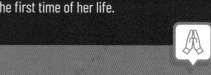

O God, Bakhita suffered extremely in her life. Help me to recognise your presence and love, especially when I encounter evil and suffering. Saint Josephine Bakhita, pray for us!

SCAN

RELIGIOUS LIFE

Bakhita was baptised and stayed with the sisters for four more years. She said: 'I was hearing more and more clearly in the depths of my soul a gentle voice drawing me to want to become a sister myself.' She was accepted and the former slave freely offered her life to the only truly good Master she had ever met, Jesus. The day of her first vows as a sister she showed how much she was convinced that a life of faith is of great value to face the difficulties of life. She prayed: 'O Lord, if I could fly to my people and tell them of your goodness at the top of my voice, oh how many souls would be won!' She felt so sorry for her father and brothers back home, and for her sister who was still a slave. She wished for all Africans to get to know Jesus.

WHERE WAS GOD?

It is easy to wonder 'Where was God' when this small child had to suffer so much as she was growing up. Looking back, Bakhita was convinced that he had been there with her throughout her life, especially when she was suffering, even though she did not know him at the time. She said: "Had I known that there was a God during my long years in slavery, my suffering would have been lessened." Knowing the love of God for you will not make you immune for suffering and pain, but your whole perspective of life will be different. That is why Saint Paul wrote: 'I consider that the sufferings of this present time are not worth comparing with the glory that will be revealed to us' (Rom 8:18).

WHY?

When people have to suffer and when disasters happen, we often ask: 'Why?' Bakhita said in retrospect: 'If I were to meet those who kidnapped me, or even those who tortured me, I would kneel down and kiss their hands. Because, if those things had not happened, I would not have become a

---

> ## GOD IS THE TRUE MASTER
>
> 'Josephine Bakhita...suffered much at the hands of cruel masters. But she came to understand the profound truth that God, and not man, is the true Master of every human being, of every human life. This experience became a source of great wisdom for this humble daughter of Africa. In today's world, countless women continue to be victimised, even in developed modern societies. In saint Josephine Bakhita we find a shining advocate of genuine emancipation. The history of her life inspires not passive acceptance but the firm resolve to work effectively to free girls and women from oppression and violence, and to return them to their dignity in the full exercise of their rights.'
>
> [Pope John Paul II, Homily at the canonisation, 1 October 2000]

Christian and would not be a sister today.' Although this is not a complete answer to the pertinent 'Why?' question, it shows that she recognised how out of evil something very good could come. She realised that without the events of her life, she would probably not have met Jesus. The presence of evil in the world is real (see #TwGOD 1.34-1.35), but so is the love of God! Her faith helped Bakhita to make sense of the terrible events in her life. It also helped her to become close to Jesus in everything. Do you want to do like she did?

> *God always sides with the oppressed and persecuted: he never leaves you alone! Created with a free will, we can accept God's love, or reject it and make others suffer badly.*

SAINT **PIO OF** PIETRELCINA – PADRE PIO

📅 1887 – 1968 🌍 ITALY 🕯 23 SEPTEMBER

Q: CAN GHOSTS AND EVIL SPIRITS GET ME?

WHAT ABOUT POSSESSED PEOPLE?

Francesco was born in Pietrelcina, Italy. When he entered the convent to become a capuchin friar, he received the name Pio, which suitably means 'pious'. He had a strong faith in the love and strength of Jesus. Many miraculous accounts are related about him, for example his 'stigmata': in his hands, feet and side wounds appeared similar to those inflicted on Jesus at the crucifixion. Various medical investigations could not demonstrate the origin of these wounds. You may have difficulty in believing such miracles *(see Saint 2.23)*. Do not worry, you are not alone. The Vatican ordered various serious inquiries into the life of Padre Pio. At one point he was even forbidden to say Mass in public. However never could any fraud be proven. His fame grew quickly.

O God, Padre Pio faced many trials, but overcame these with your help. Give me your grace to steer away from evil and grow in closeness to you in love. Saint Pio of Pietrelcina, pray for us!

Many people were attracted to the holiness of Padre Pio, and hundreds of thousands of people passed through his convent every year. They encountered Jesus through this holy man who heard their confession.

THE SUPERNATURAL

Padre Pio had many supernatural visions during his life. Not only of Jesus and Mary his Mother, but also of the devil, the enemy of God *(see Saint 1.2)*. He would see the enemy as a disgusting animal or as provocative obscene dancers, trying to frighten him or test his chastity *(see Saint 2.37)*. Padre Pio noticed that whenever he had a vision of Jesus or Mary, he was left with a great feeling of peace and inner joy. However, when the enemy of God appeared in disguise, he experienced an immediate feeling of joy and attraction, but afterwards he would feel empty, sad, and remorseful. Saint Ignatius called the first feeling consolation and the second desolation *(see Saint 1.34)*. These feelings are very helpful in distinguishing between what comes from God, and what is inspired by his enemy. It takes time and faith to learn discern between these feelings, and you need a good spiritual director *(see Saint 1.10)*.

THE HAUNTED HOUSE

There are a lot of accounts of ghosts haunting certain places. These would be evil spirits that were summoned at one point, or the souls of people 'stuck' on earth and unable to move on. Most of these accounts are pure fables. Many people have an unhealthy fascination for such dark supernatural phenomena *(see Saint 1.26)*. Unhealthy, for evil is real, and can take many forms. As Christians, we are warned to steer away from evil *(1 Pet 5:8; see box)*. Jesus and the disciples cast out spirits and demons of various kinds *(Mt 8:16; 28-33)*. In very rare cases, someone's body can be possessed. A priest can then cast out the evil spirit in an exorcism after asserting there is no medical or psychological cause *(see #TwGOD 3.18)*.

DO NOT BE AFRAID

"'Your adversary the devil prowls around like a roaring lion, looking for someone to devour" (1 Pet 5:8). Do not be afraid of the many snares of this infernal beast. Jesus is always with you and will fight with you and for you. He will never allow you to be taken and defeated. Do not fear when your heart is fighting with the one who refused the love of God. Bring all your worries to God, for he takes great care of you and his vigilant grace will always make you triumph over all the evil arts of the enemy... Choose a confessor who is learned and lives a spotless life, and... elect a good spiritual director... Open all your heart to him and let him guide you in everything.'

[Padre Pio, Letter to Annita Rodote, 29 January 1915]

DO NOT FEAR

There is no reason to fear evil spirits, though, for these cannot get you when you ask help from God: 'Perfect love casts out fear' *(1 Jn 4:18)*. Evil is real, but so is God's love! God is stronger than any evil, and Padre Pio shows that whoever stays closely connected to his love has nothing to fear. You may feel that you are still very far from God. But know that he is with you right now! Jesus has won the victory over sin, evil and death. You only have to call on him to be protected against any evil! Do you want him to be ever more part of your life?

No evil things can get to those who are close to God. Possession by the devil is real but rare. God's love overcomes every evil. Avoid an unhealthy interest in evil spirits and demons.

SAINT
OSCAR ROMERO

 1917 – 1980   EL SALVADOR   🕯 24 MARCH

Q: IS GOD'S LOVE REALLY STRONGER THAN ANY EVIL?

Oscar came from a poor family in Ciudad Barrios, El Salvador. At a young age, he wanted to become a priest. After his studies in Rome and his priestly ordination, he returned to his country. He became Auxiliary Bishop and later Archbishop of San Salvador. Now he was responsible for the spiritual well-being of all the people in his diocese. He had a deep faith and applied his strong will and mind to search for God's Will in everything.

SOCIAL INJUSTICE

It was a time of political turmoil and oppression by the military government. Many priests, who had hoped for a strong voice against the leading classes, were disappointed with Oscar's appointment. He was considered to hold conservative views and felt uncomfortable with social actions that would challenge political leaders. He preferred to quietly work for maintaining the traditions of the Church, rather than to voice his criticism of social injustice, they thought.

O God, Bishop Romero spoke up for the oppressed and gave a voice to the voiceless. Help me to always speak up against injustice in the name of Jesus. Saint Oscar Romero, pray for us!

 SCAN

Soon after Oscar's appointment, his good friend Father Rutilio Grande was killed, apparently because he had promoted self-reliance of the poor. Grande was among the many teachers, nuns, and priests killed by the government because they demanded justice. Oscar felt that he could no longer be silent, and asked the president to investigate the killings but with no avail.

VOICE OF THE VOICELESS

This situation prompted a change in Oscar. Where he used to be a rather quiet and careful man, he now quickly developed into the defender of the oppressed, speaking out publicly against the poverty, injustice and torturing of his people. He literally gave a voice to the voiceless in his Sunday homilies, broadcast on Catholic radio and published in the diocesan newspaper. He called for peace, listed the dead and disappeared, denounced injustice and asked to hear the voice of the poor. His broadcasts had the largest audience in the country and he was considered a liability by the leading classes. On 23 March 1980, just after finishing his homily during Mass, he was shot dead by unknown gunmen from a car driving past the open doors of the church. The day before, he had shouted out: 'I beg you, I implore you, I order you: in the name of God, stop the repression!'

FROM EVIL TO GOOD

The evil deed of Oscar's killing is horrific indeed. How can people get to the point of doing such terrible things? Unfortunately, the influence of evil can be seen all around us. But look at what happened after Oscar's death. The people stood up in a peaceful struggle, and eventually won. They considered Oscar to be a martyr and asked for his intercession. In turn, they felt called to continue his work. Thus his death brought forth great fruits (see box). Instead of silencing him, his voice was amplified and projected by many people. They

FROM DEATH TO HOPE

'I tried to interpret the message of the blood of a murdered priest, which reveals three things to us: first, the mystery of evil, pointing out the unjust situation of sinful structures in our country... The second point: the mystery of faithfulness - how dying in such a way does not mean a priest was bad, but rather that he was faithful, like Christ to the Father, like the Church to Christ. And third, to provide a message of hope, since this death shows us what should be the dimensions of the Church's work: to form a people made new through love and to open their eyes to the vision of the eternal that death shows so clearly.'   [Oscar Romero, Diary, 21 June 1979]

were inspired by his steadfast faith and willingness to offer his life for Jesus and his people. Just before dying he had said: 'Those who give themselves to the service of others for the love of Christ will live like the grain of wheat that dies... The harvest comes because of the grain that dies.' Oscar's death as a martyr shows how this is true. However bad the situation may seem to be, however hopeless, if you trust in God things will come right in the end. Know that life on earth is not everything; even death is not the end for those who love God. Ultimately, supported by our prayer and commitment, God's love will always prove to be stronger than any evil! How does this change your life?

It may take some time, but ultimately, God's love always has the last word. In the meantime, he needs us for reaching out to others in need and opposing evil.

SAINT
MAXIMILIAN KOLBE

2.27

 1894 – 1941   POLAND   14 AUGUST

BLESSED
KARL LEISNER

1915 – 1945   GERMANY   12 AUGUST

SCAN

Q: CAN I BE ANGRY WITH GOD?

HOW CAN I TRUST HIM DESPITE TRAGEDY?

Maximilian was a Franciscan friar who founded the successful monastery of Niepokalanów, Poland. The main focus of the friars was prayer and evangelisation. Maximilian peacefully opposed the Nazis who invaded Poland in 1939. He sheltered many refugees, and hid around 2000 Jews in the friary. He used new media like modern printing and radio to diffuse the gospel and anti-Nazi propaganda. In February 1941 the monastery was closed and the friars arrested by the Nazis. Soon, Maximilian was transferred to the extermination camp at Auschwitz. When ten prisoners managed to escape from the camp, the commander picked ten men at random to be starved to death in isolation as a reprisal. One of the selected men cried out in shock because of his wife and children. Maximilian did not hesitate, and stepped forward to offer himself in his place. Weeks of absolute horror followed, as the ten men were slowly dying of starvation.

O God, Maximilian and Karl loved you to the very end. Help me to overcome my anger and trust you with all my heart. Saint Maximilian Kolbe and Blessed Karl Leisner, pray for us!

Maximilian did what he could to keep their spirits up, and spoke of the great love of God to them. After three weeks Maximilian was one of the few survivors, and he was killed by injection. The prisoner he saved attended his canonisation in 1982.

A PRIEST FOREVER

Karl came from Rees, Germany. Already at school he formed a youth group, and loved outdoor activities like cycling and camping. He tried to avoid Nazi interference in his group. He became diocesan youth minister of Münster while studying for the priesthood. Shortly after his ordination as a deacon in 1939 he was diagnosed with tuberculosis. He was overheard making negative comments about Hitler, and arrested by the Gestapo. In the concentration camp at Dachau, where he spent most of his internment, conditions were harsh. The cold weather, small rations and regular beatings made his health deteriorate quickly. In spite of everything, and because of his fierce love of God, Karl's great regret was that he was never ordained a priest. The arrival in September 1944 of a new prisoner, a French bishop, made it possible to start preparing his clandestine ordination. Priests sewed the vestments, a Jewish prisoner played the violin, and some protestant pastors helped too. Because of his illness, Karl celebrated only one single Mass after ordination. At the liberation of the camp in May 1945, he was so weak that he died some months later.

ANGER

It seems so logical to be angry with God at times. Why did he not intervene? How could he allow disaster to happen? Something can be said in answer to these questions (see Saint 2.24). God did not create evil (see #TwGOD 1.34-1.35). But the most powerful answer is the testimony of these two men of God: they were angry with the Nazis, and fought evil as well as they could. But they never raised their voice against God. Why? Because they knew he is love, goodness, peace in himself, and would

---

OUR HEAVENLY MOTHER

'Let us be led by Mary, so that we may become more like Jesus through her. That is the safest and most perfect way. Consecrate yourself totally to our heavenly mother and you will victoriously overcome all difficulties in life and you yourself will become holy, a great saint, what I wish for you with all my heart. All saints – as one can truly say – are the work of the Blessed Virgin Mary, and special devotion to her is the common feature of the saints.'

[Maximilian Kolbe, Jedem ist der Weg Gewiesen, Ostfildern 1977, 103]

---

never leave them alone. So, you can wonder, what reason do you have to be angry at God? You can be angry with God — and he will understand — but your anger is always unfounded.

#TRUST

Karl trusted God so much that in spite of his extreme situation he only wanted one thing with all his heart: to dedicate himself to God as a priest. So great was the trust of Maximilian, that he was able to offer his own life to save another without further thought. These two men demonstrated their total trust in God. They knew that precisely in their misery God was at their side, to give them spiritual strength to bear what they were going through. Can a God of love do anything to lose your trust?

God himself is love and he will never do anything to hurt you or to deserve your anger. In spite of everything, he is by your side, hoping you will accept his helping hand and trust him.

SAINT
MARTIN
DE PORRES

 1579 – 1639   PERU, PANAMA   3 NOVEMBER

SCAN

Q: WHAT IF I AM INSECURE, SHY, OR HAVE LOW SELF-ESTEEM?

HOW CAN I BE MORE MYSELF?

Martin was born in Lima, Peru, the son of a Spanish nobleman and a freed slave from Panama. As a child he was ridiculed because of his mixed race. His father abandoned him and his mother was poor. At the age of 12 he was placed as an apprentice with a barber, where people came both for a haircut and medical treatment. He was very fond of God and especially during the night he spent hours in prayer. Legislation did not allow people of mixed race to be a full membcr of a religious order, so he joined the Dominicans as a volunteer servant. Desiring to follow Jesus in everything, he dedicated his life to the service of others. He was always seen with the broomstick with which he kept the convent clean, and which he carried as his cross. Hence his nickname 'Saint of the broom.' Even in the convent he was sometimes ridiculed and insulted as a "mulatto", to which he replied with a silent smile. Jesus's words 'They who humble themselves will be exalted' *(Mt 23:12)* perfectly apply to Martin.

O God, Martin led a humble life of dedication to you without worrying about what others would think. Help me to be more and more myself in my life. Saint Martin de Porres, pray for us!

SERVICE AND PRAYER

Eventually, Martin was admitted as a lay Dominican brother. He was assigned to the infirmary, where he cared for the sick, without fear of contagion. His skills as a barber came in very handy. He took in everyone, regardless of their background, race, or wealth. In their illness, they were all the same to him. When, during an epidemic, his superior forbade him to bring the sick to the convent out of fear of contagion, he set up an infirmary at his sister's house. During his life of humble service, he never forgot to make time for his prayers. For him, his service of Jesus came in the first place.

JESUS'S GRACE

You may struggle with the high expectations of the people around you, thinking that you will never please them. Note, however, that your vocation is not to live up to their expectations! *(Rom 12:2)*. Their opinion cannot truly hurt you when you stay close to God *(Mt 10:28)*. The following may seem like a contradiction but think about it: are you maybe too focused on yourself? Do you dare to lift up your eyes long enough from yourself in order to truly gaze at Jesus? Martin did this during all his life. He did not care what others would think of his mixed race or his broomstick. He wanted to live for Jesus alone. If you try to do the same, you will see that gradually things get better *(see box)*. The focus of Christian life is not on ourselves, our misery, our difficulty, but on Jesus and his grace!

LOVE AND TRUST

The key to becoming more yourself is to accept that God loves you just the way you are. This is how he created you, this is how he wants you! Including your possible low self-esteem or tendencies to be shy, insecure, depressed... Your fragilities can even help others and thus be a source of good. For starters, by showing that they are not alone. We all have our limits, and nobody is perfect. God invites you to see beyond your limits, for he truly loves you! Can you love him back? "Perfect love casts out fear," Scripture

---

JESUS IS WITH YOU

'Nothing prevented [Saint Martin] from achieving his dreams, nothing prevented him from spending his life for others, nothing prevented him from loving, and he did so because he had realised that the Lord loved him first. Just as he was: a mulatto. He had to face many hardships...[but] he knew how to trust. To trust in the Lord who loved him. Do you know why? Because the Lord had trusted him first; just as he trusts each of you and will never tire of trusting you... There are moments when you can feel powerless to achieve your desires and dreams. We all experience situations like that. In these moments when our faith seems to fade, remember that Jesus is by your side. Do not give up! Do not lose hope! Remember the saints who accompany us from heaven. Go to them, pray and never tire of asking for their intercession.'

[Pope Francis, Angelus in Peru, 21 January 2018]

---

promises *(1 Jn 4:18)*. We all are afraid from time to time, but with Jesus there is no reason to! He loves you and tells you: 'Do not be afraid' *(Lk 12:7)*. Obviously, you cannot change your attitude from one day to the other. But with God everything is possible *(Mt 19:26)*. If you try to live for him alone, you will step by step learn to let go of your self-consciousness and find true happiness by simply being yourself in the light of God. What could be your first step?

God loves you just the way you are, including your fragilities! Look up to him and let Jesus heal your wounds: he is always with you!

SAINT
ELIZABETH SETON

 1774 – 1821   UNITED STATES OF AMERICA

🕯 4 JANUARY

.SCAN

Q: HOW CAN I DEAL WITH GRIEF?

IF GOD IS LOVE, WHERE IS HE WHEN PEOPLE ARE IN PAIN?

Elizabeth had to live through many dark periods in her youth. She was born in New York, USA, and baptised as an Episcopalian. Her mother died when she was three years old, and a year later she lost her baby sister. Her father remarried. But after a few years the marriage ended in a separation, and the stepmother rejected Elizabeth. She and her sister were sent to live with their uncle. This was a dark period for her, partly because she missed having a mother around. She married William Seton, a handsome and wealthy businessman. They had five children, and even took in other children. All went well until the business failed, and William died of tuberculosis when they were in Italy. Elizabeth was penniless. To support her children, she started an academy for young ladies in New York.

O God, Elizabeth could accept her grief and surrender to your will. Help me to recognise your presence when I am sad, and open myself to your grace. Saint Elizabeth Seton, pray for us!

LOVE FOR JESUS

Elizabeth had much reason to become depressed and wary, but she did not. Instead, she started to contemplate what it means to accept and embrace God's Will. In Italy she had come to know the Catholic faith. When she decided to become a Catholic, she was rejected by friends and family, and lost most of the girls in her academy. Still, her love for Jesus, Mary and the Eucharist was great enough to overcome also this trial. She thought of joining the Daughters of Charity of Saint Vincent *(see Saint 2.19)*, but then decided to accept the invitation to start a Catholic girls school in Baltimore, Maryland. In the process she also founded a religious community to run the school. This was the beginning of the Catholic parish school system in the USA. After a life of hardships, Mother Seton died at the age of 46.

NEVER ALONE

Elizabeth's experience is not unlike the story of Job, who lost almost everything and had to face many trials *(see #TwGOD 1.25)*. The question why there is so much pain, suffering and grief is not easily answered *(see Saint 2.24; #TwGOD 1.34-1.36)*. We cannot simply say that it is the will of God, for he wants us to be happy and bring us what is good for us. What we do know is that we are never alone when we are in pain, suffering, or grieving. God never leaves your side, and especially at difficult moments he wants to give you his grace to overcome difficulties and hardships. When Elizabeth came to realise this, at the highpoint of her suffering and grief she asked to become a Catholic. She continued to trust in God and did not despair.

LEARN FROM ELIZABETH

Elizabeth shows that it is possible to live through grief and suffering by growing in your relationship with Jesus. In fact, precisely her grief made it possible to do so much good. You can do like she did, knowing that grieving needs time and that everyone has to follow their own path in life.

DO GOD'S WILL

'The first end I propose in our daily work is to do the will of God... What are our real trials? By what name shall we call them? One cuts herself out a cross of pride; another, one of causeless discontent; another, one of restless impatience or peevish fretfulness. But is the whole any better than children's play if looked at with the common eye of faith? Yet we know that our God calls us to a holy life, that he gives us every grace, every abundant grace; and though we are so weak of ourselves, this grace is able to carry us through every obstacle and difficulty.'

[Elizabeth Seton, Conference to the Sisters]

- First, she accepted the situation as a fact, even without understanding why these bad things happened — and without blaming God.

- Second, she got up every day, knowing that this is a new day given to her by God to make most of it.

- Third, she worked on her relationship with God, reading the Bible, praying, and receiving the sacraments.

- Fourth, the more she discovered the will of God for her, the better she could make herself useful.

- Fifth, she realised that all this did not change the past, but the way she faced the future. Instead of turning away from him, she was facing it together with God. Do you want to have such faith?

God wants to be with you in your grief! Even when the cause is unknown, he wants to help you find consolation. Seek his will for you now, and you'll find peace.

SAINT **ANTHONY OF PADUA**

 1195 – 1231   PORTUGAL, ITALY   13 JUNE

.SCAN

Q: I AM WORRIED AND DESPERATE; IS LIFE ALWAYS GOING TO BE SUCH A CHALLENGE?

HOW DO I STAY MOTIVATED AND AVOID BURNOUT?

Anthony was born in Lisbon, Portugal. As a young man he decided to give up his excellent career prospects to join the Augustinians for his studies. Ten years later he was deeply impressed by the sight of the bodies of Franciscan friars who died as martyrs when preaching the gospel to the Moors in Morocco *(see Saint 1.35)*. Now that was dedication to Jesus! Anthony asked to become a Franciscan himself. However, as he started out to preach with passion in Morocco, he fell seriously ill and had to return to Europe. He went to Italy, and was desolate, for he had so much wanted to preach the gospel, and look at him now, a human wreck! In his desperation he dedicated himself to a life of prayer and study.

O God, Anthony overcame his desperation in growing closer to you. Help me to reach out to you especially in hard times and let you console me. Saint Anthony of Padua, pray for us!

One day, no preacher was available, and Anthony hesitantly accepted the charge. Those present were struck by his passion, knowledge, and love of the Lord. This was the beginning of his new life as a preacher and teacher of theology. He was sent to the Albigensians in southern France *(see Saint 1.18)*. His preaching was very simple and very profound at the same time, so that also uneducated people clearly understood the importance of the faith. Later, he was based in Padua, from where he continued to preach.

JESUS LOVES YOU

Several legends about this popular saint may help you see beyond your desperation, and recognise how God wants to be close to you. One night, Anthony had a vision of the child Jesus visiting him and consoling him. This is why he is often depicted with the child Jesus on his arm, who touches his cheek affectionately. Jesus loves you in the same affectionate manner! A lady who had lost the key to her shop promised to give bread to the poor if Anthony would help her. This is one of the reasons why he is often called upon for recovering lost things *(see #TwGOD 4.16)*. It is an old tradition to bless bread on Saint Anthony's feast as a sign of gratitude for God's grace. This 'Saint Anthony Bread' is also a reminder that we should feed the poor. One of the best ways to break away from anxiety and despair is to turn your gaze from yourself towards God and the needs of people around you.

LOST JOY

Anthony is a great saint to turn to when you feel you have lost your motivation or joy of life. It sounds so simple, but also in the greatest desolation you may be certain that God loves you. This may ask for an act of will, a decision to trust God in spite of everything. It was the only conviction that helped Anthony to pick up his life after his life's dream was scattered. There is always hope! When things go wrong and your world seems to have been ruined, there is always a new future awaiting you. At first sight it

---

> ### *YOUR VALUE IN CHRIST*
>
> *'Christ who is your life is hanging before you, so that you may look at the cross as in a mirror. There you will be able to know how mortal were your wounds, that no medicine other than the blood of the Son of God could heal. If you look closely, you will be able to realise how great your human dignity and your value are.... Nowhere other than looking at himself in the mirror of the cross can man better understand how much he is worth.'*
>
> [Anthony of Padua, Sermones Dominicales et Festivi, III, 213-214]

may not seem as good or glorious as what you lost, but gradually you will find that your new life has value in itself, because of your new chance to live with God in love. The only fear admissible is the fear of sin *(see box)*, but also there it is important to realise that God's love is always greater than evil *(see Saint 2.26)*.

NO BURNOUT

If you stay closely connected to Jesus, you will be well prepared for facing even disaster with faith and trust. It is this trust in God that will prevent your burnout, which is often caused by you trying to do the impossible, and straining yourself beyond your forces. It is so easy to forget that God is with you at every moment, and does not ask you to do more than you can. He is the Boss, and he carries the ultimate responsibility, not you. Hence the wisdom of the old saying: 'Do your best and God will do the rest.' Do you want to trust God like this?

> *Surrendering to God's love with all your heart is the best remedy against worries and desperation. Realise that you can only do so much, and leave the rest in God's hands.*

SAINTS
ZÉLIE & LOUIS MARTIN-GUÉRIN

2.31

 LOUIS 1823 – 1894; ZÉLIE 1831 – 1877

 FRANCE   12 JULY

Q: WILL GOD PUNISH ME FOR FEELING MISERABLE AND ALONE?

Zélie Guérin was born in Gandelain, France. Her parents showed her little affection, and she wanted to do better in her life. She had a great personal faith. As she grew up, she first thought of entering a convent, but then became a talented lace maker. She set up quite a successful business for herself, and soon she married Louis Martin, a watchmaker. Together they continued their respective businesses in Alençon, France. Both Zélie and Louis came from military families: for them discipline and spirituality went hand in hand. They found much comfort and joy in their faith and their life together. However, not everything was easy. Some years before their marriage, Louis had tried to enter monastic life, but had not been able to master the required Latin language. The illness and depression he experienced as a consequence would have a continued effect. And so would his faith in God.

O God, Zélie and Louis are an example of living through misery and difficulty together with you. May I find strength to do the same and find peace. Saints Zélie and Louis, pray for us!

JOY AND PAIN

The couple had nine children, who brought their parents much happiness. The most famous of them is without doubt Thérèse of Lisieux (see Saint 2.42). However, tragedy struck, and within three years four of their children died. Zélie was mortified, and wrote to her sister-in-law: "When I closed the eyes of my dear little children and buried them, I felt sorrow through and through." Her youngest daughter Thérèse was weak and frail, and Zélie wrote: 'I have no hope of saving her. The poor little thing suffers horribly... It breaks your heart to see her.' In all her suffering, Zélie gave proof of great faith. She knew she would see her dead children in heaven, and continued to trust in the love of God for her and all her family.

AGONY

Thankfully, Thérèse and her four sisters lived and grew up. By facing their tragedies together, Zélie and Louis had further grown in love for each other, and in their relationship with God. Zélie died at the age of 45. Thérèse wrote: 'I loved mother's smile and her deep look seemed to say: "Eternity delights me and attracts me, I am going to the blue sky to see God!"' Louis continued to care for his daughters, while missing his wife dearly. Eventually, misery and loneliness took their toll and his mental state began to decline, ultimately leading him to be admitted to a psychiatric hospital. Thérèse wrote: 'Words cannot describe our agony, so I shall not try to write about it.' Father and daughters faced this trial with great faith, and continued to trust in the Lord in every moment.

GOD IS WITH YOU

Feelings of misery, sadness, loneliness, or depression, invade most of us at certain times. For some, these feelings seem to be there on a permanent basis. This is nothing to be ashamed of and you won't be punished for them! God knows what you are going through. Better still, he is with

---

> ## DO NOT WORRY
>
> *'I desire with all my heart that you succeed in your enterprises and I am sure that you will succeed if you want it; it depends only on you, the good God protects all those who trust him, there has never been a single one left behind. When I think of what the good God, in whom I put all my trust and in whose hands I gave the care of my business, did for me and for my husband, I cannot doubt that his divine providence does not look with particular care upon her children.'*
>
> [Zélie Martin, Letter to her brother, 1 January 1863]

---

you, especially at such moments. No one should have to face these trials alone, and as a Christian community we need to be attentive to the needs of others, just as Zélie shared her burden with her husband, and Louis was cared for by his daughters. Their greatest strength, however, did come from the knowledge that they were not alone at all, that God was with them at all times! Even if you do not feel his presence, God is there with you. He is miserable, sad, and even lonely together with you. Does this change your situation?

God loves you very much and is with you at this and every moment. He knows your condition and feelings better than you, without any judgement or punishment.

SAINT
JANE FRANCES DE CHANTAL

 1572 – 1641   FRANCE   12 AUGUST

SCAN

Q: IS THERE A CHRISTIAN WAY TO DEAL WITH DEPRESSION?

Jane did not always suffer from deep depression. She was a beautiful and refined woman from an important family in Dijon, France, with great human and organisational qualities. She was extremely happy in her marriage to Baron Christophe de Chantal, and they had six children, two of whom died in infancy. After seven years of marriage, Christophe was killed instantly in a hunting accident.

DEPRESSION

Jane was devastated and fell into a deep depression of darkness and interior anguish. To make things worse, she saw herself forced to go and live with her father-in-law, a great bully, with an even meaner housekeeper. In spite of her depression, she continued to care for the education and future of her children, while trying to dedicate herself also to prayer and charity to those in need. It was the darkest period of her life. About ten years after the death of her husband, Jane met Francis de Sales, who became her spiritual director (see Saint 1.10). He called her a 'perfect woman', intended in a spiritual sense. Many of their letters were preserved, and show how she too was a spiritual director to him, also because of her own emotional and psychical experiences. Thus her fragility became a source of good (see box).

O God, Jane placed all her confidence in you. Give me strength to accept the unavoidable, while finding ways to move away from depression. Saint Jane de Chantal, pray for us!

SUPERNATURAL GIFTS

Under Francis's guidance, Jane learned to live a life of prayer while being busy with her everyday tasks, and in spite of her depression. She even learned how the insults and bullying she suffered at home could help her to become more patient, charitable and forgiving, searching only to do the will of God in everything. She started to understand why Jesus asks us to be humble: spiritual humility is essential if you want to be fully available for God in everything and in every situation. Suffering and depression thus helped this naturally gifted woman to become more and more supernaturally gifted: she was able to turn her psychological weakness into a strength by letting herself be led only by the will of God. The advice of her spiritual director was very important to attain this.

KEEPING HEART

After providing for her children, Jane wanted to follow the passion that had grown in her for years. With Francis de Sales, she co-founded a Congregation named after the Visitation, the visit of Mary to her cousin Elizabeth *(Lk 1:39-56)*. Jane wanted her sisters to be like Mary, in spite of the difficulties they might have encountered in their lives. The keyword was spiritual humility: the sisters did not seek to be important or even noticed. They found their fulfilment in dedicating themselves to a quiet life of faith and prayer. Like Mary, they wanted to keep everything they heard and experienced 'in their hearts' *(Lk 2:19; 2:51)*. And Jane had much to keep in her heart. Also in monastic life she experienced grief and loss. She saw the death of almost all her children, and also that of her friend and mentor Francis. Vincent de Paul, her new spiritual director, said that Jane was one of the holiest people he had ever met *(see Saint 2.19)*. Still, she experienced periods of

---

WHEN YOU ARE DEPRESSED

'When you are experiencing some physical pain or a sorrowful heart, try to endure it before God. Recall as much as you can that he is watching you at this time of affliction, especially in your illness when very often the heart is weary and unable to pray. Don't force yourself to pray, for a simple adherence to God's Will, expressed from time to time, is enough. Moreover, suffering borne voluntarily, quietly and patiently is a continual, very powerful prayer before God, regardless of the complaints and anxieties that come from the inferior part of the soul... [God will give you] all the graces, consolations and blessings of his holy love in the measure that they will be useful in this life. In the next life he will grant you eternal bliss.' [Jane F. de Chantal, Letter DCIII to Mgr. A. Fréymot, 1625]

great depression, temptations and dryness in her spiritual and emotional life. The example of Jane shows how it is possible to endure your depression or anxiety with Jesus, and slowly let yourself be moulded into an instrument that can be of use to God and to many people. Are you ready to become such an instrument?

First of all, trust that Jesus is with you in your suffering: you are not alone! Try to see beyond your illness recognising the path that God has prepared for you. He will give you strength.

SAINT
ELIZABETH
OF THE TRINITY

 1880 – 1906   FRANCE   8 NOVEMBER

Q: WHAT IF SOMEONE THINKS ABOUT SUICIDE?

Elizabeth was known as a brat in her youth in Avord and Dijon, France. She excelled in music and studied at the conservatory. Her irritable temper was a continuous problem for herself and the people around her, and only gradually did she learn how to behave better. She enjoyed fashion, music, and dancing (see Saint 1.24, 1.27 & 1.33). At the same time, within her, a desire grew to become a Carmelite nun in the convent opposite their house. Her mother wanted to find her a husband, but at the age of 21, Elizabeth entered Carmel and received the monastic name Elizabeth of the Trinity. She had a great love for God, with whom she wanted to spend all her life: 'I have found my heaven on earth, since heaven is God, and God is in my soul.' She continued to be strong willed: when she made up her mind, she would not change it. Together with her great love, this helped her to overcome many difficulties.

SCAN

O God, Elizabeth turned to you in her prayer. May I find consolation in your great love and find ways to overcome depressions and difficulties. Saint Elizabeth of the Trinity, pray for us!

DESPAIR

Two years after entering the monastery, Elizabeth fell gravely ill. She suffered for years and was in great pain. Still, she found much consolation in the love of God, and in her prayer, and often spoke of a great joy in her spiritual life. But the physical pain combined with her loneliness, sense of uselessness, and the sensation of being empty and abandoned by God also gave her other thoughts. Especially the last months of her life were very difficult. One day she said: 'I suffer so much, that I now understand suicide.' And she added: 'But be calm, God is here, and he watches over me.' Elizabeth died of her illness at the age of 26. Her experience shows that suicidal thoughts are not something to be ashamed of. Rather, such thoughts are often the result of a desperate situation in which one sees no other way out. But there always is a way! If only they would talk about their problem and admit that they cannot face this alone.

COMMUNICATE

When you experience similar feelings, force yourself to do like Elizabeth: talk to the people around you about your suicidal thoughts. Let others help you. Let them listen, be compassionate, be loving. As Elizabeth said: 'Let yourself be loved' *(see box)*. Even if it may not always seem to be so, you are truly loved by God and many people around you. Do not hesitate to ask for help from your friends. Talk to your friends, counsellor, pastor, or someone else you trust. If necessary, they will help you find professional help. As a Church community we need to be attentive to each other. No one should have to face depression alone!

LOVE

Elizabeth knew that the greatest gift of God is his love for every human being. Everyone! That includes you. She knew that God expressed his great love for her by giving her life. Even in her darkest moments, Elizabeth did not want to hurt God by turning away his gift of her life. Even in her deepest

---

> ## *LET YOURSELF BE LOVED*
>
> *'Let yourself be loved... [God] rejoices to build you up by his love and for his glory. He alone wants to work in you, even though you will have done nothing to attract this grace except that which a creature can do: works of sin and misery... He loves you like that... He will do everything in you. He will go to the end: for when a soul is loved by him to this extent, in this way, loved by an unchanging and creative love, a free love which transforms as it pleases him, oh, how far this soul will go!... The fidelity that [God] asks of you is to remain in communion with Love, flow into, be rooted in this Love... You will never be commonplace if you are vigilant in love! But in the hours when you feel only oppression and lassitude, you will please him even more if you faithfully believe that he is still working, that he is loving you just the same, and even more: because his love is free and that is how he wants to be magnified in you; and you will let yourself be loved.'*
>
> [Elizabeth of the Trinity, Letter to her Prioress, October 1906, L337]

depression, she continued to count on God and cried out to him, in spite of her pain and doubts. You can do the same, even when life seems unbearable. Try to break out of the circle of lonely misery. Reach out to God. Pray! Pray for yourself, and pray for others. Try to thank God for the good things in and around you. God is there for you, to listen to you, to support you, to encourage you and above all to love you. Can you see how much God loves your life?

> *Such thoughts are nothing to be ashamed of. Speak to friends and people around you and let them help. Trust that God loves you just as you are and is with you now.*

SAINT
JOSEPH

 1ST CENTURY   HOLY LAND

19 MARCH (HUSBAND OF MARY); 1 MAY (JOSEPH THE WORKER); SUNDAY BETWEEN 26-31 DECEMBER (EAST)

SCAN

Q: HOW TO DEAL WITH STRESS AS A CHRISTIAN?

Joseph was a carpenter from Nazareth in Galilee (*Mt 13:55*). He was not wealthy, although he descended from King David (*Mt 1:1-16; see Saint 1.24*). Joseph loved Mary so much that he was prepared to silently separate from her when he heard she was pregnant without his involvement (*Mt 1:19*). Another in his place might have denounced her, with the result of her being stoned as an adulteress. After Joseph had thus demonstrated his compassionate character, he had a dream while he was sleeping. An angel told him not to be afraid to take Mary as his wife, and to accept her child as his own, because the child came from God and not from a man (*Mt 1:20-21*). Thus Joseph became Jesus's foster father. He must have died young, for he is not mentioned in Jesus's later life.

HE IS THE BOSS

Joseph had a lot on his plate. And so do you! 'I want so much in my life; there is always more work than I can finish!' 'I am worried about the outcome of...' 'I am afraid that something will happen to...' Do such thoughts sound familiar? Anxiety and stress are part of the life of most people. But there is no need for this at all! Ultimately, God is in charge, not you. You can only do so much.

O God, Joseph knew how stressful I sometimes let my life become. Help me leave all my worries in your hands and concentrate on the essential alone. Saint Joseph, pray for us!

Allegedly it was saint Ignatius who said that we have to work as if everything depends on us, but to pray as if everything depends on God *(see #TwGOD 4.5)*. That summarises perfectly the attitude that we should have as Christians. It is very healthy to lay the ultimate responsibility for the outcome of your work in the hands of God. He is the Boss! *(see Saint 2.30)*. Yes, he depends on you to apply your mind, your heart and your hands to your tasks, and to do so with all you can give. However, he does not ask more from you than that.

NO STRESS

Saint Joseph is a great example of how to deal with responsibility and a multitude of tasks. Did you notice what he did in probably the most stressful moment of his life, when his loved and trusted bride to be seemed to have betrayed him and all his world was crumbling down? He went to sleep, trusting God! *(see box)*. Precisely by going to sleep he made it possible for God to act (in his case through a dream). Jesus spoke of a farmer casting seeds: the seed sprouts and grows while he sleeps *(Mk 4:26-29)*. Often, our stress is making it more difficult for God to help us, as we stand in the way and do not listen!

STEPS AWAY FROM STRESS

God knows you need your rest, and just before going to sleep you may entrust everything you worry about into his hands. But what if you cannot sleep because you are too stressed? Here are a few tips.

- First, pray and communicate. Tell God about your worries, asking for his help. Speak to someone like a friend or a teacher, and write down all your worries and tasks.

- Second, prioritise: order the list in order of importance, so that you can get at least the essential things done.

- Third, ask help from others and learn to say 'no': you can only do so much by yourself *(see Saint 1.4)*.

SLEEPING JOSEPH

'I have great love for Saint Joseph, because he is a man of silence and strength. On my table I have an image of Saint Joseph sleeping. Even when he is asleep, he is taking care of the Church! Yes! We know that he can do that. So when I have a problem, a difficulty, I write a little note and I put it underneath Saint Joseph, so that he can dream about it! In other words I tell him: pray for this problem!... Like Saint Joseph, once we have heard God's voice, we must rise from our slumber; we must get up and act (Rom 13:11)... Faith does not remove us from the world, but draws us more deeply into it. This is very important! We have to be deeply engaged with the world, but with the power of prayer. Each of us, in fact, has a special role in preparing for the coming of God's kingdom in our world.'

[Pope Francis, Speech to families in Manila, 16 January 2015]

- Fourth, go to sleep. The next day you can take a brief moment of prayer for God's help and review your priorities. Then get started, beginning with what is most important.

- Fifth, work hard, but leave the rest in God's hands *(see Saint 2.30)*. If you make your relationship with him your top priority, you will find that eventually you have time for all the things that really matter. Resolve to leave the outcome in his hands. And ask Saint Joseph to pray for you. Can you believe that this will change your life?

Trust in God! Pray to him and spell out worries; prioritise; ask help or say no; go to sleep; review your priorities and work hard, leaving the outcome in God's hands.

SAINT **ELIZABETH** OF HUNGARY

 1207 – 1231   HUNGARY   17 NOVEMBER

SAINT **BRIDGET** OF SWEDEN

 CA. 1303 – 1373   SWEDEN   23 JULY

.SCAN

Q: HOW DO YOU GET OVER A BROKEN RELATIONSHIP?

WHAT DO I DO WITH A BROKEN HEART?

Elizabeth was a Hungarian princess, related to Saint Vladimir *(see Saint 2.46)*. She did not have a typical youth: her marriage was arranged almost at birth, she started her formation to be queen at the age of four, and her mother was murdered when she was six. At the age of 14 she married Louis of Thuringia, whom she deeply loved. They had three children and were very happy together. Elizabeth had another love in her life: Jesus. She was especially struck by the example of Saint Francis of Assisi *(see Saint 1.35)*. She lived a simple life, spent much time in prayer, and did what she could to help the poor and needy. Then her heart broke. Louis died suddenly of illness on his way to the Crusades *(see #TwGOD 2.31)*. She was desolate, and it was to her as if the whole world had died. She mourned for months. Then she decided to dedicate the remainder of her life to God alone, and never remarry, in spite of the demands of her family.

O God, Elizabeth and Bridget picked up their life after their great loss. Help me to recognise that your love is forever. Saints Elizabeth of Hungary and Bridget of Sweden, pray for us!

She became a lay member of the third order of Saint Francis, and lived in prayer and poverty. After some dispute, she received her heritage, which she used to found a hospital named after Saint Francis. Here she personally cared for the sick during the remaining years of her life. She was 23 years old when she died.

BRIDGET

Bridget was born in Uppland, Sweden. She married Ulf Gudmarsson at the age of 13 or 14 (yes, that was quite a normal age to marry!) and had eight children. They had a very deep and loving relationship. Bridget often prayed with her children. She became a lady in waiting to the queen. Early 1344 Ulf fell ill, and he died not long after. Bridget showed her deep love by staying with him even after death, spending hours of prayer at his graveside. Since the age of ten she often had visions of Jesus hanging on the cross to save his people (hence the title 'Saviour'). She was 41 years old when she felt that God was calling her to found a new religious order, named after Jesus the Holy Saviour. Her second daughter also became a nun, and is known as Saint Catherine of Sweden. Bridget went to Rome to ask official recognition for her order from the pope, but with the papacy being undecided *(see Saint 1.48)*, it took 20 years to get the long-awaited confirmation. She died three years later in Rome. After her death, the order spread quickly throughout Europe and into the world.

GRIEF FIRST

Bridget and Elizabeth's grief is very comparable to that of a broken relationship, for the other one is no longer at your side. Jesus knows what grief is. He cried bitterly over the death of his friends *(Jn 11:35)*. He can heal your grief – but it takes time. Elizabeth and Bridget show it is possible to pick up your life again in spite of everything and make it worthwhile for God and fellow people!

FROM DEATH TO LIFE

'The fact that some have less tribulation, and others more, occurs so that mankind may turn away from sin and may, after troubles in the present, obtain consolation in the future... As it is written: They will pass "from death into life"... Let everyone who has the grace of intelligence... fear that, because of it, he will be judged more heavily if he is negligent. Let him who has no intelligence or talent rejoice and do as much as he can with the little that he has.' [Bridget of Sweden, The Fifth Book of Revelations, Q3-Q4]

GETTING ON

There is no one way to get over a broken heart. When you break up, you'll first be shattered and see no future at all. Know that this painful phase of bereavement will pass eventually. Try to see that even though all love seems to have left you, God loves you with great affection. In other words, don't stay fixed only on your situation, look up to Jesus! Your personal path is different from that of Elizabeth and Bridget, but they show how important it is to keep busy: follow Bible classes, get a new hobby, help at the local soup kitchen... Keep seeing your friends and make new friends. In your prayer, do not only dwell on your situation, but especially open yourself to God's presence and love. Do you think these points can help you?

It will take time, but God's love can heal every wound of the heart. Search for him in everything and you will eventually find peace. He has a vocation in mind for you!

SAINT
NICHOLAS
OF MYRA

📅 CA. 270 – CA. 343 🌐 TURKEY 🕯 6 DECEMBER

SCAN

Q: HOW CAN I EVER FIND THE RIGHT PARTNER?

Nicholas was born in today's Turkey. He was known as a wise man, and as bishop of Myra he probably attended the Council of Nicaea in 325 (see #TwGOD 2.22-2.23). In spite of his popularity, also in the East, not much is known about the historical Nicholas. A beautiful legend gave him his reputation of giver of gifts. At the tragic death of his parents, he inherited their fortune, which he wanted to dedicate to the well-being of others with the sole purpose of honouring God.

THREE DOWRIES

One of Nicholas's neighbours lost all his money, and decided to give his three daughters over to prostitution for he could not afford the customary wedding gift. Nicholas was appalled when he heard this and decided to change the girls' fate. At night, he secretly threw a bag of gold through the open window. With this dowry, the eldest daughter quickly found a good husband and became happily married.

O God, Nicholas searched to do your will alone; if it is my vocation to get married, help me meet and recognise the one partner you have intended for me! Saint Nicholas of Myra, pray for us!

A little later, Nicholas threw in another bag of gold, which allowed the second daughter to marry. In some accounts, the bag of gold fell into a shoe, which is the alleged origin of placing a shoe (or stocking) at the chimney for presents. When Nicholas delivered the third bag of gold, his neighbour was waiting for him, and overwhelmed him with gratitude. Nicholas made him promise not to speak of it. This is how Saint Nicholas became the patron saint of people looking for the perfect partner.

THE GIFT OF SELF

Finding the right person to marry may seem a daunting and sometimes even impossible task. You may feel that all your friends are getting married to the most wonderful people, while you remain single. Do not despair: if it is your vocation to marry, the right partner can be found eventually. Do not be afraid! Obviously, you can and should search, but realise at the same time that finding the one person with whom you will share the rest of your life is a gift from God (whether you recognise them as such or not). You cannot take a gift by force, for then it is no longer a gift. But you can learn to be a gift to others! Life does not stop while you are waiting to meet your future spouse. Also when you are alone, your life has value for God and other people. Like Saint Nicholas, you can share your time, talents, and possible wealth with others.

STEPPING STONES

The following tips may help.

- First of all, pray *(see #TwGOD 3.1-3.4)*. Ask God to help you find the right person, to remain patient, and to grow in your relationship with him. Ask Saint Nicholas and other saints to join you in your prayer.

- Second, keep your expectations real: even the most beautiful princess or prince has some flaws... With time, you may even learn to love these flaws!

- Third, when you think you have found the one, picture yourself waking up next to them as an old man or woman: will you still be able to love them when they are all wrinkles and grey hair?

- Fourth, try to stay chaste and live apart *(see #TwGOD 4.20 & 4.22)*. Cohabitation does not guarantee that it will work, and some researches even demonstrate the opposite. Keep that beautiful gift of yourself for the one and only *(see Saint 2.37)*.

- Finally, as you are getting ready to marry, focus on preparing for married life itself, not just the wedding day! What is your vocation?

Do not despair: if it is your vocation to get married the right partner can be found! Pray, be realistic, be chaste, and remember that marriage is a life-long gift of self.

SAINT **AGNES**

 CA. 291 – CA. 304   ITALY   21 JANUARY

BLESSED
ALBERTINA BERKENBROCK

 1919 – 1931   BRAZIL   15 JUNE

Q: WHY IS CHASTITY SUCH A CHRISTIAN THING, ANYWAY?

Agnes was a beautiful girl from a wealthy noble family in Rome, Italy. At a young age, she promised herself to Jesus with all her body. About her life not much can be said with certainty, but legend comes to our help. At the age of 13, she had a range of high-ranked young suitors. As she continued to refuse their attentions, they denounced her as a Christian, which was a crime at the time. The Prefect of Rome who investigated her case also made some advances, but she said: 'I am already the spouse of a Lover much more noble and powerful than you.' Enraged, he condemned her to be dragged naked through the streets of Rome into a brothel. She was thrown into a fire, but the flames were extinguished after her prayer. Finally, she was killed with a sword. Usually she is depicted with a lamb, a sign of her purity.

O God, Agnes and Albertina defended their virginity at all costs out of love for Jesus. Help me to live my life in chastity and love for Jesus. Saint Agnes and Blessed Albertina, pray for us!

ALBERTINA

Albertina Berckenbrock was born in Imaruí, Brazil. From an early age she prayed with great devotion. At school she was known for her diligence in learning about the faith and her love for Jesus. She was very open to everyone, also to the children of Maneco, one of her father's employees. They were of African origin and often discriminated against. Not so by Albertina, who happily shared her bread with the poor family. One day, when she was 13 years old, Maneco lured her into a quiet place. He tried to rape her, but the girl fought back with all her force. He placed before her the choice of being raped or killed. In answer, she continued to fight in defence of her chastity and virtue. Maneco slit her throat and tried to cover up the crime, but was caught later.

CHASTITY

Agnes and Albertina chose Jesus over every man on earth. In doing so, they claimed their personal identity, also with regards to their sexuality, in a world where certain men think they have a claim on women. Every woman would have resisted such terrible and unsolicited attentions. At the same time, chastity is often considered puritan, and not of this world. Sometimes it is described as a sure path to staying single... So what makes chastity such a Christian thing? It is important to realise that this is not about saying 'no' to sex, but saying 'yes' to who you are in the plan of God. Chastity has everything to do with love *(see box)*. Real love, deep love for Jesus. But also love and respect for yourself and others. Living a chaste life means among other things not having sex when you are not married, and loving attention for the sexual needs of the other when you are.

FREEDOM IN JESUS

Agnes and Albertina were ready to defend their chastity with their lives because of their bond with Jesus. So it must be a big thing! Whether you are a woman or a man, defending your

---

CHASTITY AND LOVE

'There is no way to comprehend chastity without the virtue of love... To be chaste means to have a "transparent" attitude to a person of the other sex... the desire to "enjoy" is subordinated to a readiness to show loving kindness in every situation... True chastity does not lead to disdain for the body... That is the result of false chastity, chastity with a tinge of hypocrisy, or, still more frequently, of unchastity... Only the chaste man and the chaste woman are capable of true love... Chastity is a difficult, long term matter; one must wait patiently for it to bear fruit.'

[Pope John Paul II, Love and Responsibility, 154, 170-172]

---

virginity means understanding what the real gift of sexuality is about *(see Saint 2.40-2.41)*. It may seem to be very difficult to live in chastity, but it is absolutely possible *(see #TwGOD 4.20-4.22)*. The key is to recognise your deep desire to keep your chastity as a personal gift to both Jesus and your future wife or husband — so that sex will be the full and unconditional expression of self-surrendering in true love. Would you like to wait until marriage?

Chastity is not about saying no to sex, but yes to God's plan for us — in which all are called to chastity: sex is the fullest expression of self-giving between man and wife in marriage.

SAINT **PAUL** THE APOSTLE

📅 CA. 1 – CA. 67   🌍 HOLY LAND, ASIA, ITALY

🕯 25 JANUARY (CONVERSION), 29 JUNE (WITH PETER)

Q: AS A CATHOLIC, SHOULD I IGNORE GAY PEOPLE?

WAS SAINT PAUL HOMOPHOBIC?

Paul was a tent-maker and scholar of Jewish teaching in the Holy Land *(Acts 22:3)*. He was one of the most fervent persecutors of the first Christians, so as to protect 'the tradition of his fathers' *(Gal 1:13-15)*. One day, as he was travelling to Damascus, he had a dramatic encounter with the risen Lord. This deeply affected him and brought him to convert to Christianity. He is considered an Apostle, even though he never met Jesus during his earthly life *(see #TwGOD 2.15 & 2.18)*. Paul became one of the most fervent preachers of the salvation and love that Jesus wants to bring to everyone indeed.

NO HATRED

Although Paul preached God's message of love, some people say that he was homophobic. They then quote part of his letters, for example when he warned against certain sexual behaviour. As always, the context is important. For example, when Paul spoke of 'sodomites' *(1 Cor 6:9)*, he referred in particular to adults who kept boys or young men for prostitution, seeking their own pleasure at the expense of others.

O God, Paul preached his love for you with fervour. Whatever my sexual orientation, may I be faithful to the vocation you have prepared for me. Saint Paul the Apostle, pray for us!

Paul often warned against 'sins of the flesh', which lead people to addictions to alcohol, wealth, power, sex... Various saints did the same, and also offered remedies against addictions *(see Saint 2.41)*. True, Paul considered homosexual acts not to be in line with the biblical plan for man *(see #TwGOD 4.24)*. But he never gave any hint of hate or violence against gay people. On the contrary, Paul continued to preach the gospel of love *(see box)*.

HUMAN SEXUALITY

The Catholic Church teaches that sex has a specific purpose, and that it has a natural place only in marriage between a man and a woman *(see #TwGOD 4.19-4.20)*. Sex outside of marriage, including gay sex, does not correspond with the idea of how we are created by God. Everyone is called to live with their sexuality and sexual desires in a proper way — principally out of love for God *(see #TwGOD 4.22)*. Chastity is a virtue we should all strive for, whatever our sexual orientation *(see #TwGOD 4.21)*. To have intercourse is a conscious decision: we can decide not to have sex. However, sexual orientation is not just a matter of free choice. We can only be held responsible for our conscious acts, not for who or how we are.

COMPASSION

Ignoring people is a completely wrong reaction. It is sometimes forgotten — even by Christians — how the Church teaches that gay people must be accepted with respect, compassion, and sensitivity *(CCC 2357)*. They should not be discriminated against unjustly, but respected and accompanied pastorally, said Pope Francis *(27 June 2016)*. Whenever the view of the Church on homosexual acts is used to incite hatred, this is a great wrong. Many saints worked for the well-being of gay people. For example, Mother Teresa cared for many gay people and welcomed aids patients at a time when few would do so. People who uphold the Catholic view of sexuality like Saint Paul are not homophobic, but they do so in order to be honest about

---

LOVE ABOVE ALL

'If I speak in the tongues of mortals and of angels, but do not have love, I am a noisy gong or a clanging cymbal. And if I have prophetic powers, and understand all mysteries and all knowledge, and if I have all faith, so as to remove mountains, but do not have love, I am nothing. If I give away all my possessions, and if I hand over my body so that I may boast, but do not have love, I gain nothing. Love is patient; love is kind; love is not envious or boastful or arrogant or rude. It does not insist on its own way; it is not irritable or resentful; it does not rejoice in wrongdoing, but rejoices in the truth.' [Paul, First letter to the Corinthians 13:1-6]

---

the teaching of the gospel. In fact, it does not only take courage to admit one's sexual orientation, but also to explain why in the Catholic view sex is only for married life. As a community founded on love, in the Church everyone who sincerely seeks Jesus is welcome with their personalities, their talents and even their sinful nature — which we all share. Any person struggling with a just way of living his or her sexuality needs help, care and understanding. We all need a lot of support on our personal path towards sainthood, in the form of the grace of God, but also in the friendship and accompaniment by our fellow travellers. What about you?

Do not ignore! Hatred and discrimination are against the fundamental commandment of love. Saint Paul did not condemn anyone, but upheld the Christian view that sex is only for marriage.

SAINT
VALENTINE

📅 CA. 270 🌐 ITALY 🕯 14 FEBRUARY

SCAN

Q: IS SEX FOR PLEASURE BAD? DON'T LOVE AND SEX GO TOGETHER?

Valentine is very well known as a saint, but we know little about the man. He did really exist, for archaeologists found an early Roman catacomb and an ancient church dedicated to him. It is also sure that he was martyred for his faith at the Via Flaminia in Rome on 14 February in the third century. In fact, that is enough to connect him to romantic love, of which he is the patron saint: is it not the summit of romance to offer your life for the one you love? Valentine did exactly that: out of love for Jesus he was ready to give up everything, even his own life.

ROMANCE

We all need love in our lives. Valentine's wholehearted love for Jesus is easily paralleled with the love and dedication people hope to find in their partner in marriage. In the Middle Ages, his feast allowed for the expression of courtly love, often for an unattainable party.

O God, Valentine, is the patron of true love. If this is my vocation, may I find the love of my life and commit myself completely to him or her. Saint Valentine, pray for us!

Since the 18th century it has become customary to send cards, flowers, and chocolate (secretly) to loved ones. Today, it would often seem that love and sex have to go hand in hand. This is not necessarily true *(see #TwGOD 4.20)*. Love is the greatest virtue of all *(1 Cor 13:13)*. In an ideal world you could of course have love without sex, but sex without love would not exist. Sex is only real and true when experienced as a totally free gift of love. It can never be forced nor bought *(see Saint 2.38 & 2.40)*.

LOVE FOR LIFE

Only when you are fully committed to the other one in love, as expressed and confirmed in the sacrament of marriage between a man and a woman, can sex be such a totally free gift. Even if you love each other very much, without the bond of marriage your union is weaker and temporary — although you may not intend it to be so. In marriage, you make a formal commitment to each other to stay together for the remainder of your life, in 'good times and bad, in sickness and health.' In the sacrament of marriage you receive God's blessing, and expressly invite him to be part of your relationship. We all know that we are fragile, and that sometimes marriages simply do not seem to work, but is that reason enough to give up the beautiful dedication to marriage for life?

SEX IS GOOD

Sex in marriage is something very good, and established by God for the pleasure and enjoyment of the spouses *(CCCC 2362)*. It is therefore not only functional, as a means of procreation, although it is always possible that it leads to having children. They are a gift from God and the fruit of the total self-giving of the partners in marriage. In a non-formal relationship it is much more difficult to offer children a stable family with a father and mother who care for each other and their children *(see #TwGOD 4.20 & 4.32)*. The Bible encourages the spouses 'not to deprive one another' of the gift of sexuality, unless they decide together to wait for a little time for good reason *(1 Cor 7:3-5)*. Can you see the beauty of this way of living?

TRUE SELF-GIVING

'God is love and in himself he lives a mystery of personal loving communion... Christian revelation recognises two specific ways of realising the vocation of the human person in its entirety, to love: marriage and virginity or celibacy... Sexuality, by means of which man and woman give themselves to one another through the acts which are proper and exclusive to spouses, is by no means something purely biological, but concerns the innermost being of the human person as such...The total physical self-giving would be a lie if it were not the sign and fruit of a total personal self-giving, in which the whole person, including the temporal dimension, is present... This totality which is required by conjugal love also corresponds to the demands of responsible fertility... The only 'place' in which this self-giving in its whole truth is made possible is marriage, the covenant of conjugal love freely and consciously chosen, whereby man and woman accept the intimate community of life and love willed by God himself which only in this light manifests its true meaning... A person's freedom, far from being restricted by this fidelity, is secured against every form of subjectivism or relativism and is made a sharer in creative Wisdom.'

[Pope John Paul II, Familiaris Consortio, 22 November 1981, 11]

Love does not always need sex, but sex should always be an expression of true love! As an act of total self-giving, sex can be a great source of pleasure for a married couple.

SAINT **MARY OF EGYPT**

📅 CA. 344 – CA. 421   🌍 EGYPT

🕯 1 APRIL; 5TH SUNDAY OF THE GREAT LENT (EAST)

Q: WHY IS LUST WRONG?

WHAT ABOUT MASTURBATION?

Mary was born in Egypt and ran away from home at the age of 12. She went to Alexandria, where she lived a dissolute life, 'driven by insatiable and irrepressible passion.' The story of her life has been told by the Bishop of Jerusalem, Zosimus, who mixed fact and legend. In Alexandria, Mary danced, sung, and worked as a prostitute for 17 years. Apparently, she often offered her sexual favour without any material reward because of her lustful desires. One day she decided to travel to the Holy Land, willing to pay her passage by offering sexual favours.

PENITENCE

In Jerusalem, she felt held back by an invisible force when she tried to enter the Holy Sepulchre. Being very honest with herself at this instance, she realised she was not worthy to enter this holy place of the death and resurrection of Jesus.

O God, Mary struggled with lustful feelings for many years. Help me to overcome my lustful desires and recognise what true love means. Saint Mary of Egypt, pray for us!

Suddenly looking back over her life, she realised how her lifestyle must have offended Jesus: she had lived only for herself and her own sensual desires, without really caring for what her temporary partners felt, nor about Jesus. Crying bitter tears, she dearly wanted to change her ways: from now on she wanted to be pure. After confessing her sins and receiving communion, she withdrew into the desert. There she lived for nearly 50 years in complete solitude, finding profound joy in her life of prayer and dedication to God alone.

LUST

Thoughts of sex can be very exciting. The greatest difficulty with lust is that it is selfishly motivated, as Mary discovered, and that you easily can get trapped in addiction *(see Saint 2.41)*. This goes for sex with someone else, but also for masturbation. Whether you are a girl or a boy, you may often hear that it is natural to 'take care' of your body in this way, while your conscience will tell you that this is not as okay as it may seem. Lust is not the same as sexual desire, and surely not as true love. Sexual desire can be very appropriate between a married man and woman who express their love and gift to each other in their sexual relationship *(see Saint 2.39; #TwGOD 4.20-4.21)*. When they withdraw in privacy, they do so to surrender totally to each other. But if you retire to your room for masturbation this is not self-giving or surrendering, but selfish lust. Lust is motivated by selfishness, not true love. The physical joy you experience quickly turns into sadness and remorse. This is why Jesus condemns even those who look at someone lustfully *(Mt 5:28)*.

STRENGTH

Still, lustful thoughts or feelings are nothing to be afraid of. Anyone can be tempted in this way. But the question is what you do next. Mary first simply gave in to her lustful feelings, until when she realised what she had done. At that moment,

---

IS CHRISTIANITY OPPOSED TO THE BODY?

'It is neither the spirit alone nor the body alone that loves: it is man, the person, a unified creature composed of body and soul, who loves... Pure "sex" has become a commodity, a mere "thing" to be bought and sold... Here we are actually dealing with a debasement of the human body: no longer is it integrated into our overall existential freedom; no longer is it a vital expression of our whole being, but it is more or less relegated to the purely biological sphere... Christian faith, on the other hand, has always considered man a unity in duality, a reality in which spirit and matter compenetrate, and in which each is brought to a new nobility.'

[Pope Benedict XVI, Deus Caritas Est, 5]

---

her sorrow destroyed every desire. Mary's reaction to withdraw into the desert for the remainder of her life may seem a little overdoing it at first. However, if you try to place God at the centre of your life, there is no place for lust *(see Saint 2.41)*. Indulging in lustful thoughts is a selfishness which never can satisfy you truly. Mary shows that it is possible to overcome your lustful thoughts and feelings. Ask her to pray for you! Also, do not be afraid when you stumble: we all do in various ways. God does not wish to linger on our failures. The importance is to get up again, to confess your sins, and continue to live your life with Jesus. In him you will find the strength to overcome everything. Do you believe he is with you in your struggle?

> *Lust is not motivated by love: it is selfish and end up with you trapped in addiction. Only dedication to God (and loving self-giving in marriage) can truly satisfy your sexual desires.*

SAINT
AUGUSTINE

 354 – 430   ALGERIA

 28 AUGUST; 15 JUNE (EAST)

.SCAN

Q: HOW CAN I BREAK AWAY FROM AN ADDICTION TO PORNOGRAPHY OR SEX?

Augustine was a very deep thinker about God and the faith, and an important Bishop of Hippo, Algeria. He did have a dark past, however. During many years, his mother Monica was very worried about him *(see Saint 2.10)*.

WILL AND LUST

As a young man he followed various philosophers, moving to the next one when he got disillusioned by what he heard. He did the same with sex, moving from one experience to the other. From his adolescence onwards, Augustine struggled greatly with his sexuality. He felt he needed sex in his life to be satisfied, and yet never found real satisfaction. He felt he was a slave of his passions, and described in his autobiography, *Confessions*, accurately how addiction starts: 'Out of my perverse will came lust, and when lust was given satisfaction, it ended in habit, and when habit passes unresisted, it becomes a compulsive urge' *(Conf. VIII.5.10)*.

O God, Augustine gradually learned to love you. Help me to have a strong conviction and turn away from every bad habit or addiction to live for you alone. Saint Augustine, pray for us!

So when he gave in to his lustful feelings, they became a habit and when he did not correct himself this became compulsive behaviour: he felt he just had to give in to his physical desires.

A NEW LIFE

How did Augustine overcome this addiction? A very important moment was when he read in the Bible that it was time to wake up: 'Lay aside the works of darkness... Let us live honourably, not in riots and drunkenness, not in sexual excess and lust, not in quarrelling and jealousy. Rather, put on the Lord Jesus Christ, and make no provision for the desires of the flesh' (Rom 13:12-14). Before this moment, Augustine suffered from a divided will: he was afraid he could not give up his search for sexual satisfaction, while he also wanted to change his life for the better. Now he was convinced that there was only one way to overcome his addictive habit, namely by the firm and united will to change his life. His newly found faith was a great help in this. He needed to see the larger picture; it is only when he realised that Jesus was more than enough to satisfy his deepest desires that he could change his ways.

OVERCOMING ENSLAVEMENT

Saint Augustine shows that it is possible to overcome the enslavement to our passions. We all have lustful urges, but we are also more than our bodies alone: we can choose how to deal with these urges (see Saint 2.40). Sex can be very good, but it is not everything in life! Addiction usually starts with us giving in to something we know not to be good for us in the first place. For a long time, Augustine was torn between two lifestyles, and was afraid he would not able to live in chastity as he knew Jesus asked of him (see Saint 2.37). Like him, you can break free from lust: not just by resisting your urges, but by embracing the greater pleasure of a life in purity and true love with God and the people around you. You may possibly fall back many times, but do not let this worry

you: simply get up again with the resolve to do better in future and refocus your desire for a pure life. You do not have to struggle alone: it might be helpful to speak about this with your spiritual director or with a good friend. Together you stand stronger in trying to get over this. Eventually, and with the grace of God, you can prevail. Do you believe you could do this?

PASSION WITHOUT JOY

'I did not keep the moderate way of the love of mind to mind – the bright path of friendship. Instead, the mists of passion steamed up out of the dark concupiscence of the flesh, and the hot imagination of puberty, and they so obscured and overcast my heart that I was unable to distinguish pure affection from unholy desire. Both boiled confusedly within me, and dragged my unstable youth down over the cliffs of unchaste desires and plunged me into a gulf of infamy.... But where could I find such pleasure save in you, O Lord – save in you, who teaches us by sorrow, who woundest us to heal us, and dost kill us that we may not die apart from thee. Where was I, and how far was I exiled from the delights of your house, in that 16th year of the age of my flesh, when the madness of lust held full sway in me – that madness which grants indulgence to human shamelessness, even though it is forbidden by your laws – and I gave myself entirely to it?'

[Augustine, Confessions, II,2.2-4]

When you truly desire to break free from your passions, be persistent in your resolve, believe you can do it, and get up every time when you fall back. God will help!

SAINT **THÉRÈSE OF LISIEUX**

 1873 – 1897 FRANCE

 1 OCTOBER; 17 MAY (EAST)

SCAN

Q: WHY WOULD GOD WANT TO HANG OUT WITH A BAD PERSON LIKE ME?

Thérèse Martin was born in Alençon, France, of loving and holy parents who feared for her life, as her health at birth was not good (see Saint 2.31). One by one her sisters entered monastic life. Thérèse wanted to do the same, but aged 14 she was considered too young. This is when she showed her iron will. On a pilgrimage to Rome she begged the pope to let her enter the convent. When she finally was accepted in the Carmelite convent, she discovered that it was far from the romantic life she had expected. While Thérèse realised that she was imperfect herself, she also had to suffer a lot from jealousy and pettiness of her sisters in the convent. What made her a saint is the way in which she dealt with this. Thérèse died aged 24, after having been a Carmelite nun for almost ten years.

GOD LOVES YOU

You may feel that you are far from being holy, and rather a bad person in the eyes of God. That you could never apologise enough to God and to the people around you.

O God, Thérèse loved you. May I do like she did, and offer you the hardships and difficulties I find on my way through life as little sacrifices. Saint Thérèse of Lisieux, pray for us!

You may even claim that you have ruined someone's life... God is different. He does not use his power to destroy or to ruin *(see #TwGOD 1.34-1.35)*. God is love. He loves every human being. He even loves you very much! Not only does he love you in spite of your badness, but he loves you with your bad attitudes and rebellious nature. Obviously, this does not mean that God loves your bad deeds — which he abhors — but even when you commit them, God continues to love you. Whenever you come to him and ask for forgiveness, he wholeheartedly forgives you everything.

LOVE AND GRACE

Thérèse was very much aware that she did not deserve God's love and his grace *(see box)*. But she also wanted dearly to be close to him. She dreamt of being a great missionary, but knew that as a Carmelite sister her place was in the convent. 'Love proves itself in deeds' she said to herself, 'so how can I show my love, as I cannot go out and do great deeds?' She wrote in in her autobiography: 'The only way I can prove my love is by scattering flowers and these flowers are every little sacrifice, every glance and word, and the doing of the least actions for love.' Thérèse did not let herself be drowned by her feelings of badness and unworthiness. Instead, she decided to do good to others without them noticing it and to accept with joy and faith situations she could not change. You can do the same!

SACRIFICES?

Instead of feeling sorry for herself when something was difficult, unpleasant or even unfair, Thérèse decided to accept the situation without protesting. Also Jesus had to suffer so much unjustly! When she was given the worst leftovers during a meal, she would eat them without complaining. When she was falsely accused of breaking a vase, she did not protest but humbly asked for forgiveness. These small sacrifices

---

I AM WEAK AND IMPERFECT

'God made me understand my own glory would not be evident to the eyes of mortals, that it would consist in becoming a great saint! This desire could certainly appear daring if one were to consider how weak and imperfect I was, and how, after seven years in the religious life, I am still weak and imperfect. I always feel, however, the same bold confidence of becoming a great saint because I do not count on my own merits since I have none, but I trust in God who is Virtue and Holiness. God alone, content with my weak efforts, will raise me to himself and make me a saint, clothing me in his infinite merits. I didn't think then that one had to suffer very much to reach sanctity, but God was not long in showing me this was so and in sending me...trials.' [Therese of Liseux, Story of a Soul, chapter IV]

---

obviously cost her a lot, much more than big heroic deeds — especially because nobody knew about them and therefore no one praised her. She became a heroine of the faith, precisely because she did not run away from difficulties, but continued to love and serve God while accepting the inevitable suffering of life. She knew she was not perfect. Still, Thérèse did not despise herself, or think of herself as a particularly bad person. She knew that she was first of all a very much loved child of God. Can you believe that so are you?

> God loves you: he made you like this. Nothing you do can change that love. Your sin may create a temporary distance, but he always waits for you to come back to him!

SAINT **MOSES THE ETHIOPIAN**

2.43

SCAN

Q: HOW CAN I OVERCOME MY ANGER OR HATRED?

Moses was an Ethiopian slave in the house of a government official in Egypt until he was dismissed for theft. He was a tall and imposing figure, and a natural leader. He became the leader of a gang of brigands who were the terror of the Nile Valley. They raided villages, attacked travellers and killed whoever opposed them. The local governor sent out his troops to get him. One night, the gang was surprised by sheepdogs who prevented them from robbing a rich man. In his angry and revengeful hatred, Moses swam over a mile-wide river in search of the shepherd who owned these dogs. When he did not find him, he killed a few rams in his rage and carried them single-handed back to camp.

FROM CUT-THROAT TO MONK

As government troops were drawing near, Moses fled into the desert and sought refuge in a Coptic monastery to lie low until he could gather his gang again. The monks welcomed the giant man with his cruel expression without questions. Probably to his own surprise, he started to develop an admiration for the peaceful dedication of the monks.

O God, Moses knew anger and hatred before discovering the beauty of a life in peace. Help me to find the peace of heart you want to give me! Saint Moses of Ethiopia, pray for us!

Gradually their brotherly love transformed the brigand. He asked to be baptised and join the community. Monastic life proved to be difficult for the adventurer still full of anger and hate. Discipline and obedience did not come easy. One of his struggles was with chastity (see Saint 2.37). In his life he had known many women, now he only wanted to belong to God. But his body needed more time to adjust than his mind.

NON-VIOLENCE

Anger in itself is not wrong: 'Be angry but do not sin' (Eph 4:26), Scripture tells. Jesus knew a holy anger, for example when he was in the temple and saw how the house of his Father was being abused (Mk 11:15-18). In the past, a solid beating up usually solved Moses's problems with other people. Not so in the monastery, where he had sworn privately never to use violence any more. He had truly changed his ways! When he was attacked one day by robbers, he bound his intruders and carried them into the chapel before his surprised brothers, for he did not want to hurt them. When he was about 75 years old, a group of Berbers intended to attack the monastery. Moses talked his brothers out of taking up arms, and urged them to flee into the desert instead. He stayed behind with seven brothers and they all were killed by the attackers.

STEPS TOWARDS CHANGE

A holy anger like that of Jesus and the non-violent attitude of Moses are rare in us. Usually our anger is combined with thoughts of violence and hatred. A blind rage is always wrong, because then you no longer are open to the inspiration of God's Spirit. So how do you change?

- First, realise that often tiredness and stress are at the root of your anger and hatred, so try to find relaxation, exercise and rest in time.

- Second, do not hesitate to get professional help if needed.

CONDITIONS TO LIVING JOYFULLY

'One of the most obvious works of mercy, and perhaps the most difficult to put into practice, is to forgive those who have offended us, who have done us wrong or whom we consider to be enemies... To let go of anger, wrath, violence, and revenge are necessary conditions to living joyfully. I meet so many young people who say that they are tired of this world being so divided, with clashes between supporters of different factions and so many wars, in some of which religion is being used as justification for violence... Mercy is the only way to overcome evil. Justice is necessary, very much so, but by itself it is not enough. Justice and mercy must go together.'

[Pope Francis, Message for World Youth Day, 15 August 2015]

- Third, the best way to overcome anger and hatred is by letting Jesus be part of every element of your life. This may seem impossible, but try to focus on God instead of on your anger.

- Fourth, sit down to pray, especially when you are angry. Let God's peaceful presence invade you step by step, recognising that nothing is more important than his love!

- Fifth, 'do not let the sun go down on your anger' (Eph 4:26). In other words, do not let your anger turn into hard feelings, but let it go and quickly make peace with God and with those you may have hurt. Will you be able to apply these steps when necessary?

Realise that it is possible to let go of anger and hatred. Let Jesus be part of your life, and pray. Let his peace invade you and make up with God and those you have hurt.

SAINT
MARIA GORETTI

2.44

📅 1890 – 1902   🌍 ITALY   🕯 6 JULY

SCAN

Q: WHAT IF I CANNOT FORGIVE?

HOW CAN I FORGIVE MY ENEMIES?

Maria was born to a poor farming family in Corinaldo, Italy. She never learned to read or write, and was quite large for her age. One day, when she was eleven years old, Maria was mending a shirt on the outside steps of her home. Her family was away working in the fields. Suddenly her young neighbour Alessandro appeared. He grabbed her and tried to rape her. Struggling hard to get loose she yelled: 'No! It is a sin! God does not want it!' She said she would rather die than give in. Alessandro began to stab her with a knife. As she tried to run away, he continued to stab her and then left her bleeding on the floor.

HEAVEN

When she was found, she was immediately brought to hospital, but the injuries were too severe. She must have suffered excruciating pain when she woke up prematurely while the doctor was still performing surgery. Maria devoutly received Holy Communion for the last time.

O God, Maria Goretti forgave her attacker, and you forgive me all the time. Help me to forgive those who do me wrong and wish them well. Saint Maria Goretti, pray for us!

She said very clearly that she forgave Alessandro, and that she wanted him to be with her in heaven. She died the following day. Alessandro was sentenced to 30 years in prison. For many years he did not repent. Eventually, he came to realise the great gift of forgiveness that Maria had offered him. This drastically changed his life. When he was released after 27 years, his first act was to beg Maria's mother to forgive him. She did so immediately, saying that her daughter had already forgiven him.

FORGIVING OTHERS

Maria Goretti shows that it is possible to forgive. She is like Saint Stephen, who was stoned to death because of his faith and cried out just before dying: 'Lord, do not hold this sin against them' (Acts 7:60). Unconditional forgiveness, without waiting for the other to come and beg for it, is very Christian. It is also very liberating. It is very natural to feel anger, hatred, and maybe even a desire for revenge. But these feelings block us until we do like Maria Goretti, and forgive with all our heart. As a preliminary step, you may ask Jesus to forgive them in your name, hearing Jesus tell your enemy: 'I forgive you.'

STEPS TO FORGIVING

- Forgiving is not easy. You have been hurt and wronged. Admit it! That is the first step. You can tell God about your feelings, write them down, or talk with a friend. But don't stop there, or you'll only end up in bitterness and resentment.

- The next step is to put whatever happened to rest, to lay it beside you. This may be the most difficult step, but this is essential for you to move on with your life. And it brings you one step closer to being able to forgive. Accept that what happened is now part of a past which you nor anyone else can change.

- Third, remember that God has forgiven you so many smaller and bigger wrongdoings. He has no resentment against you for your sins, and simply loves you. Pray that he helps you to forgive in turn.

MERCY AND FORGIVENESS

'Maria Goretti was a girl whom God's Spirit endowed with the courage to stay faithful to her Christian vocation even to the point of making the supreme sacrifice of her life... Her forgiveness of the man who killed her and her desire to be able to meet him one day in heaven deserve special attention. This spiritual and social message is of extraordinary relevance in our time... Forgiveness, in the Church's opinion, does not mean moral relativism or permissiveness. On the contrary, it demands the full recognition of one's sin and the assumption of one's responsibilities as a condition for rediscovering true peace and for confidently resuming the journey to evangelical perfection. May humanity start out with determination on the way of mercy and forgiveness!'

[Pope John Paul II, Message for the centenary of Maria Goretti, 6 July 2002]

- Fourth, decide in your heart that you want to do like God does to you, and forgive. You may need to come back to this step a few times, before being able to say with all your heart 'I forgive you.'

- The fifth step is that you pray for the person who did you wrong. Pray that they will recognise God's great love for them. Wish them well. And go on with your life, liberated from the heavy feelings that bore you down. Do you want to forgive like this?

It takes time and dedication to forgive! Acknowledge the pain, accept you cannot change the past, realise that God continuously forgives your sins, pray, and decide to forgive!

SAINT
MARGARET OF CORTONA

📅 1247 – 1297   🌍 ITALY   🕯 22 FEBRUARY

SCAN

 2.45

Q: I AM SO BAD, HOW CAN I EVER FORGIVE MYSELF?

Margaret came from a farming family in Laviano, in Italy. She was very beautiful and she knew it. Her parents spoiled her terribly, and she grew up as a wilful and dissatisfied child. Margaret's mother died when she was seven, and her stepmother made life horrible for her. And she was so in need of attention and love! In her poverty, Margaret realised that her beauty was her only possession. She learned to bend young men to her will, and gave herself over to a life of pleasure and indulgence. Soon she became known as an 'easy girl.' When she was 18, Margaret took a position as a maid at the castle of a nobleman. With her skills, she soon became his mistress, and he treated her as the lady of the house. But he would not marry her, and when Margaret bore a child, he never accepted it as his heir. At first, she loved her lavish lifestyle, the presents, and being waited upon. However, somewhere in herself she started to realise that she was living a lie, not in accordance with the plan of God. She felt enslaved by the situation and by her lover. But she saw no way out.

O God, Margaret knew of sin and of redemption. May I too see my sins and turn to you again. Saint Margaret of Cortona, pray for us!

DEATH CHANGES ALL

One day, when Margaret was 27 years old, her nobleman did not come home. When his dog showed up, it led her to the body of her murdered lover. His sudden and violent death changed her life overnight. She was shocked to realise that others had murdered his body, but she had done worse: she had led him to a life of sin (see Saint 2.40). Would he now go to hell because of her? The same could happen to herself! Mortified of what she had done, Margaret decided to spend the remainder of her life trying to make up for the wrong she did. She vested in rags, lived in poverty, and hid her beauty. She became a lay member of the third order of Saint Francis and set up an institution of women serving the poor and suffering. Margaret is sometimes called the Second Magdalene (see Saint 1.47). Her body is still intact today, interpreted by some to mean that God has forgiven all her sins.

HOPE

Margaret experienced that sin can leave deep wounds in your heart. But she also shows that there is always hope! It is never too late to change your ways. God loves you, no matter what. Nothing you do can change that. He is always waiting for you, hoping that you will turn to him. You may feel that you are no longer worthy to be called his child (Lk 15:21). You may feel as if you can never forgive yourself. Still, he wants to welcome you with open arms and celebrate your return! Forgiveness is not a feeling, but a reality, a gift of God. You can receive that gift at every moment: just ask for it!

A CLEAN START

- Forgiving yourself can be most difficult. It is not just about making amends: in many cases you cannot really make up, and you realise: 'My sin is always before me' (Ps 51:3).

- Realise that compared to God's perfect love, we are all losers who never meet the mark without his help. But he loves you right now, even though you have a tendency to sin!

- Note that you'll probably remember your mistake longer than others, and think worse of yourself than they do! At any rate, know that God only wants to forgive you!

- Confess your sins (see Saint 2.15), and receive God's forgiveness: accept that you do not deserve such goodness and love, but that he still takes away all that is wrong (1 Jn 1:8-10).

- Even if you cannot understand it (no one can, really), God's deepest desire is for you to turn to him and receive his mercy (see Saint 2.47): Do you dare to believe he wants to give you a clean start?

God loves you, no matter what you do. Certain scars will remain on your soul for life, but God's forgiveness offers you a new start. Ask God's strength to embrace that start!

SAINT
OLGA OF KIEV

📅 969 🌐 UKRAINE, BELARUS, RUSSIA 🕯 11 JULY

SAINT
VLADIMIR
THE GREAT

📅 1015 🌐 UKRAINE, BELARUS, RUSSIA 🕯 15 JULY

2.46

Q: ARE EVIL PEOPLE LIKE MAO, HITLER, STALIN AND SADDAM HUSSEIN IN HELL?

Olga was married to Igor of Kiev, ruler of the large Rus Federation in today's Ukraine, Belarus and Russia. When her husband was slaughtered while collecting taxes from the Drevlian tribe, she became ruler as regent on behalf of her son Svetoslav. She swore to avenge her husband and prepared a punitive expedition against the Drevlians. It became a true genocide, the mass murder of an entire people. Some years later she converted and was baptised in Constantinople. This changed her completely. She took the name Helena and became known for her wise governance of the country.

VLADIMIR

However, her grandson Vladimir stuck to the pagan way of life. He erected shrines to pagan gods and is said to have had some 800 concubines and wives. He killed his half-brother Yaropolk and raped his sister-in-law. Thus he became the ruler of Rus. He was known for his cruelty and immorality.

O God, Olga and Vladimir came to recognise you eventually and brought many to the faith. May I do the same, in spite of all my sins. Saints Olga and Vladimir, pray for us!

.SCAN

Eventually, however, he was influenced by the religious convictions of his grandmother and converted to Christianity. He became as fervent a Christian ruler as he had previously been cruel. He invited missionaries to preach the gospel and declared Christianity to be the religion of his entire realm. Vladimir promoted education, built churches, instituted courts, and set up systems to aid the poor and needy.

UNLIKELY SAINTS

So, here we have two very unlikely saints who mass-murdered, committed genocide, killed their brother, raped, abused… What does this say about the value and morality of the saints? First of all, like each of us, the saints are people who struggled in their lives, learning only step-by-step to live as good Christians. Think of Saint Paul, who was a fervent persecutor of Christians before his conversion (see Saint 2.38). Not the sin, but the conversion and subsequent total dedication to Jesus makes a saint. Like Jesus on the way of the cross, we all stumble from time to time under the weight of sin. What makes saints different is that they get up again — with the help of God's grace — aware of their fault and full of remorse. Like them, we too can get up, over and again, sincerely ask for God's forgiveness, make up for what we did as far as possible, and continue our lives as Christians. Our past is always part of us, but does not have to define our future (see Saint 2.40).

HELL FOR CRIMINALS?

But, you may object, the evil we did has still been committed. That is true, and it cannot simply be erased. It is easily imagined that God would not want to forgive terrible sins like those of Mao, Hitler, Stalin and Saddam Hussein. The extreme horrors they caused have greatly disturbed and hurt God. They — and sadly many others — have knowingly and willingly ignored their inner conscience (see #TwGOD 1.46, 4.9 & 4.12-4.13). They seem to have abandoned themselves totally

---

BAPTISM OF EUROPE

'At the origin of Slavo-Byzantine Christianity was the famous mission of Saints Cyril and Methodius (see Saint 2.16), who had gained the understanding and support of my predecessors in the ninth century. The baptism of Prince Vladimir in 988 was a very important step in the development of Christianity in the European continent… Full religious freedom, freedom of conscience and profession of faith…is a plenary right for the peoples of the former Kievan Rus' – Ukrainian, Belarussian and Russian peoples – baptised in the salutary waters of the Dnieper, while in faith in Christ the Church remained one and undivided.'

[Pope John Paul II, To the participants of the Slavic-byzantine symposium, 5 May 1988]

---

to evil and permanently turned away from God. Still, in the case that they might have changed heart, even at the last second of their lives, and turned to God full of remorse, God would welcome them too — after being purified in purgatory (see #TwGOD 1.47). His love and forgiveness is greater than any evil (see Saint 2.44 & 2.47). Can you imagine how vast his love is?

God is greatly saddened and hurt by every act of evil. Still, he cannot deny himself: until the last moment he hopes that we turn around and accept his love, so we can be with him forever.

SAINT
FAUSTINA KOWALSKA

 1905 – 1938   POLAND   5 OCTOBER

SCAN

Q: ARE THERE SINS THAT EVEN GOD CANNOT FORGIVE? WHAT IS DIVINE MERCY?

Helena came from Głogowiec, Poland, and had but one desire when she was very young: to enter religious life. However, her family was poor and could not afford to pay for her habit. So she started to work as a housekeeper in a convent in Warsaw until she could save enough. Her persistence finally brought her the life she had dreamt of. At 20 years of age she received her habit and the religious name Sister Maria Faustina of the Blessed Sacrament. One day she had a vision of Jesus, who told her he was the 'King of divine mercy.' Later, she had a painting made of this vision *(see Picture)*. Her confessor insisted she be checked by a psychiatrist, who confirmed that Sister Faustina was completely sane.

SACRIFICE AND MERCY

Sister Faustina dedicated her life to the imitation of Jesus. She was especially close to him in the great sacrifice of his life on the cross, which he suffered solely out of love. While offering her own suffering to Jesus, Faustina tried to live her daily life in service and mercy towards others *(see Saint 1.39)*. Thus she became herself an example of the message that Jesus gave her. She wrote about her visions of Jesus in her diary *(see Box)*. The prayer that she was given in one of her visions, the divine mercy chaplet, can be found in the *Tweeting with GOD* app *(Pray > Catholic prayers > 4. Other prayers)*.

O God, Faustina dedicated herself entirely to your divine mercy. May I recognise your mercy in my life and accept your love and forgiveness. Saint Faustina Kowalska, pray for us!

DIVINE MERCY

In the dictionary, 'mercy' is compassion or forgiveness. Divine mercy is the love of God for every human being. His mercy is greater than our sins, than any of our sins. Whoever tries to reach out to God or calls out to him with trust, can encounter his love, mercy, and forgiveness. Hence the prayer 'Jesus, I trust in you', which Faustina prayed very often. Obviously, we do not receive God's mercy just for ourselves, but to share it with others, like Sister Faustina did. Forgiveness is the beginning of new life. There is no way in which we can erase the past. Often we are frustrated and angry about what we or others have done. But remember that God does not love you because you are good; you can be good because he loves you first (1 Jn 4:19). This love is freely given, and totally undeserved. And so is his forgiveness.

SIN AND FORGIVENESS

You may sometimes wonder 'Does God stay in my life even if I commit a really bad sin?' To find an answer, we can turn to Jesus. On the cross, after all he had suffered from the hands of people, Jesus said: 'Father, forgive them; for they do not know what they are doing.' What is worse than killing God's own Son, who came to bring us his love and forgiveness? If you sincerely ask for it, God is ready to forgive you every sin, and he does so unconditionally! As long as you repent with all your heart, there is no sin that God cannot forgive. Precisely for that reason Jesus gave us the sacrament of reconciliation: through the words of the priest it is God himself who forgives you your sins. For that forgiveness to take effect in your life, you need to acknowledge your sin with remorse, and accept God's forgiveness with all your heart. That is not always easy! (see Saint 2.44). But God's divine mercy is so great that he wants to help you even with that (see #TwGOD 4.14). Do you want him to forgive you?

GOD'S WORDS TO YOU

'Be not afraid...do not run away from your Father; be willing to talk openly with your God of mercy who wants to speak words of pardon and lavish his graces on you. How dear your soul is to me! I have inscribed your name upon my hand; you are engraved as a deep wound in my Heart... My mercy is greater than your sins and those of the entire world. Who can measure the extent of my goodness? For you I descended from heaven to earth; for you I allowed myself to be nailed to the cross; for you I let my sacred heart be pierced with a lance, thus opening wide the source of mercy for you. Come then, with trust to draw graces from this fountain. I never reject a contrite heart. Your misery has disappeared in the depths of my mercy. Do not argue with me about your wretchedness. You will give me pleasure if you hand over to me all your troubles and griefs. I shall heap upon you treasures of my grace.'

[Faustina, Diary, 1485]

God wants to forgive every sin. His mercy and love are greater than any sin. He is always waiting for you, hoping you will turn to him and say sorry: he'll wholeheartedly forgive you!

SAINT
BERNADETTE SOUBIROUS

📅 1844 – 1879 🌐 FRANCE 🕯 16 APRIL

SCAN

Q: WHY DOES THE VIRGIN MARY HAVE SO MANY NAMES AND TITLES?

Bernadette was an ordinary girl from a poor miller family in Lourdes, France. In spite of her ill health, she had a happy childhood. She did not go to school, could neither read nor write, and spoke the local dialect Occitane rather than French. On 11 February 1858, she was gathering firewood with her sister when she heard a rushing sound, saw a light and the figure of a lady in a grotto. Her sister saw nothing, so Bernadette thought she must have been mistaken. But a few days later she saw the lady again. Eighteen times in total Our Lady appeared, and she said in Occitane: 'I am the Immaculate Conception', meaning that she was conceived without sin *(see box; see Saint 2.50)*. Bernadette did not have enough education to make it all up, and her answers to inquiries about the appearances were always the same. One day, the lady told Bernadette to dig in the earth, and a spring welled up. Soon, people realised that various miraculous healings took place. A great sanctuary was erected in honour of Our Lady of Lourdes.

O God, Bernadette was doing her duty when Mary appeared to her. Help me to go about my duties, knowing that you are with me at all times. Saint Bernadette, pray for us!

Bernadette did not like all the attention, and eventually joined the Sisters of Charity at the mother house at Nevers. Here she lived a simple life of service and prayer until she died while praying the rosary. Her body never corrupted and is as beautiful today as when she died *(see #TwGOD 1.36)*.

CHANGE YOUR VIEWPOINT

The only true name of the Mother of God is Mary, so you can wonder why she is venerated under so many names. In fact, all these 'names' are, rather, titles with which we honour her as the Mother of God and our Mother. When you first enter a splendid church, for example, you get an overwhelming impression, but to take it all in you need to walk around, considering the architecture and art from various angles, looking at details, thinking about God, hearing the music, praying with your heart, smelling the incense, feeling the heat of the candles... Similarly, the Marian titles seek to help us look at the message Jesus wants to give us through his Mother from various points of view. With each title you cast a fresh glance at a certain aspect of our faith.

EVENTS AND POETRY

Some titles are related to events in Mary's life, like the Annunciation by the Angel Gabriel. She is the Virgin Mary or the Blessed Virgin, because of the way Jesus was conceived without the intervention of a man *(see #TwGOD 1.40)*. Events alone are not enough to express Mary's fundamental role, so that also poetic and theological titles are used *(see Appendix 3)*. 'Star of the Sea', for example, reminds us that Mary points the way to Jesus, just as sailors can navigate by the stars. Then there are many titles related to places, like Lourdes or Fatima *(see Saint 2.49)*.

MISSION AND DEVOTION

Other titles are related to Mary's personal life and mission, like Our Lady of Sorrows, which reminds us of the painful experiences in her life *(see #TwGOD 1.38)*. Furthermore, some titles express our faith that Mary's mission continues to bring our petitions to Jesus in her prayer: 'Comforter of the Afflicted', 'Help of Christians', or 'Refuge of Sinners'. Again other titles are related to devotions that can help us in our life as Christians, like 'Our Lady of the Rosary' *(see #TwGOD 3.12)*. The aim of all these titles is to help us consider specific aspects of the faith so that we can grow in our unique relationship with Jesus. How can Mary help you?

The only name of Our Lady is Mary. Because of her role in making our salvation by Jesus possible, she received may titles, both to honour her and for us to learn about the faith.

SAINTS
FRANCISCO
& JACINTA

 1908 – 1919 (FRANCISCO)

 1910 – 1920 (JACINTA)

 PORTUGAL 20 FEBRUARY

Q: WHY ARE THERE SO MANY DIFFERENT IMAGES OF MARY?

WHAT IS THE USE OF ALL THESE SANCTUARIES?

Francisco and Jacinta were siblings from a village near Fatima, Portugal. They were illiterate. Together with their cousin Lúcia they witnessed the apparition of an angel in 1916 while herding their sheep. On 13 May 1917 they saw a lady, 'brighter than the sun', who invited them to pray the rosary, to do penance and pray for the conversion of sinners, as well as for peace. She introduced herself as 'Our Lady of the Rosary.' For six months Mary appeared on the 13th of the month. At the final apparition on 13 October many people saw the sun move in a miraculous way. Soon, people praying to Our Lady of Fatima were healed in ways that science could not explain (see Saint 2.23). Lucia became a religious sister and lived to old age, but Francisco and Jacinta died young from influenza. Their task on earth was complete, and they pray for us in heaven. They are buried in the sanctuary that was erected at the place of the apparitions in Fátima.

SCAN

O God, you gave children the grace to see our heavenly mother. Help me recognise your presence in my life, and ask Mary to pray for me. Saints Francisco and Jacinta, pray for us!

ONE PERSON, MANY IMAGES

At Lucia's description, a statue of Mary was made. This statue started to travel in order to bring Mary's message about Jesus to the world. She does not only have many titles (*see Saint 2.48*), but also many faces. The Virgin of Lourdes looks different from the Virgin of Fatima, for example. These images have been made by artists on the basis of the description of the visionaries. Other artists were entirely led by their artistic imagination. As she is Mother of us all, it is quite appropriate that there is not one single image of Mary, but that she adapts to culture, race, and time in order to be as close as possible to our daily lives. Her message is one for today, and she only desires that we will grow in our relationship with Jesus.

PLACES

Fatima, Lourdes and Guadalupe are among the most popular Marian shrines in the world (*see Saint 2.23 & 2.48*). But there are many more places where God is worshipped through the example and at the intercession of the Virgin Mary. These shrines are not always erected after a miraculous event, but also simply because the people wanted to ask Mary for her intercession, like is the case of Our Lady of Lebanon or Kevelaer, for example. All these shrines or sanctuaries are holy places of prayer, which are worth visiting if you want to grow in your faith and closeness to Jesus. In the case of a miraculous event like a vision, the Church first thoroughly investigates whether there can be a natural or evil explanation for these events. Only when the conclusion is that their origin must be supernatural (heavenly), is the place recognised as a place of pilgrimage. We are strongly invited to believe, for these places can help us in our faith, but this is not obligatory (*see Saint 2.23; #TwGOD 1.39*).

> ## MARY'S FIRST WORDS AT FATIMA
>
> *'Please don't be afraid of me... I want you to return here on the 13th of each month for the next six months, and at the very same hour. Later I shall tell you who I am, and what it is that I most desire... [Your friend Amelia] is in purgatory. Will you offer yourselves to God, and bear all the sufferings...in atonement for all the sins that offend him? And for the conversion of sinners?... Then you will have a great deal to suffer, but the grace of God will be with you and will strengthen you.... Say the rosary every day, to bring peace to the world and an end to the war.'*
>
> [Lúcia, The first apparition, 13 May 1917]

MESSAGE

The message of Our Lady at the various apparitions around the world can be summarised as a call to grow in our faith in Jesus and to deepen our prayer life in order to advance in our relationship with him. Pure as she is, Mary knows how ugly sin makes us, and in her messages she often called to do penance and pray for the conversion of sinners. On the cross, Jesus gave Mary to all of us as our mother: she wants to console us and promises her help by praying to Jesus as she did in Cana, for example (*see Saint 2.50*). Do you want to ask your Mother Mary to pray for you now?

> *Mary is the mother of all, and we can all see her in a different light. Sanctuaries are special places of prayer where we can go on pilgrimage to be helped in our faith.*

HOLY **MARY, MOTHER OF GOD**

2.50

 CA. 18 BC   🌍 NAZARETH, HOLY LAND

🕯️ (SEE APPENDIX 3)

SCAN

Q: WHAT IS THE SECRET TO MARY'S TOTAL TRUST IN GOD?

Mary, the Mother of Jesus, was with her son during his entire life on earth. Her husband Joseph must have died in Jesus's youth. Mary's presence in the Bible is constant but quiet: only on a few occasions do we hear her speak in her own words.

MARY'S VOCATION

We first hear her speak when the Angel Gabriel comes to tell her that she will be the Mother of Jesus. Mary is shocked and cannot understand: 'How can this be?' *(Lk 1:34)*, she asks. But her faith in God overcomes her doubt: without understanding what nor how, she is able to declare with all her heart: 'I am the servant of the Lord. May it be to me as you have said' *(Lk 1:38)*. This is the beautiful way in which she said 'yes' to the will of God. The way in which Mary surrenders herself to God with all her heart and all her life is the greatest inspiration for each of us. Obviously, we all have a different vocation than she had. Her vocation is unique. And so is yours! Whatever your vocation may be, be ready to embrace it with all your heart, even when you do not understand everything.

Holy Mary, Mother of God and of the Church, pray for me, a sinner, now and at the hour of my death. Amen.

MARY'S ANSWER

In the Bible, Mary is always present in the background. Others speak much more than she does, like Saint Peter, who received a vital task when Jesus made him the first pope. So you could ask why Mary has been given such an important role in our daily faith. Why do you find at least one statue of Mary in every church? Why are the months of May and October dedicated to her? Why there are so many hymns, prayers, and rosaries in honour of Mary? The secret of Mary is her wholehearted answer to the call of God. Without Mary's 'yes', Jesus could not have been born the way he was. She was chosen and prepared for this role by God, but only by her 'yes' did she allow God to act through her. On the cross, Jesus confirmed that she is the mother of the entire Church community, a feast celebrated on Whit Monday. So she is also your Mother! Do not hesitate to call on her when you need her help!

MARY'S PRAYER

The last time Mary speaks in the Bible is at a wedding in Cana, which she attends together with Jesus. She notices that there is a problem and tells Jesus: 'They have no wine' *(Jn 2:3)*. Jesus says rather rashly that this is not the right moment, but she is not disturbed. She says to the servants: 'Do whatever he tells you' *(Jn 2:5)*. And indeed, at her request, Jesus does the impossible and changes water into very good wine. That wedding in Cana is the first moment Jesus speaks and acts in public. It is significant that after this episode, the Bible no longer records any words of Mary. She knows that this is not about her, but about Jesus. From now on, he will announce the love of God to everyone in a very powerful way. In spite of her being chosen from all humanity to be the Mother of God, she realises that she is just an instrument of his grace. She withdraws into the silent presence of prayer. Mary's prayer is very powerful, even when the timing may seem to be wrong. She tells Jesus of all the needs she sees and hears.

MARY CALLS TO ACTION

Mary's words in Scripture call to action in at least four ways.

DISCERN: Mary's question 'How can this be?' *(Lk 1:34)* invites you to find out how Jesus is present in your life, to do what you can to grow in your relationship with him, and to discern your vocation.

ENGAGE: Mary's answer to God 'I am the servant of the Lord' *(Lk 1:38)* invites also you to engage and get involved according to your personal vocation. There is no need for false humility, but realise that this is not about you but about God. He calls you!

PRAY: Mary says: 'They have no wine' *(Jn 2:3)*, and continues to bring her prayers to Jesus. You can do the same. Pray for your journey to God, for the people you meet, for those in need... And do not forget to ask Mary to join you in prayer!

DO GOD'S WILL: Mary says to you at this moment: 'Do whatever he tells you' *(Jn 2:5)*. Your faith, however variable it may be, calls you to action: to share God's love with others and to discern his will for you every day.

When you ask her to pray for you, you can be sure that she will pass on your petitions to Jesus. But you have to join her and the other saints in prayer, however imperfect your prayer may be. What is your answer to God's call to holiness?

Mary's secret is her total abandonment to the will of God: only thus he could perform the greatest expression of his love, giving us his son Jesus who opens the way to eternal life.

SAINT _____

(your name)

DATE OF BIRTH: _____

DATE OF BAPTISM: _____

PLACE: _____

Saint to be _____

(your name) was born in _____ (place).

S/he is searching for the truth. These pages, are about her/his story of a life with God, with the struggles, achievements and above all the gifts of God received.

MY JOURNEY WITH GOD SO FAR

_____

_____

_____

_____

_____

_____

_____

_____

DISCERNING HOLINESS IN OUR LIVES

'When, in God's presence, we examine our life's journey, no areas can be off limits. In all aspects of life we can continue to grow and offer something greater to God, even in those areas we find most difficult. We need, though, to ask the Holy Spirit to liberate us and to expel the fear that makes us ban him from certain parts of our lives. God asks everything of us, yet he also gives everything to us. He does not want to enter our lives to cripple or diminish them, but to bring them to fulfilment. Discernment, then, is not a solipsistic self-analysis or a form of egotistical introspection, but an authentic process of leaving ourselves behind in order to approach the mystery of God, who helps us to carry out the mission to which he has called us, for the good of our brothers and sisters.'

[Pope Francis, Gaudete et Exsultate, 175]

_____

_____

_____

_____

_____

_____

O God, I thank you for my life. You love me very much! Help me to grow in sanctity with your grace and the example of the saints. All saints in heaven, pray for us!

_____

_____

_____

_____

_____

_____

_____

_____

_____

_____

_____

_____

_____

Everyone is called to holiness; also you can grow every day a little more. The saints pray for you to follow your personal journey to God; if you do, you'll meet them in heaven!

APPENDIX 1: **THE BOOKS OF THE BIBLE**

Old Testament

Gen	Genesis	Prov	Proverbs
Ex	Exodus	Eccl	Ecclesiastes
Lev	Leviticus	Song	Song of Solomon
Num	Numbers	Wis	Wisdom of Solomon
Deut	Deuteronomy	Sir	Sirach (Ecclesiasticus)
Josh	Joshua	Isa	Isaiah
Judg	Judges	Jer	Jeremiah
Ruth	Ruth	Lam	Lamentations
1 Sam	1 Samuel	Bar	Baruch
2 Sam	2 Samuel	Ezek	Ezekiel
1 Kings	1 Kings	Dan	Daniel
2 Kings	2 Kings	Hos	Hosea
1 Chr	1 Chronicles	Joel	Joel
2 Chr	2 Chronicles	Am	Amos
Ezra	Ezra	Ob	Obadiah
Neh	Nehemiah	Jon	Jonah
Tob	Tobit	Mic	Micah
Jdt	Judith	Nah	Nahum
Esth	Esther	Hab	Habakkuk
1 Macc	1 Maccabees	Zeph	Zephaniah
2 Macc	2 Maccabees	Hag	Haggai
Job	Job	Zech	Zechariah
Ps	Psalms	Mal	Malachi

New Testament

Mt	Matthew	1 Tim	1 Timothy
Mk	Mark	2 Tim	2 Timothy
Lk	Luke	Titus	Titus
Jn	John	Philem	Philemon
Acts	Acts of the Apostles	Heb	Hebrews
Rom	Romans	Jas	James
1 Cor	1 Corinthians	1 Pet	1 Peter
2 Cor	2 Corinthians	2 Pet	2 Peter
Gal	Galatians	1 Jn	1 John
Eph	Ephesians	2 Jn	2 John
Phil	Philippians	3 Jn	3 John
Col	Colossians	Jude	Jude
1 Thess	1 Thessalonians	Rev	Revelation (Apocalypse)
2 Thess	2 Thessalonians		

APPENDIX 2: **DATES AND FEASTS**

Calendar of saints in this book

4 January – Saint Elizabeth Seton
14 January – Blessed Petrus Donders
16 January – Saint Peter (East)
21 January – Saint Agnes
22 January – Blessed Laura Vicuña
24 January – Saint Francis de Sales
25 January – Conversion of Saint Paul
31 January – Saint John Bosco
31 January – Saint Marcella of Rome

1 February – Saints Perpetua and Felicity (East)
8 February – Saint Josephine Bakhita
10 February – Saint Joselito Sánchez
14 February – Saints Cyril and Methodius
14 February – Saint Valentine
20 February – Saints Francisco & Jacinta
22 February – Chair of Saint Peter
22 February – Saint Margaret of Cortona

3 March – Saint Cunegunde of Luxembourg
3 March – Saint Katherine Drexel
7 March – Saints Perpetua and Felicity
14 March – Saint Benedict of Nursia (East)
17 March – Saint Patrick
19 March – Saint Joseph husband of Mary
22 March – Saint Nicholas Owen
24 March – Saint Oscar Romero
5th Sunday of the Great Lent – Saint Mary of Egypt (East)

1 April – Saint Mary of Egypt
12 April – Saint Teresa de los Andes
16 April – Saint Bernadette Soubirous
23 April – Saint George
28 April – Saint Gianna Beretta Molla
28 April – Saint Peter Chanel
29 April – Saint Catherine of Siena

1 May – Saint Joseph the Worker
5 May – Saint Nunzio Sulprizio
6 May – Saint Dominic Savio
9 May – Saint Christopher (East)
16 May – Saint John Nepomuk
16 May – Saint Vitus (East)
17 May – Saint Thérèse of Lisieux (East)
26 May – Saint Philip Neri
30 May – Saint Joan of Arc

3 June – Saint Charles Lwanga and 21 martyrs
6 June – Saint Norbert of Xanten
7 June – Venerable Matt Talbot
13 June – Saint Anthony of Padua
14 June – Saint Lidwina of Schiedam
15 June – Blessed Albertina Berkenbrock
15 June – Saint Jerome (East)
15 June – Saint Augustine (East)
15 June – Saint Vitus
19 June – Saint Jude Thaddeus (East)
21 June – Saint Aloysius Gonzaga
22 June – Saint Thomas More
24 June – Birth of Saint John the Baptist
29 June – Saints Peter and Paul
1st Sunday after Pentecost – All Saints (East)

4 July – Blessed Pier Giorgio Frassati
5 July – Saints Cyril and Methodius (East)
6 July – Saint Maria Goretti
7 July – Blessed María Romero Meneses
7 July – Blessed Peter To Rot
11 July – Saint Benedict of Nursia
11 July – Saint Olga of Kiev
12 July – Saints Zélie & Louis Martin-Guérin
13 July – Saint Henry II
14 July – Saint Kateri Tekakwitha

15 July – Saint Vladimir the Great
22 July – Saint Mary Magdalene
23 July – Saint Bridget of Sweden
24 July – Saint Charbel
25 July – Saint Christopher
26 July – Blessed Andrew of Phú Yên
31 July – Saint Ignatius of Loyola
3rd Sunday of July – Saint Charbel (Maronites)

1 August – Saint Alphonsus Liguori
1 August – Saint Peter in Chains
4 August – Saint John Vianney – Curé of Ars
8 August – Saint Dominic
8 August – Saint Mary MacKillop
9 August – Saint Teresa Benedicta of the Cross – Edith Stein
12 August – Saint Jane Frances de Chantal
12 August – Blessed Karl Leisner
13 August – Saint John Berchmans
14 August – Saint Maximilian Kolbe
15 August – Blessed Isidore Bakanja
23 August – Saint Rose of Lima
25 August – Saint Louis IX
27 August – Saint Monica
28 August – Saint Augustine
28 August – Saint Moses the Ethiopian
29 August – Death of Saint John the Baptist

5 September – Saint Teresa of Calcutta
16 September – Saint Andrew Kim Taegon
17 September – Saint Hildegard of Bingen
20 September – Korean Martyrs
23 September – Saint Pio of Pietrelcina – Padre Pio
26 September – Saint Paul VI
27 September – Saint Vincent de Paul
29 September – Archangels
30 September – Saint Jerome

1 October – Saint Thérèse of Lisieux
2 October – Guardian Angels
4 October – Saint Francis of Assisi
5 October – Saint Faustina Kowalska

9 October – Saint Henry Newman
11 October – Saint John XXIII
15 October – Saint Teresa of Avila
19 October – Saint Jean de Brébeuf
19 October – Blessed Jerzy Popiełuszko
21 October – Blessed Charles of Austria
21 October – Saint Laura of St Catherine
22 October – Saint John Paul II
28 October – Saint Jude Thaddeus
29 October – Blessed Chiara Luce Badano

1 November – All Saints
3 November – Saint Martin de Porres
5 November – Blessed Marije Tuci & The Albanian Martyrs
8 November – Archangels Michael and Gabriel (East)
8 November – Saint Elizabeth of the Trinity
11 November – Saint Martin of Tours
12 November – Saint Martin of Tours (East)
13 November – Saint Homobonus of Cremona
13 November – Saint Stanislaus Kostka
17 November – Saint Elizabeth of Hungary
22 November – Saint Cecilia
25 November – Blessed Luigi & Maria Quattrocchi-Corsini
30 November – Saint Andrew the Apostle
30 November – Venerable Suzanne Aubert

3 December – Saint Francis Xavier
6 December – Saint Nicholas of Myra
9 December – Saint Juan Diego
29 December – Saint David the King
29 December – Saint Thomas Becket
Sunday between 26-31 December – Saint David the King (East)
Sunday between 26-31 December – Saint Joseph (East)

––– Venerable Matt Talbot (†7 June)
––– Servant of God Henry Dormer (†2 October)
––– Venerable Carlo Acutis (†12 October)
––– Venerable Fulton Sheen (†9 December)

Feasts of Mary

Many Marian commemorations are celebrated around the world, the following are the ones that are part of the universal General Roman Calendar.

1 January – **Holy Mother of God (solemnity)**

11 February – **Our Lady of Lourdes (optional memory)**

25 March – **The Annunciation of the Lord (solemnity)**

13 May – **Our Lady of Fatima (optional memory)**

31 May – **The Visitation of the Blessed Virgin Mary (feast)**

Monday after Pentecost – **The Blessed Virgin Mary, Mother of the Church (memorial)**

A few days after Corpus Christi – **The Immaculate Heart of the Blessed Virgin Mary (memorial)**

16 July – **Our Lady of Mount Carmel (optional memory)**

5 August – **Dedication of the Basilica of Saint Mary Major (optional memory)**

15 August – **The Assumption of the Blessed Virgin Mary (solemnity)**

22 August – **The Queenship of Mary (memorial)**

8 September – **The Nativity of the Blessed Virgin Mary (feast)**

12 September – **The Most Holy Name of the Blessed Virgin Mary (optional memory)**

15 September – **Our Lady of Sorrows (memorial)**

7 October – **Our Lady of the Rosary (memorial)**

21 November – **The Presentation of the Blessed Virgin Mary (memorial)**

8 December – **The Immaculate Conception of the Blessed Virgin Mary (solemnity)**

These are the major Marian feasts in the Greek Catholic Church.

2 February – **Purification of the Most Holy Mother of God (minor feast)**

25 March – **Annunciation of the Mother of God [Theotokos] (great feast)**

15 August – **Dormition of the Mother of God (great feast)**

8 September – **Nativity of the Mother of God (great feast)**

1 October – **Protection of Our Most Holy Lady Mother of God and Ever-Virgin Mary (minor feast)**

21 November – **The Entry of the Most Holy Mother of God into the Temple (great feast)**

9 December – **Feast of the Conception of the Most Holy Mother of God (minor feast)**

26 December – **Synaxis of the Mother of God (minor feast)**

Lord have mercy.
Christ have mercy.
Lord have mercy. Christ hear us.
Christ graciously hear us.

God, the Father of heaven,
have mercy on us.
God the Son, Redeemer of the world,
have mercy on us.
God the Holy Spirit, *have mercy on us.*
Holy Trinity, one God, *have mercy on us.*

Holy Mary, *pray for us.*
Holy Mother of God, *pray for us.*
Holy Virgin of virgins, *pray for us.*

Mother of Christ, *pray for us.*
Mother of the Church, *pray for us.*
Mother of mercy, *pray for us.*
Mother of divine grace, *pray for us.*
Mother of hope, *pray for us.*
Mother most pure, *pray for us.*
Mother most chaste, *pray for us.*
Mother inviolate, *pray for us.*
Mother undefiled, *pray for us.*
Mother most amiable, *pray for us.*
Mother most admirable, *pray for us.*
Mother of good counsel, *pray for us.*
Mother of our Creator, *pray for us.*
Mother of our Saviour, *pray for us.*
Mother of mercy, *pray for us.*

Virgin most prudent, *pray for us.*
Virgin most venerable, *pray for us.*
Virgin most renowned, *pray for us.*
Virgin most powerful, *pray for us.*
Virgin most merciful, *pray for us.*
Virgin most faithful, *pray for us.*
Mirror of justice, *pray for us.*
Seat of wisdom, *pray for us.*
Cause of our joy, *pray for us.*
Spiritual vessel, *pray for us.*
Vessel of honour, *pray for us.*
Singular vessel of devotion, *pray for us.*
Mystical rose, *pray for us.*
Tower of David, *pray for us.*
Tower of ivory, *pray for us.*
House of gold, *pray for us.*
Ark of the covenant, *pray for us.*
Gate of heaven, *pray for us.*
Morning star, *pray for us.*
Health of the sick, *pray for us.*
Refuge of sinners, *pray for us.*
Mother of divine grace, *pray for us.*
Comforter of the afflicted, *pray for us.*
Help of Christians, *pray for us.*
Queen of Angels, *pray for us.*
Queen of Patriarchs, *pray for us.*
Queen of Prophets, *pray for us.*
Queen of Apostles, *pray for us.*
Queen of Martyrs, *pray for us.*
Queen of Confessors, *pray for us.*

Queen of Virgins, *pray for us.*
Queen of all Saints, *pray for us.*
Queen conceived without original sin,
pray for us.
Queen assumed into heaven, *pray for us.*
Queen of the most holy Rosary, *pray for us.*
Queen of families, *pray for us.*
Queen of peace, *pray for us.*
Lamb of God,
who takest away the sins of the world,
spare us, O Lord.
Lamb of God, who takest away the sins
of the world, *graciously hear us, O Lord.*
Lamb of God,
who takest away the sins of the world,
have mercy on us.

Pray for us, O holy Mother of God.
*That we may be made worthy
of the promises of Christ.*

Let us pray.
Grant, we beseech thee, O Lord God,
that we, your servants, may enjoy
perpetual health of mind and body;
and by the intercession of the Blessed
Mary, ever Virgin, may be delivered from
present sorrow, and obtain eternal joy.
Through Christ our Lord.
Amen.

APPENDIX 4: **LECTIO DIVINA, PRAYING WITH A BIBLE TEXT**

There are many ways of praying with the Bible. An ancient method which is often used is called Lectio Divina, meaning "Divine Reading", or in other words: reading with God. The intention is not to perform an in-depth academic Bible study, but rather to grow in knowledge of God by reading and praying with his living Word, the Bible.

PREPARATION

- Choose a place, and set aside a time for prayer. Start with five or ten minutes; later you may pray longer. Be faithful to the time you decide to pray, also when nothing seems to happen. Your first gift to God is your time.

- Take your bible and choose a passage to pray with, for example from the daily readings for Mass. You can also read an entire Bible book, every day a bit. Any text will do, but keep it short, and be careful not to pick only texts which you like.

- Choose a position in which you will pray: sit, stand, lay down... If this is helpful, you can do a brief breathing exercise to calm down *(see Saint 2.5)*.

- Now place yourself in the presence of God: tell him that you are here to listen to his Word, and ask the Holy Spirit to help you pray.

STEP 1: READ (LECTIO)

- Calmly read through the entire passage, with great attention to what you read. Take your time to really grasp what the text is about. Reading slowly is important here.

- 'Listen' to the text, and observe what it does with you. Be aware of your emotions: which words, phrases or concepts grasp you, move you, make you happy or angry, for example?

- Now read the passage again and stop at the points where you are touched. You may repeat the word or phrase several times, as if you were chewing on them, or saying them aloud.

STEP 2: MEDITATE (MEDITATIO)

- Use your mind and imagination in this step. Take time to ponder on what the passage means, what its message is for you at this moment.

- You may try to imagine yourself to be part of the scene that is described. Reflect on how the message applies to your life: what could God want to tell you through this text?

- Slowly read through the text with these points in mind. Pay attention to your emotions, for God does not only speak to your intellect.

STEP 3: PRAY (ORATIO)

- Now you can give a response to what you read and meditated on. You can speak to God about what you experienced so far, about what he may be telling you...

- You may read the passage one more time, but this time without attention for the words, only for God.

- This step is not about thinking or imagining, but about speaking to God from your heart: praise him, thank him, ask him...

STEP 4: CONTEMPLATE (CONTEMPLATIO)

- This final step is not about doing something like reading, thinking, or praying. Rather, the idea is that now you simply try to be in the presence of God. Try to let go of your ideas, desires, and thoughts.

- Simply be with God, let him speak to you. Try to let yourself be transformed by his presence in your life, and try to see things from his perspective.

- Especially in this phase you may notice that you are easily distracted. Do not worry, but simply refocus on being in the presence of God *(see Saint 2.5)*.

CONCLUSION

- Conclude your prayer with a word of thanks, and maybe an Our Father or another standard prayer.

- Briefly look back over your prayer, with special attention for what you experienced, for your emotions: how did you feel, at which point were you touched, bitter, angry, at peace...?

- Jot down a few words about your experience, so that you can look back on your prayer life later, and help yourself prepare for meeting your spiritual director *(see Saint 1.10)*.

- Bring your faith in action in your daily life.

INDEX OF SAINTS

INDEX OF SUBJECTS

HOW TO
GROW IN FAITH

A LIFE-CHANGING COURSE TO EXPLORE THE FAITH, SEARCH FOR ANSWERS OR PREPARE FOR THE SACRAMENTS

What if growing in faith were just as easy, natural, and contemporary as interacting on social media? The course *How to grow in faith* shows that it is just that! You will find an opportunity to ask questions, search for answers in groups, and discover how God loves each of us very deeply!

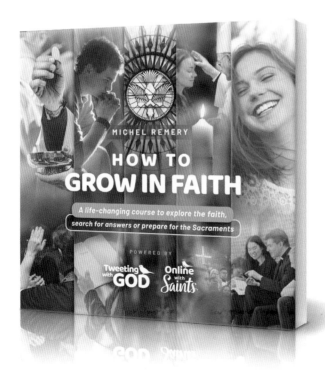

MULTIMEDIA RESOURCES

Online resources, videos, mobile apps, social media, and manifold activities make this a very interactive course. Every meeting begins with a question which helps the participants to explore their personal faith, through interactive exercises and profound dialogue. This results in a very interactive program that challenges the participants to truly participate while searching together for answers that will reveal the truth about life, love and faith.

www.howtogrowinfaith.com

PERSONALISED PROGRAM

The proposed course consists of 18 meetings on the sacraments and Christian life. If you need more than the proposed meetings, you can add some related questions from the *Tweeting with GOD* book and find more suggestions for themes in the appendix. The program can be spread over one, two, three and even more years, with extra material available. Free downloads make the course complete!

A COURSE FOR PEOPLE OF ALL GENERATIONS

The course can be used by schools as a program for religious education, by communities as a catechetical program to grow in faith, or by parishes to support those preparing for the Sacraments of Confirmation or First Holy Communion, catechumens seeking Baptism (RCIA), or couples preparing for Marriage. Think also of the personal development of teachers, health and social workers...

"This course is intended as a joint adventure for people who are searching, questioning, doubting... and above all desiring to grow."

Father Michel Remery - Author

POWERED BY

www.onlinewithsaints.com